Clean Your Own House,

Princess

Angel Christine

NEWMAN SPRINGS PUBLISHING
320 Broad Street
Red Bank, NJ 07701

First originally published by Newman Springs Publishing 2021

ISBN 978-1-63881-186-2 (Paperback)
ISBN 978-1-63881-187-9 (Digital)

Printed in the United States of America

FOR MY CHILDREN, EARL and Zina, who are my biggest accomplishments, and to my grandchildren Riley, Jessica, Bradyn, Ethan, Emily, and Miles, who have taught me that love is completely unconditional. I love all of you to the moon and back and thank God each and every day for you. I would also like to thank my husband, Khris, for inspiring me to get this book from my head to paper.

T HIS STORY IS THE culmination of events in my life of which I had little control. The end result of these events forced me to become a single mother, which made me a strong survivor, and ultimately, I would thrive.

As I look back over my small business of cleaning homes, I realize I should have charged $250 an hour for my services; after all, I was a therapist to each and every client!

However, on the flip side, I would like to thank all my former clients for making this book possible. It was like *Knots Landing, Dallas, or Falcon Crest* in every neighborhood. These events are the never-ending drama that I lived through in real life, over seventeen years running my small business in the greater Denver, Colorado, area, also known as the Front Range.

All names have been changed to protect the innocent and those who are not-so innocent.

Sammy

THIS BOOK HAS TO begin with Sammy because she was the first Realtor I contracted work for, and she sent me to the person who, I believe, saved my life, and that is a whole different book.

Sammy found me from an ad I ran in a small newspaper in Louisville, Colorado, or should I say, her stepmother found me through Sammy, so I must speak about Joan. I would do a handful of jobs for Sammy's stepmother, Joan, before ever meeting Sammy.

Joan was a short and stocky woman with short graying hair, late sixties, and not well-dressed for a Realtor but rather frumpy instead. One would look at Joan, and think perhaps, she was not successful at being a Realtor. I mean, they always say, show how successful you are by what you wear and drive.

Perhaps she had already proven herself to the area, she has been a Realtor for many years now, over thirty-five. Joan didn't speak up when she spoke, you had to really tune in to what she was saying; it was always like, turn up the volume, please! She reminded me of a little short and stocky typical grandmother from the Rockwell paintings. You know, one who would feel her way around the kitchen and just a pinch of salt, never following a recipe. Just a grandma.

Joan, as it turned out, had been a Realtor her entire life and did very well, all the while raising five children, and these five children were not her own. Sammy's dad was a widower and had met Joan when Sammy was just six years old.

I met Joan at her home on a hill overlooking Boulder from the east. Sammy had directed me to the house by texts; at one point, I lost my signal. I came upon an older ranch home that had been built onto. A very nice home indeed. This home, if on the market today, with the five acres of land it sat on, would go for over a million five easily. All the rooms had large windows in order to bring in the outside and enjoy the views.

At the time I met Joan, she had hired a furniture placement specialist. What is a furniture placement specialist, you're thinking? It is a person who repositions or places your furniture to make the rooms look bigger. They come in, take all the furniture out, and then bring it all back into the rooms in a more suitable way to make the flow better in the home, some use feng shui. *Feng shui* means "wind water," which are two of earth's flowing elements. Placement of furniture such as beds, even doors and colors, along with water features, keep the good energy flowing in one's home. Because of feng shui, my bed always faces the door.

Joan had absolutely no talent for decorating, could be because she bought and sold their family homes each year, constantly moving on. I mean, I don't know about you, but whenever I move into a new home, it takes me at least two years to get situated and begin the decorating. They had actually been in this home for two years—unusual for this family.

In the months to come, I would do quite a few jobs for Joan, easy jobs for move-in and move-outs real estate deals. It was always a pleasure to see her sweet face, and she was so nice but somehow uppity. And then there was always the argument to get the money I wanted out of the jobs I did for her; yes, this old gal was about as frugal as one could be, a shrewd businesswoman. But oh, how she loved to vacation in Mexico three to four times a year. Perhaps she was shrewd because she raised five kids pretty much on her own. Soon I would meet Joan's stepdaughter Sammy.

Sammy was a very thin, extremely pale, thirtysomething single mother of two small daughters. Sammy appeared to have never been in the sun much and always, always wore black. Sammy's clothes were never fit to her body but always loose; you could see she was thin, but you couldn't make out her body shape at all. She was pretty but sported a very large nose. I mean, you had to work hard not to stare at her nose. She had short black hair and never wore shorts, dresses, or skirts but always black pants with some sort of blazer. I would discover why she covered up her body later on.

Sammy hired me on to do several jobs for her as she worked under her stepmother, as a Realtor herself. Becoming a Realtor was how she survived her divorce. I would later discover that Sammy pretty much was handed $500,000 real estate deals from Joan on a continual basis. She didn't have to go out and get her own clientele. It was easy peasy for Sammy, except for the fact that she had to do all the math on every deal and do the open houses on the weekends. She said the math was the hardest part of real estate, trying to make the property worth what the selling price was, hence, she would begin going to older men in the business to help her do this math but at a personal cost—a very high personal cost.

Sammy complained about everything, and I mean everything under the sun. Soon after we met, she went to work for a large brokerage company and left Joan's wings of protection, saying, "I don't like it that she always knows where I am and what I am doing, and then there are all the errands she is constantly nagging at me to run for her." I thought to myself, *Oh, you poor little thing, so spoiled, must be rough.*

I was still doing work for Joan, but more work for Sammy. The only time I would see Joan was to pick up a check. Joan began to tell me little secrets about her stepdaughter and how they fought all of the time over the years. I, of course, just had my usual listening ear to offer. It was clear that Joan was more than a little upset that Sammy had left her brokerage firm. But lo and behold, Mommy still handed her $500,000 deals on that silver platter.

Sammy and I soon became friends who talked about everything in life, and it would not be long before she realized my marriage was on the outs. She directed me to a divorce counselor, the one who, I believe to this day, saved my life; yes, indeed he did. I will always be grateful to Sammy for that.

Sammy was a single mother of two small girls, Stacy and Jax, ages four and six. Sammy had been married to an ex-policeman who had gotten caught up in drugs and alcohol. The marriage had finally ended after years of mental and physical abuse, and then there were all his visits to rehab that never worked out. He still saw their girls when he was sober and sometimes when he was not.

Sammy would complain about how hard life was for her as a single mother, but personally, I thought she had it made. A nice $300,000 house, a stepmother, and siblings that would watch her girls at the drop of a dime, always catering to all her needs, and she got along with her four siblings well.

She was still close to her ex-father and mother-in-law, reaping benefits of the bounty. Her ex-father-in-law was a retired airline pilot and his wife, a retired airline stewardess. They lived outside of Aspen in a beautiful home they built along the river. Sammy would go up often to play tennis. I suppose she sported shorts then, or maybe not, I will never know but only imagine. I mean, she had to wear shorts to play tennis, right? Who plays tennis in pants, really? She had to put on a skort or shorts, one would think.

I soon began cleaning Sammy's personal home. What a mess of a home it was, no other way to put it. Picture a grown woman raising kids in a home where it appeared a teenager, out of control, resided, only the teenager was Sammy, the mother. It was such a beautiful ranch-style home, but Sammy had no idea how to keep it organized or clean. I knew it before I got inside the house, as the yard was not kept up at all, and yes, I could smell that a cat lived there. The yard was mostly straw, the grass had gone long, long ago. There were weeds, tall weeds. Picture a field out in the plains—that was the yard.

As I entered the front living room, you could see all the stains on the cream-colored carpet, as if it had not been cleaned in years. The curtains were worn and old, looking like they had been hanging there for fifty years. Furniture was sparse in this room, which was connected to the dining room, an open floor plan. The couch looked as though it was purchased from a cheap hotel lobby, no other way to explain it. Again the furniture was sparse in the dining room as well. The furniture appeared to have been bought at an auction house or garage sale, worn. I don't know how to explain that type of furniture, except it was just like horrible hand-me-downs. The dining room set was dark weathered cherry wood with dark-green upholstered seats, something you would expect in an elderly person's home.

The kitchen was small but open to another living area, which made it appear larger than it actually was. The kitchen had minimal cabinets, not even in the small island. No stools to sit on around the island and only a small round glass-top table in the eating area. You could barely move around in this kitchen.

Another small living room was off the kitchen. This home seemed like a young bachelor lived in it. It was as though nobody spent much time there except to crash and eat a meal or two. And yes, the sink was full of dirty dishes, and the gas stove covered with all kinds of food and grease. This gal didn't love her nest.

You could not see the floor of Sammy's bedroom; this is usual for a teenage girl, but I had never seen this in a woman's bedroom prior or even to this day. Well, there was the alcoholic mother I had worked for prior, you couldn't see her bedroom floor either. The mirror on her dresser had not been cleaned for years, no doubt. I thought to myself, *How could any grown woman live like this?*

The girl's bedrooms were the same. The laundry room, down the hall, well, you couldn't see any floors due to all the laundry piled up, all along the way in front of the rooms and in the rooms.

I knew that Sammy didn't take after her stepmother, whose house was immaculate, with everything in its place. I wondered why.

The first time in, I knew it was going to be quite a job, a job that took the entire day. What a workout my body got that hot sweltering summer day. I was soaking wet with sweat the entire time, as Sammy had no air-conditioning, no fans, zilch. Now keep in mind, I am like a well-tuned machine at this age of my life; a job like this would take the normal person three days to do. And please tell me why a Realtor who turns $500,000 jobs all month cannot afford air-conditioning! I mean, really!

Sammy began having small affairs with much older men in the new brokerage firm she joined. She felt safer with older men. She said, "Older men are more mature, and they have money and lots of it." One of the men she saw owned half of Louisville, Colorado, and the building his brokerage firm was in, and yes, he owned the brokerage that Sammy worked at.

I kept telling Sammy that what she really needed was to spend more time with her two girls and stay away from men for a few years. She didn't feel that was necessary; Sammy was needy for a man, and she never went long without one in her life or in her bed. There was a reason for this, I would soon learn. We all know women who don't have fathers in their lives, or at least interacting with them during their childhood, seek out acceptance from men.

Soon we began to have dinners and lunches together, and with other gals, we even took up hiking together. She, her friend Nina, and I became good friends, and we three did quite a bit together. I was newly single and liked friends to hang out with. It all worked quite well at the time, we were all single. Sammy would encourage me to become a Realtor, but I wanted nothing to do with that life. Working weekends and nights did not appeal to me at all. I had been to real estate school a few years earlier and knew that there were about one thousand different ways that a Realtor could be sued, and those awful hours, no thanks, not for me! But oh, how I love to go through beautiful homes, so much fun!

For the first year or so of our friendship, we were seeing the same divorce counselor, and he—the divorce counselor—had warned me that Sammy leads quite a risky lifestyle. I had no idea what he was talking about until we and some other women went up to Vail for a gals' weekend getaway together.

One of the older men she had had an affair with gave her his condo for the weekend, so it cost us zero to stay there, otherwise none of us could have afforded it. It's Vail, Colorado, and we were right in Vail Village, where only the rich live and only the rich visit, unless several people rent a place together. I had a friend years ago whose daughter became a chef in Europe and had worked in a restaurant in Vail, but could only afford to live there by sharing a house with six other people. She didn't stay in Vail more than a year.

So off the five of us went to Vail and out to dinner on the first night. Sammy was drinking quite a bit; I myself am not a drinker at all. I ended up taking a shuttle bus back to the condo with a few other women to relax and go to sleep, we were taking the gondola up the mountain and hiking down the next morning, followed by shopping. And yes, there are a few places us regular people can afford to shop for things like T-shirts and purses in Vail, Colorado. And what fun it is to sit outside a café in Vail Village and look up at the mountains, so incredibly beautiful. Who knows, maybe we would get a glimpse of Mary Hart, a former host from *Entertainment Tonight*; she had a condo right above Vail Village. President Ford and his wife, might they stroll by? No, I had my doubts on that one. But you never know who you're going to spot in the mountains.

Before we knew what was happening, we were all woken by Sammy and two strange men she brought back with her. We were all quite shocked. These were men from out of town, were in Vail for a conference, and they were obviously thinking they were going to get lucky. They said they were married and out for a fun time, their wives would never know. The night ended badly with the rest of us gals telling Sammy to please get the men out of our condo. Sammy became angry and violent with us. I later heard her vomiting in the bathroom. The next morning, we woke up, had breakfast, and went back to Denver, no hiking, no shopping, everyone was upset with Sammy and her behavior. The trip was the quietest car ride I had ever taken down the mountain. I was just so shocked by this young mother's behavior! I mean, she always had the buttoned-up blouse-and-stiff-collar look. Who'd have thunk! She was reckless and didn't mind imposing her recklessness on others. This was just the tip of the iceberg, as far as Sammy's promiscuous behavior went.

After the weekend, I began getting stood up by Sammy quite often. "Angel, can you please go to this party with me, or can you please attend this dinner with me." Just to have her never show up. She became more and more sporadic with her behavior. I didn't answer her call often; I would wait for a message or text to see if it was work-related.

Over time, Sammy began bragging about sleeping with married men to "seal the deal" when trying to sell them houses. These men came in from out of state looking for a home to buy, and Sammy was the Realtor to see. Sammy became increasingly hard to be around and to do work for, as she had so many headaches and was always complaining about how hard her life was.

I would soon find out from Joan that Sammy was bulimic, throwing up everything she ate from the time she was around thirteen years of age, hence all the trips to the bathroom after eating a meal with her at a restaurant, the headaches, the bad moods; suddenly I understood. I felt horrible for her, but at the same time, I disliked her behavior. She was such a miserable person to hang with, and I couldn't talk to her about her bulimic condition because Joan had sworn me to secrecy.

Sammy had low self-esteem, and I think this was why she threw herself at men. She thought her worth was in having sex with a man, she even had a crush on our divorce counselor, the guy that saved my life. Sammy shared with me that she secretly had an affair with our counselor, but only in her mind. I told her she didn't stand a chance because he was professional, in love with someone; plus, I was thinking he knew all her garbage.

Her relationship with her father was difficult, to say the least. Sammy's father was a tall thin much-older man with wavy graying hair that clearly had children later in life, or this man was aging rapidly. He was always polite when I was around him, but extremely quiet. Sammy confided in me that her mother died at the side of the road, while she and her father were sightseeing in the mountains of Colorado, the car had slipped out of gear. They were both standing outside the car, looking at the scenery, when the car took her mother's life. It was like something you would see in a movie. They were alone, the children were not with them.

Sammy was not sure her father was innocent of the incident, or perhaps guilt ate him up his entire life, and she thought that this was why he drank so much. Either way, Sammy didn't want to talk much about her dad, and she never seemed close to him.

Her father was an alcoholic that had started many businesses with the help of his new wife, Joan. He failed at every business, and each and every time I saw him on a job, he had a glass of whiskey in his hand. Yes, he would pull up in his Mercedes and be sporting a glass of whiskey.

It was obvious that Joan had taken care of him and all five of his children all on her own. Yet Sammy had a certain hate for her stepmother, I never understood it. This woman gave her a great childhood, handed her real estate deals that most Realtors would die for, and watched her girls whenever she needed a sitter. Joan had always made her life so easy.

Sammy, now she wanted to play more than she wanted to work, and she obviously wanted to land a rich Realtor. She found one, slept with him, but he rejected her because he was still in love with someone else, who no longer wanted him. He was a much-older man as well, by at least thirty-five years.

She would call me and say things like, "Oh my god, you should see the house! He lives up in the foothills! It is to die for." Oh, and then, "I slept with him the first night, even though I hadn't shaved my legs or armpits in like, forever, do you think he noticed?"

Then there was the time she told me that this man was still in love with his ex, but she didn't care, she thought she could sway him her way. "The ex clearly doesn't want him anymore," she said. "He is so pathetic that he cried to me about it, he's an easy catch." *Never going to happen*, I thought, and it didn't. He dropped her after two months of her just showing up at his house last minute, what do you call that? A bootie call, I believe. I told her over and over again not to date, or take a break from men or find someone to have a real relationship with, but it was like talking to a wall. You could see the destructive behavior, but she never listened to anyone. She would conduct an interview with men on the first date. If they didn't drive a BMW or Mercedes and have tons of money, they never got a second date. It was all about the money.

I began seeing a painter at jobs that Sammy and her mother used on their properties quite often. I would go in to see a house in order to give an estimate on cleaning, and he would occasionally be painting while I was there. He was quite a nice older man, tall and stocky, good-looking. Soon Sammy began bragging that she was having an affair with this man. "Did you see him today, Angel? Isn't he hot? I'm sleeping with him."

She said she had run into his wife, a psychiatrist, at the grocery store and had quite a conversation with her, stating to me, "How funny it is that this woman had no clue that I am sleeping with her husband," she would boast. This man was soon climbing through Sammy's bedroom window at night and leaving before the morning. She even bragged about him doing this on Christmas morning. Sammy became disgusting to me. I kept telling her what she was doing was wrong, but she didn't care, she liked the thrill. I don't know, perhaps in her mind, she thought he may one day leave his wife for her. She wanted an older man with a ton of money.

I became more distant from Sammy by raising my prices or telling her I was booked and declined invitations to go anywhere with her. I mean really, who wants a gal friend in her life that you can't trust to be around whoever you're dating, or who has such low morals. I saw Sammy in church years later, and she had approached me, asking me to please be her friend again, that she had changed, said she was dating a guy that I would never believe her to be with. She said, "Oh, you'd be surprised at who I'm dating now, he is a complete nerd."

I listened for a few minutes, and then I replied with "I'm sorry, but I just can't be your friend. I wish you the best in life." I walked away, never regretting it. I have never seen Sammy since nor her daughters, but I wouldn't doubt that one or both have an eating disorder because of their mother.

Tonya

I MET TONYA AT A dinner party at Sammy's house. Tonya had bought a townhome through Sammy. We all started hanging out together early in our friendship, going on walks and hiking, off to lunches and dinners, things like that. I would clean for Tonya off and on when she had a party or surgery.

Tonya is a large woman, unkempt, like a hippie from the day, midthirties. She had dropped out of college to follow the Grateful Dead around the country, doing as many drugs as she possibly could. I say she was unkempt because she would show up to go out to a nice restaurant to eat with us, and it was obvious, she had not brushed her teeth, food stuck all around in them; it was nasty, to say the least. It was as if someone coated the whole front of her teeth with pastry dough or something. Yes, you guessed it, I'm gagging right now.

Her hair would be greasy at times, and when she ate and talked, food would fly across the table at you. She wore eyeglasses that I often wondered how she could see through, she didn't clean those either. How do you tell a grown woman to brush her teeth and wash her hair? You don't. I mean, especially someone you had just met. Sammy and I would discuss it in private, but neither one of us knew how to deal with it. I mean, Tonya was thirty-three years old. Sammy said that ever since she met her through real estate that there was no way she could just blow Tonya off. She just wouldn't go away.

We remained friends because you just couldn't shake Tonya. Guess why? It became clear to me that she was one of the most codependent people I would ever come to know.

Tonya had spent the past eight years trying to hold on to a guy that would drop her, go back to her, and literally treat her like trash while he lived off of her. When I met her, this guy had just dropped her once again and was taking up residency with another woman in a town thirty miles away in Fort Collins, and Tonya was falling apart all the time. It wasn't the first time he had left her, moving in with another gal.

Sammy and I would tell her, "Move on with your life, be happy someone else has to put up with him now, you can do better." Even though we both questioned whether she could do better. Tonya just couldn't move on. We both suggested she go to our therapist, but Tonya always said she had no money.

It was only about six weeks after I met her that she would tell me she drove to the ex-boyfriend's new house, looked in the mailbox, steal his mail, just to see what he was up to. I told her that was a federal offense. Tonya said, "No, it's not a federal offense, unless you get caught, I go at night so nobody can see me, I have even looked in their windows a few times."

I again told her to seek counseling to get over this guy. She never did.

In a few months, Tonya would get laid off and have only unemployment to live off. It was then that she began mooching off of Sammy and myself.

"I don't have any money to go out," she would say. So Sammy and I would split the tab between ourselves and pay Tonya's way everywhere we went, bars, nice restaurants—you name it—we paid for Tonya. It got old really fast because she would order several glasses of alcohol at dinner or lunch. Sammy and I were getting fed up, but we pitied her—that sums it up, we honestly pitied her. I mean, aren't we, as women, supposed to lift one another up and help one another?

Tonya needed to have surgery before her insurance ran out, and at this time, I kept her house clean for free for her while she recovered. She never disclosed to Sammy or me what the surgery was for.

It would be a year or so before Tonya would file for bankruptcy and confided in Sammy and me that she had no choice, her finances were in ruins.

"Do what you have to," we both advised her. But then the big bomb hit.

"I have $4,000 in my bank account that I have to hide per orders of my attorney."

"What!" Sammy and I both blurted out at the same time. And when I looked at Sammy's face, well, it looked like I felt—like she was going to blow like the steam from a teakettle any second. Her face beet red and puffed up, not normal at all for the pale Sammy. I felt a heat stroke come over me. I mean, we had both been paying her way for well over a year! I had kept her place clean for her when she had surgery! Both of us listening to her pity party all the while!

"Where did you get that kind of money?" I asked her.

Her reply, "Well, you know, my mom, dad, and my stepmother have been helping me out, and I'm pretty frugal when I have to be."

And what did she do with the $4,000? She took a cruise to Greece and pocketed the rest of the money! Said she needed a cushion to fall back on. Well, this was the end of Sammy and me paying her way, and quite frankly, we never told her when we were going out any longer. We were both done pitying her. And so we just drifted away, rarely including her in hikes, and letting her pay for her own lunch and beer afterward. We had always taken early Saturday morning hikes in the mountains, followed by great lunches and nice cold beer afterward, in various small-town restaurants up in the mountains.

Tonya eventually landed a job as a secret shopper and would invite Sammy or me to go to restaurants with her to spy on the help. We both took her up on it because we felt we paid her way so many times prior. And besides, she could bring a person to every restaurant or bar she was spying on. That person got a free meal and two alcoholic drinks on the company Tonya worked for. Tonya would just turn in the receipts and get reimbursed. It was fun actually because we would go to nice restaurants on the Pearl Street Mall in Boulder and enjoy great food. We would be there spying on the bartender, who was presumed to be stealing from the register, or the waitress who was giving friends free drinks or how the food was and was the place clean.

There were times the three of us would go together, and Tonya would pay the entire tab. "Never mind either one of you paying, I figured I owe you."

Ahh, yeah, yes, honey, you do, we both thought. The friendships were never the same for many reasons, but Tonya always kept in touch. It came down to none of us hanging out any longer as time flew by.

Tonya would call me and tell me she had met an old classmate from high school on an online site where former classmates chatted. This fella's wife had died in childbirth, and he had a total of four kids, one of which was a six-month-old baby. Next thing I knew, Tonya had moved in with the guy because—guess what—Tonya was pregnant! *Unbelievable*, I thought, I mean she moved in with him within a few short weeks, and then they were married in six months and off on a Greek island cruise for thirty days—yes, thirty days. Unreal, especially since he was just a school teacher, with no master's degree, making little money.

I have seen Tonya from time to time since at sporting events when I went to watch one of my grandchildren play football or baseball. Tonya now had three boys in sports, the instant family.

One day, my daughter and I were sitting in our lawn chairs, watching my grandson's football game, and we heard, "Angel, my golly, is that you?" As we looked and saw her running toward us, no bra on and an old Grateful Dead T-shirt.

My daughter goes, "OMG, she doesn't have a bra on." Tonya had remained the same, hippie-looking, unkempt, teeth not brushed, hair greasy and uncombed. I was embarrassed for her.

Tonya is a photographer now, does a lot of weddings and senior pictures in the small farm town she lives in. I see her work on Facebook from time to time, as this is where she advertises her business. Still taking elaborate vacations every summer, for three weeks at a time, because she can; I mean teachers have all that time off in the summer months. Good for Tonya. And you know what, there really is someone out there for everyone!

Ellen

O NE OF MY VERY first clients is still retaining my services to this day, my counseling services, that is. Her name is Ellen.

Ellen will say to me, "Thank God you answered the phone, you're the only person who picks up when I call." And with the two to three calls coming in from Ellen, at least three days a week, I do not answer more than one a week. Sometimes I don't answer at all because Ellen is like a full-time job! So many times, when I hang up, I feel as though I have been insulted the entire conversation. I wonder, does she call me to belittle me because in her money-driven world she isn't allowed to insult anyone around her? But no, I have learned over the years that Ellen insults everyone she comes into contact with, very nonchalantly but somehow quite brutally.

We met on a hot summer day, and like so many clients to come, Ellen heard about me from a neighbor. There were three children—all girls—in the kitchen: one child screaming, one climbing in the dishwasher, and one on Ellen's hip. "I need your help!" she screamed out to me.

Ellen looked to be the spitting image of the infamous Ellen DeGeneres, go figure. This is a woman who had her children in her midthirties. Not a feminine build at all and not a pretty woman. This woman had a negative energy that I could feel as I listened to her complain about how she hated Colorado and everything about it. Hated her husband traveling and on and on.

I knew right away that nothing in her life was as she wished it could be. She lived in a neighborhood full of young mothers, so to speak, because I knew of no other mothers that were not in their early twenties. Ellen had become a mother later than most, and it showed; she was completely overwhelmed.

Shoot, I recall back when I had my three little ones, and I was teaching high and low-impact aerobics classes along with body-firming classes at the YMCA, all with my kids in tow. Having your babies when you're young is the only way to go, as far as I am concerned. I canned tomatoes, peaches, beans, and froze corn, roasted peppers, and made twelve apple pies for the winter, along with making all of my children's clothes, blankets and afghans, and stuffed animals. I think it is a different energy when you have your children in your early twenties instead of your thirties. I look back today and realize just how much I juggled and how much pure energy I had had, and I sure wish I had that energy today at age sixty-one.

Ellen thought you should have babies when you're older, after you have lived life some, yet she had absolutely no energy and seemed to hate her life in general.

Her house was a small newer home that would be an easy clean, and like so many clients to follow, her husband, Mick, traveled frequently, going to Japan and Germany for his work, and would be gone as long as two weeks at a time. Of course, I always loved these clients because I knew they were a constant income for me every week or every other week. A life without her husband at home so frequently was too much for Ellen to do it all, and so voilà, I knew I had a consistent client in Ellen. I would later discover that she was raised by extremely rich parents, so getting your house cleaned was the norm.

Ellen and Mick had moved from Phoenix, Arizona, where Ellen said the weather was nicer, the houses bigger, more affordable, and everyone was friendly. There had been many dinner parties, and the ladies in her previous neighborhood got together often for coffee, lunches, and hiking outings, at least that was what Ellen's story was. Her group of mothers in Arizona helped one another out with babysitting and borrowing a few eggs whenever they were out, that kind of thing.

She was not experiencing this in Colorado, stating, "The people here just suck!" Yeah, Ellen is extremely blunt, painfully blunt! "The weather sucks, everything about this place my husband moved us to sucks!"

As you entered Ellen's house, the steps leading to the upstairs almost hit you in the face, that is how small the foyer was, if one would call that a foyer.

The home was like a starter home, small. Her home looked as though they had just moved in, as though things needed to be put away, yet they had already lived there a full year. The house was not decorated, no pictures on the walls, no paint color, just the stark white from the builder grade. There seemed to be no personality to this home. Nobody had made it their own yet. There were no pretty things sitting on end tables or shelves. No fresh flowers like so many of us have in Colorado at all times, it's just a thing for Colorado women!

You have to realize that Colorado is full of happy people, the sun shines more than in Florida, at least three hundred days out of the year, and the tone is happy all around. Life was celebrated every day, at least it was back then, and it is today, just in fast motion. Today that is called the rat race.

The rooms were small, especially the kitchen. Ellen hated the house and said, "This is nothing like the home we have left in Arizona, this house is embarrassing." She described the house in Arizona as a big home with lots of character and all the upgrades you could imagine for very little money compared to what homes in Colorado cost. Ellen said that this home was all they could find when they moved to Colorado, and it was like starting all over again, like when they were young. She was very unhappy in it, and it showed with every breath she took. The unhappiness showed all over the home. The girl's rooms were not pretty little rooms like other homes, it was if they were staying in a cheap rental until they found something better. Ellen was just waiting to get another home.

Nobody talked to Ellen in this neighborhood. No one had dinner parties, and there were no groups of mothers getting together to do anything. I had told Ellen I experienced the same problem when I moved from South Carolina to Colorado. I quickly learned that people were not outwardly friendly.

I myself still recall the shock of the six-foot fences around every yard, where in South Carolina, there were white picket fences, if any fence at all. I learned in Colorado that if you want to make friends, you had to get involved with the YMCA, exercise with young moms there, take your kids to swim lessons, or join a book club for young mothers. At the time I moved to Colorado, there were bumper stickers on cars everywhere that read "IF YOU'RE NOT A NATIVE, GO HOME!" Well, you can't get more blunt than that.

I had shared with Ellen that it would be a good idea to put a notice up on the group mailbox area stating that she would like to start a group for mothers with their toddlers. I don't know that she ever put that notice up. Ellen just wanted out of that house and out of the neighborhood that she felt to be so unwelcoming.

It would only be a few short months, perhaps eight months, after we met that Ellen would move across the highway to a much bigger (four thousand square feet, to be exact) expensive house. This house was a beautiful house that had all the upgrades that Ellen loved such as granite countertops, large bathrooms—and plenty of them—a mudroom, and an enormous master bedroom. The three girls' bedrooms were large, and she would have murals painted on the walls.

This house was a new build in a new neighborhood with alleyways designed for people to meet and talk while taking out the trash. The alleyway theory didn't work, not for Ellen. People were still not friendly enough for her.

Ellen's life was empty, even though she had just moved into this new house and had the perfect husband and three girls to take care of. Nobody seemed to be able to give her enough of their time; this is still the case today, seventeen years later. Again in this neighborhood, there were no dinner parties, no hiking groups, and no sharing of eggs or milk, and most mothers seemed to work.

If Ellen did a favor for anyone, she expected something in return, if this did not happen for her, she was extremely hurt to the point where she would cry and shout insults about the person to me.

Ellen would say things like, "I wouldn't want to hang out with her anyhow, my god, her husband is a mechanic, and this is her second marriage, the kids aren't even his." Or, "That little bitch, I bought her two pounds of pine nuts, do you know how expensive those are? And now she tells me she can't babysit my girls so I can go to a damn yoga class for one lousy hour!" Nobody could help Ellen enough, and believe me, these people would feel the wrath of Ellen time and time again. Ellen was blunt to a fault.

Before long, it seemed all my other clients in the same neighborhood were avoiding Ellen.

They would complain to me, saying, "She's so needy, she demands so much of my time, and she constantly weighs and measures everything we do."

Ellen once invited me to her jewelry party, along with some of her neighbors. I was introduced as the cleaning lady. I have now been Ellen's secret best friend for seventeen years. God forbid if anyone knew that we spent time at lunches together.

According to Ellen, a person is what they do for a living, nothing more, even though a person can be making a living at cleaning houses, having an active life besides. She once stated, "I have no time for anybody who has no college education, I cannot even tolerate being around them."

I was a full-time college student when I met Ellen, and I volunteered at MADD (Mothers Against Drunk Driving). Later I cofacilitated a grief workshop at my church, am a grandmother and mother, and worked out at the gym two hours practically every day. My time also belonged to a book club, a divorce group, and a hiking group. I considered myself a full-rounded individual but would never be anything more than the cleaning lady to Ellen, and she would remind me of this throughout the years to come. As I think back, it was as though I was the underdog that she wanted to study. I don't know, come to think of it, maybe she was writing a book about me because I did have quite an interesting single life.

Ellen had a bachelor's degree for teaching but no longer taught. She had become a babysitter and kept about four kids at a time. If the parents were not on time to pick them up at the end of the day, she would sit them on her front porch alone to wait for their parent, even if the child was only four years of age. I found this shocking. Ellen did not seem to enjoy doing day care, and I often wondered what kind of school teacher she had been. After doing daycare for about two years, Ellen was ready to move on to massage therapy and went to school for it. I scored big time when this took place.

In order to graduate massage school, Ellen had to give one hundred hours of free massages, and I was fortunate enough to be a participant. The massages were given in her large master bathroom. This new bathroom had a huge walk-in closet, a twelve-foot counter with double sinks, a large soaking tub, and a shower. In the center of the bathroom was plenty of room for a massage table. This bathroom was beautiful.

I had another client who had the same model home, and in her bathroom, she placed a large round ottoman in the center, I'm talking six feet in diameter. It was beautiful as well, I mean, who has a bathroom that big? Not too many people, as I would discover over the years to come.

All you had to do for the free massage was show up and give Ellen a tip at the end of the massage, in the amount of what she would suggest, of course. The trouble with getting a massage from Ellen was that she could not be quiet while giving a massage. She would go on and on about everything in life that upset her, from her alcoholic mother, who adopted her and treated her like Cinderella throughout her childhood, to the love of her life who dumped her in college.

Oh, how I would have enjoyed those massages more so had she just kept her mouth shut and been quiet. I mean, isn't that mentioned in the school of massage? I would soon begin going home immediately after the massages and taking a long bubble bath with soft music playing in order to completely relax. Spending time with Ellen in any capacity is like being traumatized, you feel the effects for hours afterward. Her negativity remains that strong to this day.

Ellen once told me during a massage that she had turned to alcoholism after her college lover broke up with her. She recalled waking up in people's yards in the mornings, not knowing where she was. The breakup was devastating to her. She cleaned up her act because her grades were suffering, and her parents threatened to quit paying her tuition, but she never fell out of love with him.

Ellen went on to meet Mick, whom her roommate told her if she did not go out with him that she would certainly pursue him. Ellen gave Mick a chance, saying that she didn't want her roommate to snatch him up, that he seemed fun, and that she knew he would make good money one day and be a good provider.

During another massage in her home, one evening, Ellen told me that she had found the man from college, that she still loved him, and had contacted him, wanting to fly to the East Coast just to have lunch with him and talk. This man turned her down and told her he was happily married and had no desire to see her. Ellen was angry and devastated and did not understand why he would not see her. I could not believe she found him and contacted him. I thought it to be stepping out on a ledge since he had ended the relationship.

She told me the sex had been incredible with him and that sex rarely happened with her husband. I lay there on the table, wondering if her husband, Mick, could hear the conversation through the vents that night; he was right downstairs.

I left her home through the kitchen that evening with her perfect husband handing me a latte. I recall how terrible I felt for Mick, thinking that there was a great possibility that he heard every word, but as always, Mick had that smile on his face. "How was it, Angel, are you relaxed now?" Smiling at him while thinking, *Hell no, now I need to go home, soak in my tub, and drink wine.*

Mick is a tall, slender, attractive, dark-haired, intelligent man who had a six-figure income and loved his family. Mick was involved in the church choir, played many instruments, collected instruments from around the world, and was active in a band. He cooked all the family's meals, helped with laundry, and was a hands-on dad. Those three girls love their dad. If ever there is a perfect husband and father, it would be Mick.

Mick grew up in Fort Collins, Colorado, and his parents had divorced when he was young, both remarrying. He was happy to be back in Colorado, unlike Ellen. I always thought it must be hard for

Mick to be married to a woman who did nothing but complain 24-7. He is quite the trooper; I give him a ton of credit.

Now when it came to massages, Ellen would always tell me to send people to her. "But no fat or hairy people," she would say. I sent some clients and friends her way, but none wanted to return because they could not enjoy the massage due to her constant talking. I came to the conclusion that she should not be in this kind of business because of how she viewed people's bodies and the fact that she never stopped talking while giving a massage. I have never referred another person to her.

Ellen has not been successful with her massage business over the years. She always says the same thing when I ask her how business is going, "They never come back, and I can't figure out why."

Why? Because nobody wants to receive a massage and be a personal therapist to Ellen at the same time! I mean that's what therapists do, right? Listen to someone's problems, hoping that what little advice they give them will someday soak in and help them.

Ellen was always looking for a thrill, always bored with everyday life. It was as if raising the girls and being married to Mick was a stage in life that you just do. There was this weird disconnect. Perhaps I was the only person who saw this because of all she disclosed to me.

One winter day—and winter seemed to be the worst time for Ellen—she asked me if I had ever thought about going down to where the prostitutes hung out on Colfax Street in Denver. She then told me she went down there and actually spent an afternoon on Colfax Street and that she just needed to experience something different. "Be away from the same everyday people," she said, "all my neighbors are the same," she said.

Of course, I said, "Why on earth would I ever do that?"

Then she said she had lunch at a strange restaurant and felt superior there, stating, "It was one of the most interesting afternoons I have had in a long while."

Ellen was intrigued by the life of prostitutes and the type of individuals who lived in that area of town. I don't know, perhaps it made her feel better in her neighborhood when she returned home. She was already bored with the area and the people, after only living there a year. Or maybe she turned a trick or two, who knows, you never know what this woman will do to fight the boredom of every-day life. Ellen never really laughed, she examined everything philo-sophically, it was never like bursting out laughing with her.

I began to observe Ellen's wild behavior in different ways. She would want me to come clean on a Saturday. I would arrive, and she would be alone ironing in the living room, watching porn on her television. Clearly the normal life Ellen had just was never going to be enough. This was the time I began to write down things that hap-pened with her, and this process would continue with other clients to come.

Mick's work transferred him to Australia, and the family would be there for two years. The phone calls to me continued, and she would beg me to go visit her in Australia.

"Everyone is so happy here, it's so beautiful here. We walk every-where, the grocery is right around the corner, and we have a saltwater pool, you just have to come," she would say.

When I told Ellen I had decided I may make the trip to Australia, it was clear that she did not want "the cleaning lady" to go. She said to me, "The women I have lunches with are so snobby that they would never eat lunch with a cleaning lady." I did not answer my phone for many months after this. The calls kept coming in until I finally gave in and answered. Again, *More for my book*, I thought to myself.

I answered mostly because of the messages I was receiving from Ellen. She was again saying that she had no friends, now in Australia. I have always felt that if I did not answer the phone one day, that she may go into an even deeper depression than she seems to always be in. I mean, you can be talking to Ellen, and one minute, she is telling you about all the trips the family is going to take, and the next, well, she just hates life.

Ellen would return from Australia after two short years and come to Denver while transitioning to Austin, Texas. Ellen would visit with me, telling me how horribly depressed she had become having had to return to the United States. Ellen said everyone in

Australia was happy, nobody drove cars, and she thought that was why everyone was so happy there.

For some reason, she felt she had to apologize for not coming back to Colorado because a gal friend, Tippy, was upset with her for moving to Texas. At the same time, she would slam everything about Colorado that she could. This was her personality—who or what can I slam today. The negativity constantly flowing from her mouth. Ellen again had her mind made up to be horribly depressed because life just wasn't going her way. She would move to Texas to please Mick, but I knew she would despise living there every day of her life, and yes, she does, always stating, "If Mick came home today and told me we had to move, I would have this damn house packed up by the end of the day."

Over the years, Ellen would complain to me about the pain her adoptive mother, a functioning alcoholic, would cause her. Of course, not getting enough attention from her, sending her very small sizes in clothing, knowing full well that Ellen was at least three sizes bigger, and never giving her enough of their money.

Her mother would send $5,000 to Mick and her for Christmas, and she would say, "Really, you would think the bitch could do better than this, I mean they're rich!" It was shocking, simply shocking, to hear such comments. She would say this each and every Christmas.

Ellen was adopted and was raised by millionaires who lived in Canada. They were both alcoholics who were not always present in her childhood because they traveled so often. She was raised by the nanny and always said her mother treated her like Cinderella. An example, Ellen said that whenever her parents were in town, it was she who had to clean all the bathrooms; the cleaning gal was dismissed when they arrived, until they departed once again. Ellen said that her mother would make her clean the bathrooms with a toothbrush, you know, like in boot camp.

Ellen had an adoptive brother, but then the mother was later able to give birth to two more sons. Ellen would complain that she never felt love from her mother and neither did her adoptive brother. She said her father gave her mother all of his attention, along with his natural sons.

Ellen would later go searching for her biological mother and find her and a half sister. This mother informed Ellen that she was a rape baby. This was when I began to see a completely different side of her. She began taking trips without her family, girlfriend weekends, going to see women she knew all over the country, college friends.

You would always know when she was coming to town because she would ask to stay at your home. "Oh! I'm coming to Colorado, and I would just love to come and see you while I'm there, perhaps stay with you? You're the only one I really want to see!" she would say.

I recall one trip where she asked me if she could use my home for a party to gather all her friends at Christmas. Of course I said no, and then I did not hear from her for a period of four months. Everyone I knew wanted fair warning when Ellen was coming to Denver so that they could avoid her, much like the plague.

She made a trip back to Colorado to go to the mountains for a weekend with me. Now when this weekend began, she told me that I was not to post anything on Facebook, showing that she was with me in the mountains. She said, "If all my other friends here know I came and didn't visit them, they will be angry with me." Once again I was reminded that I was Ellen's secret friend, ya know, the cleaning lady that didn't fit into her world.

The trip began with her wanting to shop at Macy's before heading to the mountains. This shopping extravaganza ended with me leaving her in the store after several hours and heading across the way to have a drink. Off to a bad start—as usual, everything was about Ellen.

And of course the room my travel agent gal friend secured for us was not good enough for Ellen. I wanted to stay in the mountains at little expense. It was Estes Park, I was there all the time. We ended up renting an Airbnb for $189 a night, ridiculous! And what did she want to do in this double master suite townhome? Sleep with me! No, thank you, Ellen! And when I said this was not something I wanted to do because I was so accustomed to sleeping alone, she pouted. It was weird, the entire trip was just bizarre, and I found myself wondering why I had yet again let Ellen push her way into my life. She insisted we put our bathing suits on and get into the soaking tub, pretending it was a hot tub. There were times with Ellen that I felt she had unwelcome affections toward me. Ellen could make me feel extremely uncomfortable.

At this point, Ellen and her family would be taking up to six vacations a year, not including her girlfriend getaways. To be home was just too boring. Life never seemed good enough or exciting enough for Ellen, thus many, many trips.

Mick once rented a home in San Diego for four weeks in the summer because Ellen said it was too hot in Texas. Two of her girls had passed out at a farmers market the summer prior, so the new deal was that if Mick wanted to live in Texas, then he had to rent a home somewhere cooler every summer, and that he has done.

One week after returning home to Austin from living in San Diego all summer, Ellen was calling me, telling me how bored she was and how she wished she was back in San Diego. Two weeks later, they were at the beach in Galveston.

Poor, poor pitiful Ellen, I had always thought to myself. *What would this woman do if all the money were gone, and she had to stay at home and be a regular housewife? Shoot herself?* I would suppose.

It came as a shock to me when Ellen sent out a group e-mail asking friends to please donate to trips her daughters would be taking in the summer months, mission trips. When I did not reply to these e-mails, she would call me and let me know she was unhappy that hardly anybody contributed to her daughters' trips.

I told Ellen, "Maybe if you did not take so many vacations, that perhaps then you could afford to send the girls on these trips yourself."

Again I did not hear from Ellen for several months. I learned that with Ellen, if I stated my opinion, that I could get several months break from her constant whining about life in general. Ellen never knows how well she has it, how blessed she is, yet she attends church every week.

Mick told Ellen that she could do anything she wanted for her fiftieth birthday, anything at all. Guess what Ellen picked—going to a treatment program in Arizona to deal with the fact that she was a rape baby. There at the center, she would hold baby dolls and tell them what she would have wanted someone to say to her when she was a baby.

Now her "secret friend," myself, was told about the trip, but everyone else was told that she was at a yoga retreat; she even bragged about the retreat on Facebook. I couldn't believe my eyes. Who does that?

Does this woman have two personalities? I thought to myself. How weird does it get with her?

Ellen's half sister would reach out to her a few years after she met her bio mother. This woman went to visit her in her home in Austin, Texas. Ellen called me, dreading the visit, and I told her to get the most out of it that she could.

"After all," I said, "you have always wanted a sister."

The sister came and went, and Ellen sent me a photo of them together, and I told her they looked like twins, only different-colored hair. Ellen was insulted and told me she looked nothing like her, that her sister had no class whatsoever, and that she was a complete drag to be with.

Ellen stated, "This is going to be awkward now because I never want to see or talk to her again."

I felt my heart sink for her newly found sister, how Ellen must have belittled her the entire visit. Go find your long-lost sister, dig into her life and invite her into yours, then just throw her away. Ellen has never mentioned her sister in conversation again. Yep, just dropped her out of her life, just like that.

The next major disappointment in Ellen's life was that her sister-in-law, Mick's sister, a twin, had been shot and killed by her husband, and then the husband killed himself, thus leaving two small boys behind. It was a tragic heartbreaking story to hear.

The family went to San Diego to help out. Ellen soon learned that Mick wanted to go back to San Diego the following summer and spend it with his dad and the family because everyone had such a helpless feeling over the loss and was just devastated. The two young boys would be raised by their aunt. Ellen told the story to me so nonchalantly that I felt a deep dark coldness in her voice. What did she do, Ellen? Steal your spotlight?

It was heart-wrenching, and the entire ordeal gave me chills. It was so sad. She called me, inquiring if she could visit with me in my home that coming summer, saying that she needed places to go because she would not be with Mick in San Diego and all that sadness. She is so self-absorbed that it was making me sick. She wasn't going to be there for the family or for her sweet husband; after all, Mick was only there to serve her needs.

It brought me back to a time, many years prior, that I had a devastating loss in my family, and Ellen came to visit me, and during the visit, she stated, "Why in the hell could this have not happened to my mother?"

My mother had been shot and killed. I was paralyzed beyond belief, but after that statement, I was unable to even speak. Ellen had appeared to me as even more of a monster now. She wanted her parents' money so badly that she wished her mother had been murdered, I had no words.

I don't answer my phone much from Ellen these days as she has become completely angry with me. Ellen has always wanted to live on an acreage but never could afford it. Perhaps she could if she didn't insist on taking so many vacations all year round.

I now live in New York State on fourteen wooded acres, on top of a mountain, with a wonderful man that I waited for seventeen years to come into my life. Ellen seems to hate me for finding this new life I have and has even called me, making statements about how selfish some people are that they think they can just go wherever they want to live and leave their families behind. Perhaps I was selfish moving here and leaving my daughter and her kids behind, but I was there for them for so many years, now it was my turn to live my life, and I did move here to be near my son.

Ellen and her husband finally upgraded to a large horse property home forty-five minutes from anything she knew, even the simple trip to the grocery store. She had finally obtained everything she ever wanted. The large home in which to host dinner parties and barbecues, the acreage for her horses. Yet it was soon to be that she would call, complaining about how large the home was.

"I'm shutting doors to close off rooms in the house, I wish we had gotten this property when the girls were still here." Now all three daughters were off to college. There were no friends nearby to visit with or receive favors from. The trips to the grocery were wearing Ellen out. Mick was traveling for his work, and she was afraid to be alone out in the middle of nowhere. One horse soon died, and they sold the other because the girls were no longer home to take all the jumping classes nor go to all the competitions. It was one complaint after another on each phone call. The calls were harder and harder to answer, but Ellen seemed to be on her last leg, in a panic about life. There I was, still being the never-ending listener to this needy person.

Then the pandemic hit our world. Ellen was so happy that her three girls were moving back home until everything went back to normal. But this happiness would not last for long. The phone calls became more and more bitter toward her daughters. "They are just pigs, just trashing the house and making me wait on them hand and foot, I don't know how much more I can take." I didn't answer the phone calls for months, I just couldn't take her constant ups and downs—with plenty of the downs, let me tell you.

This is a woman who is always taking trips around the country, can't stand to stay in her own home, she was losing it at a high rate of speed. Ellen just couldn't enjoy her time in her new home, it had become a prison. Here I was, just out of knee replacement surgery, had just gotten back to work for only two weeks when the shutdown came. It was hard on me also, but I had to keep being grateful to have more time to heal and more time with my husband, enjoying our nest.

The last phone call from Ellen, well, it was the kicker, the final blow for this gal. Ellen was upset, complaining about the two small donkeys she had purchased, saying, "They're cute, but I can't ride them. It's so much work to take care of them, all the feedings and cleaning their stalls." The girls were finally gone from being home all through the pandemic months, and she was hating being back to work as a teacher's aide, virtually. Yes, Ellen was now being chained to her computer eight hours a day, trying to teach kids with disabilities. She had tried, time after time, to be a private teacher to small groups of families but was never hired for these positions. She did not want to be a teacher's aide any longer, not virtually.

And then Ellen stated that the boyfriend of her middle daughter showed up at her home to do some yard work for them. He showed up sad. She asked what was wrong, he told her they had broken up. Ellen was devastated and had no prior knowledge of the breakup.

Now keep in mind, this is the boyfriend that Ellen had shared with me, weeks prior, that she could not tolerate any longer. Ellen had stated, "This guy has no job and wants to live off my daughter, he needs to go back East and live with his family."

So now he shows up all sad. She had cried with him the entire day, stating, "I actually sobbed for hours, Angel." At one point, she told me she was going to call her daughter and tell her she needed to take him back, that she had made a wrong decision. Yes, she was going to tell her daughter who to date. Unbelievable! Well, this phone call went on and on about how depressed she has become over everything in life. She now wants to sell the new home and move to a property somewhere on a lake, or as she put it, "I want to get the hell out of here and move to a lake home, or a mountain home in Arizona, or just buy two homes, anywhere but Texas." She told me she now missed her three girls, was tired of Mick's one-hour commute to and from work. Mick had worked from home before and was now gone ten to eleven hours a day. The property was just too much to keep up. Now keep in mind, they had only been at this new home for less than a year.

Ellen then went on and on until she stated, "I was suicidal yesterday, honestly I just don't see the point of living most of the time." I then asked her if she was feeling suicidal now. Ellen said, "No, I guess I'm all right for now." I listened a little longer, and then I told her I was having a few turmoil in my life. Well, guess what, this worked, per usual. As soon as you tell a narcissist you're having a problem, well, they just got to go. "Oh my, hate to cut you off like this, but I just got to the store." It works every time with Ellen.

Whenever Ellen called, I tried my best to fit in what was going on in my day-to-day life, but she just talks over me. She has never been able to deal with the fact that I am happy and thriving, living in Upstate New York. This gal cannot be happy about one little thing in her life, so it literally rips her to pieces if someone else is happy. Thus, the statement, "Oh thank God you answered the phone, Angel, nobody else answers when I call." Gee, I wonder why.

How did I unfriend Ellen? It wasn't hard. I began to tell her I was having all these problems. I made them all up and used reverse psychology on her. My degree is in behavioral science, it was easy. I have not heard from her in months. You see, it's all about Ellen. I may answer the phone again when Ellen calls, I may need more for this book. Who knows, there ends the story of Ellen.

Olivia

I WOULD MEET OLIVIA THROUGH Ellen, at her jewelry party. I had not remembered her, but she remembered me. It seemed the entire neighborhood was at the party I had attended.

She had called me and wanted to set up cleanings right away.

"I heard you are just wonderful at cleaning, and I have this new job now, and please, please come and see my house and talk to me."

It was a full-of-life voice that came across the telephone, that of one like a young girl, lots of happy energy. When I arrived at her house, there were steps, many, many, concrete steps leading up to her enormous house.

I thought, *Is this entire neighborhood built above all these steps?* And yes, the answer is yes, many of the homes had these steps. Steps that were icy and snow-packed in the winter. Most people never shoveled prior to my arrival, knowing damn well that I was coming, but Olivia would!

I would soon learn that Olivia is a power chic, like my beautiful daughter. There to greet me up on the porch was this tiny bubbly blond who seemed to have a greater amount of energy than myself.

"Oh my gosh, I love your hair, who does your hair? Do you remember me from Ellen's party? Well, I still remember her introducing you as her cleaning lady! No mention of your name at all! I was appalled! Nobody likes to hang with Ellen, we are all obligated to go to parties, you know. That's just how this neighborhood works."

As I walked up the stairs she asked again, "Who does your hair?"

I answered with, "I color it out of a box and get it cut now and again, thanks," with a big smile on my face.

Everyone always loved my box-colored hair, I thought it to be quite funny. And then the next thing out of her mouth was, "Well, you need to go to my girl Brooke you will love her."

And so, I went on in the house, and it was like so many others in this neighborhood. Actually a carbon copy and sparsely decorated. I wondered how long she had lived here. The thing that stood out right off the bat was that there was wood, then carpet, then tile. I'm that crazy, these types of things drive me batty, the floors didn't flow. Turned out it drove Olivia batty as well. Over the next few years, all the floors would be replaced with wood.

Now Olivia sports very short blond hair. The type that you can just wash and run with, and it looks great on her small face. Olivia is as petite as you could possibly be but dresses herself in baggy clothes. She has huge blue eyes and is rather plain, but she does plain well. She goes into this big story about how she needs help cleaning because she used to be a stay-at-home mom and babysat her niece, but now she has a sales job where she travels and sells heart machine equipment.

"Traveling was not in my plan at all, but it is what it is, all I really want to do is go back to school and become a gym teacher, but my husband won't let me," she said.

As we walked through the home, I felt as though nobody really lived there, nobody really enjoyed that house. It was like a magazine, not in any way decorated that way, but I mean, everything in its place as if it were positioned that way for show. I thought to myself that she may have done this because I was coming to look at the house, but as the years went by, I realized it was the norm, and that my new client was a severe type-A personality. The walls were all painted dark. The kitchen red, living room navy blue, and every other room dark brown, very depressing. This was not a fun house at all. It was a sad house; I could tell right away.

Over the years to come, her neighbors would say to me, "You realize she cleans the house again as soon as you leave right?"

I always replied with, "Yes, I know she does." Then I would giggle.

It was a pretty clean home, the bathrooms and the floors were dirty, but other than that, pretty kept up and stark.

Two bubbly boys would soon appear. I wondered where they played. The yard outside was the size of a large living room, much like all the yards in this neighborhood, extremely small or no yard at all basically. It seemed like a bedroom community where people didn't spend much time at their residences except to sleep. Typical in the communities that were built on what used to be farmland. Everyone spent their days commuting and working, thus bedroom community was born.

The basement was unfinished but soon-to-be finished, moving the laundry room down there with a bathroom, living room, and bedroom with plenty of area left for storage. Who moves the laundry room from the main floor to the basement? Olivia did. Perhaps she wanted the exercise of running up and down all those stairs to do the laundry, I don't know. This is the normal cookie-cutter house in that neighborhood, nothing special.

What stood out was that when you were looking through the dining room window, you were looking right into the neighbor's window, maybe ten feet between. In their window were neon signs that you would see in a bar. Olivia would soon ask them to keep their blinds shut so that she did not have to see the signs. That's Colorado for you, all the homes are so close together. Claustrophobic to me now, but I didn't know the difference then. That's how we had all lived.

So we came together on a price, and I began cleaning for Olivia. I felt I was there basically because all the neighbors used my service, the house really never needed that much cleaning. As the months would fly by, I would come to meet Olivia's husband, Sam.

Sam looked like Ken, the Barbie doll, and I am not kidding! He kept in shape by riding his bicycle in competition races throughout the mountains and working out at the gym. Sam was the brunette Ken doll. He was tall, about 6'3", almost as if Olivia had picked him out for being perfect or ordered him right out of a catalogue.

But it was his personality that she complained of almost every time I was at the house. Sam, it seemed, did not parent or intermingle with the boys, nor did he help around the home. It was not shocking to pull up to the house on a bitter-cold winter day and see Olivia crawling around on the roof, putting up Christmas lights. "Well, someone has to do it, that asshole I'm married to won't."

The typical conversation was always, "Sam can't do anything right, so why would I even bother to ask him for help with anything?"

And yes, she would say these words right in front of Sam. I felt bad for him. Once a man, or anyone for that matter, is shot down so many times and told so often that they are incapable of anything, well, they usually quit trying or asking if they can help. Olivia would even get upset when Sam wanted to go on a long bike ride on Saturdays.

Sam would look at me and say, "You understand the addiction, don't you, Angel, because you used to run?"

I would always reply with, "Yep, Sam, I do understand."

I felt such pity for Sam; he was belittled on a daily basis to the point where he would end up in the extra bedroom in the basement. It really became his apartment, and this went on for around six years.

He had an office space down there, complete with a living room, bathroom and workout area for his spin bike, which he rode throughout the bitter winter months to keep in shape for the next race. He even had a coffee station. I imagined him having his coffee in the mornings and then making a mad dash out the backdoor to work. It was so odd to see two people living together but living apart really.

I was working in the kitchen one day when Sam popped his head in from the garage asking, "Is she here? Where is she?"

"Upstairs, I believe," I answered.

Then he would make the dash for the basement.

Olivia wanted me to clean on Saturdays many times, and so this is how I saw the family unit operate. It became obvious to me, almost right away, that the oldest son, Wally, was a gay young man.

There were times that Sam and Wally would fight, and then the day would come when Sam would push Wally, and he went flying through the kitchen. I always felt that Sam could not come to terms with the fact that he had a gay son, but it was always like there was a white elephant in the room; nobody really acknowledged that Wally was gay.

Wally had a hair lip and had had many operations to correct it as a very young child, and I felt all these differences caused friction between the two boys and Sam. And this is why I felt Olivia babied Wally so much, I mean he was so small when the surgeries began.

Tommy, the youngest son, was the all-American boy, who is his father's twin. Both boys were chubby and full of life, always happy, but heavy sibling rivalry was always present. The boys never got along well, especially as they got older. Perhaps Wally was always angry because he was the gay one, I don't know, but he was mean to Tommy at every turn. And Wally, he didn't look like anyone else in the family. It was strange, and everyone in the neighborhood talked about it.

Christmas would roll around, and there would be the perfect Christmas tree that had blue ornaments adorning it, always the same, never different, as if it were taken out of a box every year and then put right back in the same order it had arrived.

Olivia would receive homemade cookies from the neighbors, and those cookies would go right in the trash because, as Olivia would say, "You never know how dirty their kitchen is and if they wash their hands after they go to the bathroom."

Yes, that was Olivia. She couldn't relax enough at Christmas to eat a cookie sent over by the little girls next-door.

Things were changing even more because Olivia began to travel frequently for her work, and when she did, her mother would move in for that week because she said she could not count on Sam for anything.

There was even the trip where she said she lost her wedding ring.

"Must have lost it washing my hands," she said.

She would say how hard it was to live life on the road with all the other people in the company she worked for. Going out for drinks and dinner, having so much fun, then coming home and being in a completely different role as a wife and mother. She said sadly, "When I come back home, it's so different."

I found it to be odd, especially when she lost her wedding ring, then replaced the ring with a bigger diamond. I could see Olivia changing. She enjoyed the attention she received from other men when she was on the road for work.

Olivia's closet was filling up with the most beautiful business wear for women, and shoes, so many shoes! The shoes were organized in her closet with pictures of the shoe on each box. This was Ms. Organization to the max. But hey, who wouldn't want that!

There would be Thanksgiving dinners in the home, and then soon, Olivia would want to have the dinners at a fancy expensive restaurant in Denver somewhere.

Sam would be upset, saying, "Can't we please just come back down to earth and eat Thanksgiving dinners at home!" I really don't know if this happened out of necessity for Olivia traveling so much, or if she just became that way from making so much more money. I mean, everything about her was changing rapidly.

Soon her income surpassed what Sam was making, according to her, and the role kept on becoming even more stronger with her being the boss of the entire home. Sam was depleted down to pretty much nothing, as far as his manhood was concerned.

There would be vacations where they would have family photos taken on the beach, and they would all be smiling, one would think it was a happy normal family from the outside. The ski vacations to the mountains would happen more and more, but then Sam began to take trips alone without the family. If Sam did take the boys with him to ski the mountains, they would complain to their mother that they never saw their dad the entire trip! They were on their own, Daddy disappeared.

The boys were growing bigger, and soon Sam would ask Olivia for a divorce. Olivia told me she had informed Sam that there would not be a divorce, and that he would remain in the home until the boys were raised. Olivia would say, "If he doesn't like it, tough, he can just suck it up."

This went on until the boys were in middle and high school, and Sam would then one day pack up all of his belongings and be on his merry way. He had bought a home down the road, in a much-older neighborhood. Sam had met a young waitress with small children and fallen in love. It seemed Sam lusted for a much more normal slow-paced life, with perhaps someone who treated him better. I always thought, *Good for him, a second chance!*

There would still be fights; Sam did not want Wally to have a convertible for his first car. Olivia bought it anyhow, so Sam did not pitch in.

Then the day would come when Olivia would come to me, saying to brace myself. "I have something to tell you that you cannot tell anyone."

"What is that?" I replied.

"Wally has come out, he is gay." She looked down with the saddest face.

I replied with, "Well, hell, Olivia, I have known that since he was six years old, I don't know how you could not?"

I know, not very sympathetic, but my golly, I couldn't believe the white elephant had lived this long in the house! She looked shocked, but I pretty much speak what is on my mind.

She said, "You knew, how could you possibly have known?"

I told her, "How could you have not known?"

That was the end of that subject for a time, and I do believe our relationship was forever changed as friends from that day forward. Some people you just can't be open and honest with, it pisses them off to no end. Oh, they want to be honest with you, to a fault, but you had better not be. That's pretty much Olivia.

Olivia would soon be crawling through Sam's doggie door at his new home, wanting to see what it was like.

I couldn't believe what I was hearing when she told me. She said, "Do you want to go see, you can fit through the door too."

I declined, of course. I couldn't believe what I was hearing. She couldn't stand the fact that he had moved on. She could not believe he had fallen in love with a waitress from Applebee's with small children. She would go on and on about what a horrid father he had been to their two boys and how anyone could date a waitress. Yes, Olivia had changed.

It would not be long before Wally would be wearing finger-nail polish, losing tons of weight, sporting scarves around his neck. He became the supreme gay boy almost instantly. It was as if he just had to burst out with his gayness. He acted out by driving fast through the neighborhood, and when I saw him doing so, I told him he needed to tell his mom what he was up to. He was revving up his car right there on the street while I was talking to him. There were so many small kids in this neighborhood running from house to house. It was scary to me that he would drive in such a way, but he had a sports car, and he acted the part.

Next time I went to the house to clean, I asked him if he told his mom what I saw him doing, and he said no, and so I told him to tell her in front of me.

It was the oddest thing, Olivia just said, "Well, I guess he drives like his mom." And then she laughed.

I found this to be quite shocking for a mother. It would not be long at all before she was sitting in traffic court with her son Wally. He had gotten a ticket for speeding, in a school zone of all things. But to Olivia, this was no big deal at all.

Sam pretty much donated all his time to his new family and didn't spend much time—if any time at all—with the boys. Wally would graduate high school, and Olivia would whisk him off to London for a graduation present.

This present was charged to Sam's credit card before he had moved out; seemed pretty bad to me because Sam had no idea at the time, but Olivia said, "He deserves to pay this." The entire trip, compliments of Sam.

It was so very hard to listen to all the negativity that Oliva was feeding her sons about their father on a regular basis.

She would tell them, "Your dad is an asshole, he pays for nothing, and he doesn't care about you anymore."

I thought to myself, *This is hard enough for these boys, why poison them against their father, they lived it, they knew.* I never got that one. I mean, the kids already lived through the fighting, the uncomfortableness of Sam living in the basement, separate vacations. They knew all he had done and not done, but he is their father, and they should be able to respect him and love him and where they come from. It was brutal, at every turn she condemned Sam to the boys, just shameful, really. So hard to watch!

Sam came from a very good family up in Longmont, and I was sure that very soon, Olivia would end the relationship between them and the boys as well. Why do I know this? Because once she and Sam divorced, she said that the family was not wanting her around any longer.

Well, that's kind of what happens when you divorce; of course, it would be fantastic if everyone still got along for the kids' sake, but it rarely happens.

Olivia had shown up at the hospital when Sam's mother became ill, and Sam politely asked her what she was doing there and to please leave. She didn't take it well at all. They were divorced, and he had moved on. I am sure his parents and siblings had witnessed her condemning Sam throughout the entire marriage.

I would later see Sam and his new wife at the gym together, and once at the movie theater, and I would just look at them and see that Sam was now so wonderfully happy. It was good to see that. He just wanted a normal life with this new gal. A gal that seemed so sweet to him and would look adoringly at him every time I saw them together. I thought to myself that they must have Thanksgiving dinners at home; it was a good feeling.

Soon Wally wanted to go to college, not just any college but Denver University, a very expensive private college. Sam objected once again, stating that Wally was an underachiever who had to be pushed to do any schoolwork at all, and that he was not paying that high tuition. Sam wanted Wally to go to a community college for his first two years.

Well, guess what, Olivia enrolled him into Denver University anyhow, and then complained because Sam would not help with the tuition costs. Olivia never told either one of her boys no, never, ever! Wally, of course, flunked out his first year there, stating that he had social problems because he was gay, people were picking on him.

It was nice around this home while he was away for his first year of college, it was clean in the basement, the boys weren't fighting, and

Oliva seemed more relaxed and finally happier, like when I first met her. But at the same time, she was with Wally two to three nights a week and spent every weekend with him, like she was afraid of letting him go; she was so protective of him because he was gay. I understood her fear, but I didn't understand the suffocation.

Now by this time, Olivia and I had become close friends, and we did a lot of things together, shopping, eating out, going to the movies, you name it, we did it. We had fun. I was single, and she was not dating yet, she had no time for dating between work and being a single mom. She was always such a good friend to me, gave me great gifts on Christmas, and I would give her birthday gifts, but let's face it, I could not give as much to her. I didn't make the same kind of money, and it began to show in our friendship.

Soon she would tell me that I was not getting my Christmas gift any longer, which was a big tip, why?

"Because we are friends, I shouldn't have to tip you on Christmas," she stated.

I missed it because I counted on my tips at Christmastime. What really hurt was that I knew she was still tipping our hairdresser on Christmas, and they hung out together as friends as well, we all hung out together. She began to make it clear that I was the lesser one. The one that needed to move on up in the world, but it wasn't happening, and I began to feel quite judged by Olivia.

Olivia could be quite cruel; I had witnessed it many times. I had inquired about a job in which she needed filled at her work, she pretty much told me, in not so many words, that I certainly was not qualified.

I couldn't believe it. Her degree was in nutrition, and mine behavioral science. It was selling heart monitors. How hard could it be! And I wanted to use my degree and change my life as far as work went.

Olivia's own sister-in-law asked for the job, and she turned her down, saying, "What does she know, all she has done is raise her kids, mow the acreage." So cruel.

Before Olivia got this job, she was babysitting her niece at home, raising her boys. Now she had climbed up in the world to district manager of the Western United States. I felt she had become unusually cruel to everyone around her. Money changes people, indeed, and it certainly changed Olivia.

The house and Olivia had become an uncomfortable place to be after Wally came home from college. So many times, I would tell Olivia that something had to be done about Wally's bathroom shower before I came, as he was vomiting in it, and this was sure not my responsibility to clean up after.

Wally had gone from a husky young man to a very thin man within a short period of time. He had changed his entire diet to gluten-free, and his excuse for the vomit was that he did it when he ate gluten. I was feeling he was doing the vomiting to lose weight. Olivia felt embarrassed at first but then became combative toward me for bringing it up. I mean, really, who vomits in the shower!

Soon she began to complain of everything I was doing while cleaning, and it just was not working for me any longer, mainly because the vomit in the shower continued.

Wally had moved into the basement and was having male friends over, and it was becoming quite the mess in the basement where he now had taken over. Olivia was crying all of the time. She was having an extremely difficult time with her son being gay and having sex in her home. She knew he was having sex because he would shut the door to the basement and tell her not to come down for the rest of the evening. She was scared to death of him contracting a disease and/or getting his heart broken. I felt so badly for her because she had gone through so much. But at the same time, if it were my son, he wouldn't give me the rules in my house.

By this time, Sam was out of the picture completely and had remarried to his new younger gal friend and went on with his new life, having no time at all for either of his sons. It was all so difficult to watch, I had never seen a father reject his family and just go off and begin raising someone else's children. I'd heard of it but never witnessed it firsthand. It was all sad. Olivia watched every move they made on Facebook by watching Sam's new wife's page. And she was so angry with Sam. She told me, "I'm the only parent, and I just can't go out and date or move on, this isn't fair."

It all became too much, and I ended the cleanings because she kept changing her cleaning day, and I couldn't move people around for her every time her life wasn't working the way she wanted it to; nobody could make her happy. I had even heard from our hairdresser that she had been in the salon screaming because her appointment time was not working for her. There was a ton of screaming now in that house, a lot of tears and sadness.

Olivia and I still remained distant friends who were there for each other, but with her, if you are not intermingled in her life, with her every day, then she fades away. One close friend of hers and mine from the neighborhood moved only forty-five minutes south, and Olivia said, "That's it, I'm done being her friend, she moved too far away."

I personally never got that myself. It was difficult to be close friends with her, as she acted so strangely about her son being gay. I could never put myself in her shoes, we all walk through our own journey, and all journeys are different.

Olivia now has a man in her life. They travel the country, and she looks happy. I wish her the best. And I hope this man can step up to the plate. Now that I have moved across the country, I never hear from Olivia at all. She will remarry in the fall. I wish her the best, but most of all, I wish her happiness and contentment in life, and I hope she allows this man to hang the Christmas lights up on the roof.

Lana

L ANA, I PICKED UP, as I had many clients, by hanging fliers on the neighborhood homes that I knew people had the money to spend on housecleaning. My son and I would put on roller blades, and he would hit one side of the street while I hit the other. I would pick up Lana in one such neighborhood.

It was a neighborhood where the homes started out at $250,000 and raise up to $450,000. Lana lived in the $250,000 home, which would be then considered as a starter home in Colorado. As I approached the front porch, I could not help but notice that the yard was covered with round white circles, no doubt from dogs relieving themselves, the only house on the block that had such a yard. I picked up an odd smell as I knocked on the door, a smell I would encounter many times to come at many more homes—they smell of cat urine. Ugh.

I was greeted by a clearly worn-out twentysomething woman who, again, said, "I just can't do it all myself." The conversation then led to the fact that she worked for her in-laws who owned a large party rental business in Denver, and that she was giving herself a raise in order to afford my services.

Lana was short and not a pretty gal, but a cute gal. She sported freckles all over her face and her hair was straight and shoulder-length. Lana didn't dress up, just your normal stay-at-home mom who pretty much always dressed in sweats, pulling her hair back in a ponytail, wearing no makeup. The two little girls—well, they were cute as buttons—always dressed to a T and had every toy in the book.

This small home was clearly a disaster each and every time I walked through the front door. Clothes on floors of each bedroom, toys thrown everywhere in every room. The kitchen and bathrooms always filthy to the point where I could not see the countertops. I would constantly wonder how a house could get so dirty in just two weeks' time. Then it dawned on me—Lana did nothing to clean up or pick up the house within the two-week period before I returned. Everything that dropped onto the kitchen floor was left there until I came back. I'm talking about spilled milk, which turns into concrete! I'm talking about ketchup and oatmeal, pieces of hot dogs, chips, and whatever they spilled during the two weeks. I did not know how any person could walk on a floor that filthy, and then I realized that Lana lived in slippers. But what about the baby that crawled around? I mean, really?

Every time I cleaned, Lana would try to get me to talk about the other clients on my schedule that she was either acquainted with or people whose lives she just wanted the dirt on. It always came down to me saying, "I just really don't have conversations with other clients, they're never home when I am there."

Lana would spend quite a bit of time on the telephone with her mother and gal friends instead of interacting with her children, at least while I was there, the girls were always begging her to look at them and pulling on her legs while she walked around the house talking on the phone. Keeping the house up or preparing healthy meals and snacks, well, that didn't seem to be the game plan. The family lived on mac and cheese out of the box and processed foods that were easily put together, along with the daily trips to fast-food restaurants. And yes, there are still people out there feeding their children this way, even with all the nutritional information that is available almost everywhere we look these days.

It became clear early on that this young couple had tremendous problems. Lana began calling me occasionally from the mall. She had left her home with the girls in tow because of the husband's abuse of marijuana and alcohol. She would be frantic, asking me what she should do next. I would inform Lana that I felt that no woman should leave her home with her kids in tow and to go home.

That a woman who is married to an irresponsible man that abuses marijuana and alcohol should remove the man from the home, at least temporarily, do an intervention, or get help from his parents on what to do, especially since he was driving the girls around under the influence. Lana did not heed my advice yet would leave again and again in the future. Returning each time to tell me that Ed was doing better. Each return home would include either new furniture, a trip somewhere, or more Disney figurines for her collection.

Lana's husband, Ed, was raised by very well-to-do parents in Denver, Colorado, and lived a privileged life. They met while Lana was working at his parents' party rental business as a clerk at the front counter. Ed was not an attractive young man really, but fair-looking, not built well, skinny, with glasses, sloppy-looking, to say the least. Ed was always quiet when I was around. I think he knew that Lana was always telling me their problems, and that embarrassed him.

Lana, on the other hand, came from a divorced family home where her father had nothing to do with her upbringing. She and her mother, along with her sister, had lived in a basement apartment most of her life. She said, "We never had a pot to piss in." And then she would always laugh. Lana said she knew she was going to land Ed the minute she laid eyes on him for the first time; she knew Ed was the owner's son.

Ed would drive the girls around in his vehicle while smoking marijuana, and he would stay out late and party with people he went to high school with. Lana just wanted him to settle down and be a good husband and father, and isn't that what every woman wants?

Lana's mother also worked at the rental business and seemed to be highly involved in the marriage and the business of raising a family. Lana's mother lived in a bad part of town, and Lana gave her a raise in order for her to move near her in a more expensive townhome than she had had. Lana's mother had a long-term boyfriend who lived off of her income. And if she needed work done on her home, the boyfriend did the work but charged her for it! It was beginning to look like the entire family lived off the rental business that the in-laws started many decades ago.

There would be huge birthday parties for each family member, complete with the food catered in, trips to Disney World and California. The neighborhood began gossiping about how Lana and Ed could not afford any of the lifestyle that they were living. Lana wanted the life of the mother-in-law but didn't seem to understand that you work your entire life building a business to get to that point. Lana wanted everything instantly because she married into money, only it was her husband's parents who had the money, a concept that she never quite understood.

Even though there were tremendous problems in her marriage, Lana would soon start throwing huge fits, fighting with him, in order to force her husband into moving across the highway, into the bigger, more expensive home. "If we can't afford it, we will give ourselves a raise," she would say. They sold the home for far more than it appraised for because back then, more people were moving into Colorado than there were homes, thus affording them to move into the bigger, better home but not realizing that they had to keep up the high payments and high HOA dues.

Lana and her husband were now living beyond their means in a $550,000 house in a wealthy neighborhood, and so was her mother. Both house poor, champagne diet with a beer income, like so many do in Colorado. Everyone had to keep up with the Joneses. The more they kept up, the more miserable their lives would become. Now this wealthy neighborhood was finely groomed with the most beautiful trees and landscaping one can imagine. Lana and Ed bought the biggest house and on the golf course. Now at this point, I was thinking they had to have forged paycheck stubs in order to get into this house. Now I am just guessing here, but do the math. They had an even bigger house than a CEO next-door to them. Ed was still working for his parents, and so was Lana. At this time, I had another client who knew Ed's parents, and they were telling everyone that they had no idea how the two of them could possibly afford the house, let alone the HOA fees (homeowner's association) in that neighborhood.

The fighting would continue, the use of marijuana and alcohol rose, Lana wanted new breasts because she said, "My breasts look like hot dogs, do you want to see?"

Of course I declined. TMI! Lana said she deserved the new breasts because her mother-in-law has a face-lift whenever she felt like it. Again keeping up with the parents who worked their entire lives to live the lifestyle that they did.

Lana wanted her neighbor to promise his son to her daughter, both ages five. Lana said that this would be good because his dad made tons of money, and her daughter would always be well taken care of. The friendship soon ended because Lana was so insistent about the kids being promised to each other, and Lana was a needy friend who needed to be sitting in your kitchen all day or talking to you on the phone.

The family rental business was sold in order for the in-laws to set themselves up for retirement. Lana and Ed were soon unable to afford my services and the house. Everything was sold, and the family moved to Virginia where Ed was able to obtain a job outside of the family business. I have never heard a peep from Lana since, and this leaves a smile on my face. I never miss Lana.

Now with clients moving across the highway into the newer richer neighborhoods, moving on up, as they would say, I began to get more and more clients who lived near one another. A client would pick me up and then refer another client to me and on and on and on.

Soon I had the option of turning people away. You had the huge houses that were horrific to clean and the snobby women who wanted me to crawl on my hands and knees to clean the kitchen floors. I'm sorry, isn't this why mops were invented? I would always quote an outrageous price and not worry about those people calling me back. There were the women who would follow me around, asking me *why oh why* I would do this for a living, and oh my, isn't it just awful! "Why on earth are you always smiling?" they would ask. They were not on my schedule for long. And why was I always smiling? Because I could work four to five hours a day and still make big money. It came easy to me.

"You're fast and thorough, like a machine or train moving through the house," the male clients would say. "Man, if only my wife would work like you do and be happy about it." Well, some of my clients figured that if they had the money, then why should they clean their own homes, who could blame them? I mean, I even had a client that would pay you to sew a button on for them.

I cleaned houses like it was a workout. I knew other women out there cleaning that took five hours to do one house where it took me two to three hours to clean the same house. They smoked cigarettes, took breaks, and hated what they did, but I did not. I loved sweating and the money that came after.

Emma

WHEN I FIRST MET Emma, she had already obtained the bigger, more expensive home, but Emma wanted to be across the highway like all of her friends, and within a few short months, that's where she was. Emma convinced her husband to move from a $235,000 home to a $350,000 home and on to a $550,000 home, all within a five-year period. How did they do this? They would build up a little equity, which was easily done at this time, and move to the bigger home. The more equity you had on your home, the more you had to put down on the new home.

Emma was very normal-looking in a plain way, dark hair, blue eyes, light complexion, and thin. She was born and raised in New York State and moved to Colorado with her parents. Emma was full of energy, yet she ate at McDonald's all day long. Emma graduated from Colorado University where she met her husband, Paul. Emma said she took one look at Paul when he walked in the classroom one day and knew he was the one.

Paul was a tall teddy bear type of guy who became very successful in the business world quickly. The family took many vacations every year, and Emma could buy anything she wanted any time she wanted. It was clear that Paul made a ton of money.

There were two children, Johnny and Patty, and they both took after their daddy in the looks department. Two little teddy-bear-looking children full of laughter, always happy-go-lucky children.

The home was full of the nicer furniture and nicer things you can buy for a home. Beautiful drapes, pictures on the walls, and just a finished house from the time they moved in. Emma wasn't great at decorating, and so her mother, who lived in the same neighborhood and worked at a store that sold beautiful French decor items for the home, decorated for her. Of course, she received a huge discount at the store in which she worked.

When I first met Emma, she had a few close friends, but as the next few years would pass, she would lose most of her friends. Emma was prejudiced and didn't mind stating her opinion about it. She was also selfish, my other clients in the neighborhood called her a self-centered bitch that had no empathy for anyone but herself. Emma had four miscarriages, and she actually had to deliver stillborn babies, at five months into pregnancy, four times, never giving her body time to heal. There was a chromosome problem that was hit and miss with every pregnancy. Emma wanted to keep taking the chance for another baby, Paul did not.

After each baby, Emma would get an urn to put in the book-shelf at the bottom of her bed so that was the first thing she would see in the morning and the last thing at night. This practice is not healthy in any way. Emma was constantly in a state of depression and wanting to get pregnant right away after each miscarriage, depleting her body before building it back up again.

Walking up to this enormous new home, as you approached the front porch, there would be a walking stone with each baby's name and date of death. It was an eerie feeling as you walked up to the door, quite a statement is made right there. Around Emma's neck, she wore several necklaces with small heart-shaped lockets con-taining each baby's ashes inside so that every time she looked in the mirror, she would see the lockets, reminding her of all the babies she had lost. She basically was tormenting herself every day, all day long.

Each time Emma would miscarry, she would go into a deeper depression and then turn around and get pregnant again. I had expe-rience in grief counseling at this point, and I had lost a child when she was fourteen years old, and tried to help Emma. I knew it was unhealthy for her to have memorials around her neck and inside the house, but she would not listen to anybody, not her husband, not her mother, not even her father, whom she was very close to.

When my child died, I had two surviving children. I was told to place pictures of my deceased child around the house in order for her siblings to feel more comfortable about her being gone from our lives. Just gone, just like that. That was painful for me because I wanted her home, not in a picture. And the pictures reminded me of my loss each and every day, but I did it for my children. Now twenty-seven years later, I can have her picture out, but not in a place where I walk by it all day; it can take you right back down. There is no worse pain in this life than losing your child.

Emma eventually had a healthy beautiful baby girl, Amy. Amy was the cutest fattest baby in the neighborhood and always had a smile on her pretty little face. The family was so happy to have the new baby in their family, what a joy she was after all the heartache before.

Within six months, Emma wanted to have another baby. Her husband got snipped so that she could not continue this practice. Emma managed to talk herself into yet another depression because she could not have any more children. She became more and more bitter, and all she could ever talk about was wanting to give love to even more children.

Emma would say, "It's not fair, we have so much love to give and more bedrooms to fill."

Emma became introverted and did not leave her home very often, kept the blinds shut all day. It became a chore to collect money from Emma. She would never have the money to pay me, could never find her checkbook; therefore, I would have to go back and knock on her door many times before she would finally pay me.

In the end, I left this client due to the fact that she became so hard to be around with her depression, collecting money owed me, and then there was the affair with the construction man.

Emma and Paul were having their basement finished, and Emma began flirting with the head of the crew. I couldn't help but notice how much this guy resembled Emma's husband, only thin and younger. It wasn't long before they were having a full-blown affair right there in her home. I think her intent was to get pregnant again by this man and somehow fool her husband into thinking it was his—insane! This construction fella would sit in her kitchen and flirt with her right in front of me, it was unreal to watch. I would hear him tell his other workers, "Her ass is to die for, I have never seen such a great ass on a woman." And Emma ate it all up. This behavior was easily performed by Emma, the kids were in school all day, and the new addition was only six months old. Watching her with this man, it was like she had no husband at all to consider. You see, Paul was away on business quite often, so it was easy. I have no idea what went on after I left, and I don't want to know.

Waverly

I MET WAVERLY ON A cold winter afternoon. I can still recall climbing up the many icy steps that led to her front porch. There would be many more times I would climb up those steps with ice and snow because nobody seemed to give a damn that I was coming and unloading my car to pack everything into their house. The laziness of some people shocks me to this day. I quickly learned to bring my snow shovel with me when I had to get into this house after a storm. Waverly was referred to me by a client who had known her a decade prior, when their husbands were in grad school, Angie and her husband, who you will hear about later.

Waverly looked like an overweight blond Barbie doll, was from Canada, and had the accent of a Canadian. I found her accent hilarious. Waverly was tired when we met, and one child was a lot of work for her. She loved being a mother, but like so many other young mothers, her husband traveled for his job, and he traveled often for long periods of time, sometimes up to three weeks at a time. Being a young mother was overwhelming to this gal, and she was still so young to be so tired, but she was on her own quite a bit.

Waverly's house was in a neighborhood that was upcoming and new, with homes ranging from $450,000 and up. When I walked into the home for the first time, there was not a ton of furniture to make it homey, no upgrades, curtains, blinds, you name it, the house was all around sparse, cold. This was a house that was just getting established. Waverly had a background in design, and that is what she went to college to study, so I knew it was going to be fun watching what she did with the future. I have learned so much from clients like Waverly. To this day, people walk into my home and say it looks like something they would see in a magazine, I love the compliments.

Waverly had one little girl, Angela, who was only two years old when I met them. Angela was a chubby gal with locks of golden-blond hair, a toddler with tons and tons of energy who liked to have tea parties over the phone with her grandmother in Canada.

Now little Angela's room looked like a designer had furnished it; this room was indeed finished, what a beautiful room it was for a little girl! A pink crystal chandelier adorned the ceiling, walls painted with pink and cream strips, a beautiful white overstuffed rocking chair with ottoman, table and chairs to have tea parties, the most beautiful floral rug in the middle of the room, and many, many clothes filled her closet. It looked like something you would see in a high-end magazine. Waverly had the touch, and it showed in this toddler's bedroom but nowhere else in the house, not yet.

Waverly's husband, Brett, worked for the meat industry and made a good income. "Buy all your meat at Costco, Angel, they have the best meat," he would say to me. Brett was not a tall man nor was he built, but he was handsome in his own way. Brett seemed to me, like a small-town boy who had come from a good family. He always had a big smile on his face, as if the world was his. He was easy to be around, and oh how his wife and little girl were happy when he was home.

Waverly would often complain to me how lonely she was and how difficult it was for her to be alone with a toddler day after day. Waverly was tired of Brett always traveling, and so he quit his prestigious job, within a year of my knowing them, in order to find another local position where he did not have to travel. Now keep in mind that Brett was making a ton of money working for the meat industry, no doubt in the $250,000 range. This house was just getting established when he quit his job. And when Brett quit his job, the money was going quickly out the door on bills. Any planned decorating came to a halt, and the fights would soon follow.

At first Waverly loved Brett being home, but she would soon begin complaining about him being home, in her way, wanting sex all the time. "He wants sex all the time, I can't stand it anymore," she would say. Many months would pass without Brett being employed, and so he began looking at different options, like starting his own business so that he could be his own boss. Waverly was getting worried because she said the money they had saved had dwindled away.

Brett needed investors, and that was his mission for the time being, finding the investors to start his own business, but what was it to be? Nobody knew yet, including Brett, what this new business might be. He was still researching.

Waverly was always forthcoming and wanting to share all her problems with me. She was the most talkative client I had ever picked up, following me all over her house while I cleaned. I could tell there was a void in her life, no doubt missing her mother in Canada and her husband because he began traveling again, looking for investors. She had a ton to talk about and seemed insecure, nervous, and unorganized about what to do each day with her time.

Waverly confided in me that her husband had filmed them making love, while she was pregnant with their daughter, without her permission, and she was upset about it. She told me Brett put a movie in one night for them to watch, and that was the movie. She told me that the whole thing made her feel dirty, and she was wondering what else he was capable of. She was afraid of her own husband, and she didn't trust him. Well, this gal just listened because quite honestly, I didn't know what to say about the entire ordeal. Why would any man want to film his wife while they're having sex, while she's pregnant!

Waverly said Brett was not the man she preferred to marry, but that he was nice to her and his family had money. "I knew I had to marry someone who would have money, Angel, his family is loaded. I mean, isn't that why all us women go to college anyhow, to get our 'Mrs. Degree?'" Well, okay then. This was the first time I had heard that phrase.

Waverly's boyfriend in college had dropped her, broken her heart, and she said she knew the best thing to do was to marry Brett. She explained that she wanted to marry someone from money, she did not want to struggle her entire life as her mother had, being married to a policeman, and then divorcing. As she would put it, "My mom doesn't have a pot to piss in."

One day Waverly found a name and phone number in Brett's pocket and asked a friend to call the number. Turns out the number belonged to an escort service in Atlanta where Brett had previously traveled to for work quite often. Waverly confronted Brett, and he admitted to seeing a regular woman there at the escort service, stating that he needed someone to talk to, and that all they did was talk, no sex. He told Waverly that all she ever did was complain and that he didn't feel loved.

The marriage survived this hiccup, I think because the couple received extensive counseling. Waverly always had a difficult time trusting Brett after this, even after therapy. She would have a complete meltdown every time he was out of town, no doubt thinking he was up to no good.

It was obvious to me that Waverly was very unhappy yet accepting of her situation, perhaps she felt stuck. What is a woman thinking in her mind after this happens? It must be total betrayal and confusion about her entire life. And what on earth would she do on her own? Every time he touched her, did she think about him being with another woman, and an escort at that! It had to be draining, to say the least.

Waverly and Brett ended up filing for bankruptcy before it was all said and done but were able to keep their home. Brett was not finding investors quickly enough. Brett's parents in Canada had already begun funding their son months earlier in order for them to survive. Waverly constantly complained that she could not shop at the grocery stores, with all the organic foods to choose from, buy the best makeup, and get her hair done.

Eventually Brett found investors to help him start his own business selling a healthier charcoal to burn for grilling your food that he began promoting through health food stores locally and throughout other states. Brett began traveling more and more to market his new business, and Waverly would return home to Canada for visits, with her daughter in tow. Waverly would stay with her mother or father and have a wonderful time visiting old friends while in Canada. She began to be happy again. And she began to make the trips quite frequently.

While on one particular visit to Canada, Waverly ran into her old college flame who had dropped her. She claimed to fall in love with him all over again after seeing him just once. Returning from that visit, she came home with a whole new outlook in life, began working out on her treadmill two to three hours a day, and dieting until she looked like a white-faced mime, so pale and so thin.

Now this old flame from college was now an elevator repairman who didn't come close to giving her the lifestyle in which she was accustomed to. Waverly said she could not fight what she felt, and that she had to go back to see him and tell him how she felt. This trip did not take place until she got in shape and had breast implants— yes, breast implants!

Waverly stated, "My breasts have to look like they did in college so that I can be with him." My goodness, she had lost her mind! And following the breast implants, she had a buttocks lift. One day it had dawned on her that her ass didn't look the same as when in college either!

Waverly would lose about twenty or more pounds. She kept spending hour after hour on the treadmill and began barrowing clothes from wealthy girlfriends, such as three-hundred-dollar blue jeans to wear when she would travel to Canada to see this guy. She started looking like a movie star or a model, not like prior days when she wore baggy sweatpants and pulled her hair back in a ponytail with no makeup on. I mean back then, this gal had no zest for living. But she did now. The excitement factor before each trip back to Canada was off the scales.

Suddenly I was observing a whole new Waverly who had reinvented herself; it was as if she wanted to be in college again and doing everything she did in college, at least that was how she was dressing.

And so a long-distance affair was ongoing. The two began writing love letters back and forth as she could not visit Canada as often as she wanted. She had a shoebox full of letters that she kept at a girl friend's home so that her husband would never find them, this gal friend was my client Angie. She would soon find a way to make numerous trips back and forth to Canada, borrowing Angie's entire wardrobe, along with her Luis Vuitton purses, jewelry, and expensive shoes and boots. All this for the elevator repairman, what was she thinking? And what was this guy thinking? No doubt he knew that he could never afford her, he had to be in it for the thrill.

Waverly, a wife and a mother, was making love to this man behind Brett's back. This was no longer a fantasy in her real life, but she was living out what time she had spent with this guy back in college. It was crazy to watch, and when her husband was home, well, I could not look him in the eye when he spoke to me. I knew he could be quite an ass of a guy because of all Waverly told me, yet I felt such guilt and pity for him. Had everything she told me about Brett been a lie? I mean, it was Waverly that was doing the crazy things in her life. I had never seen Brett do anything but nice things. It wasn't right what she was doing. And I mean, really, what the hell was she doing? This guy who repaired elevators would never be able to give her the lifestyle she wanted. If anything, this guy had to be thinking that he could never keep up with her lifestyle, if he knew anything at all about what her wardrobe cost. He had it made. This married woman came and went from the United States and never hung around, interfering with his life there, really.

Perhaps she thought her husband had had an affair or perhaps it was the escort service ordeal, this was all I could come up with, revenge maybe? If it was, she never shared that with me. I kept thinking revenge because what future would she have with this man? Had her dreams of having money her entire life vanished? Was she just looking for love now? I don't know.

And as history repeats itself so many times, the love affair ended just as it had in college, the elevator repairman dropped Waverly yet again. Waverly went into a deep depression, gained the weight back, let herself go, as they say. No more makeup and keeping up with the hair color. No more trips back to Canada but instead began flying her mother in from Canada, and often. I mean, someone had to take care of the toddler because Waverly was taking a huge nosedive. The next thing I knew, Waverly was pregnant. I couldn't help but wonder who the father was. I mean, it had not been that long since she was sleeping with the old college fling.

The joy returned in Waverly. She glowed as if she was in love all over again. She began cooking great dinners and baking again, the house became more important. She was actually decorating and designing rooms that had never been finished.

Brett was making more and more money, and they were doing well. There were trips that not even my richest clients could or would take. Trips to the most expensive resorts in Mexico and Hawaii. The new baby boy, Jacob, was born, and life was good. But all this joy wouldn't last for long.

Like with so many Canadians that move to the United States, Waverly and Brett had come to Colorado on visas. Canadians only had so many years that they can live here in the United States before they have to return to Canada, unless they are married to an American, and Waverly and Brett were both Canadian.

Waverly was very upset that they had to return. The winters were long, cold, and gloomy in Canada, and they would have to live in a small bungalow house. They wouldn't have the same lifestyle as in Colorado. It is quite expensive to live in Canada; a small bungalow home costs triple in Canada what it would in Colorado at the time. Again I witnessed Waverly going into a downward slope physically and emotionally. I had seen another client have to return to Canada as well. These women cry constantly while preparing to move; they hate Canada, it's almost as if one's watching them prepare to go to prison or some god-awful place. Who could blame them? Colorado has more sunny days than Florida. Canada has short summers and gloomy, cloudy, bitterly cold winters.

It was not long before the house would be sold, and they would return to Canada for two years. Angie informed me that Brett would continue traveling back and forth for the business. After two years in Canada, the family returned and bought a home with an approximate value of $800,000. Angie was appalled. Here these two had filed for bankruptcy just a few short years prior and had a more expensive house than Angie, whose husband was a high-end attorney. Angie would later find out that the house was purchased with the help of Brett's investors. Angie felt a little better about that!

My service was not retained after their return from Canada. There were rumors that they were house poor, living beyond their means, they still had to make the house payment for an $800,000 home. Their children were even in private schools. They went on to have two more children. Waverly had always said that she was going to space out her children so that she would never have to work at "a real job." I guess all her dreams did come true, that is, except for the elevator repairman.

I did see Brett in the health food store in my neighborhood one afternoon, but I could not look him in the eye because I had felt so much guilt about what I knew had happened in their family.

I had never seen a woman come back to life so many times because of life situations; here they were, back in Colorado. I was always grateful that she never called me again, and I didn't have to worry about seeing her at Angie's house. They had had it out over the Canadian affair, which disgusted Angie.

Lena

I WOULD MEET LENA WHILE her husband, Brad, was cooking a spaghetti dinner along with their friend Tasha who had just moved in with them after an accident left her penniless. I was asked to stay for dinner, but I declined. My first thoughts were of what kind people they were, and how easy they were to talk to, I felt comfortable with them right away.

Lena was a very tall blond with hazel eyes, very naturally beautiful, a young mother. When you first meet Lena, you know right off the bat that she has a beautiful gentle heart of gold. Brad was a shorter man, good-looking, and a teacher working on his PhD in order to get a better-paying job. They had met while Brad was in college and fell in love, but he would return to college, breaking up with Lena. Brad would later appear and do his very best to win back Lena, knowing apparently that he had made a mistake after playing the field in college. Lena said, "I made him work really hard at getting me back because he really broke my heart."

Lena grew up in a trailer park, and she had told me she dreamed of getting out of there and that someday she knew she would just fly right out of that trailer park, and she did because now, she lived in the big beautiful house, one of the biggest houses in the neighborhood.

Brad grew up with a contractor for a father and a stay-at-home mom. He had a good upbringing and lived in a middle-class neighborhood. Both Brad and Lena would tell me at dinner parties later on that neither one of them are really smart and that they had to work hard to get where they were. Nobody helped them. I think they did pretty good! Their dinner parties were always fun to go to. Such nice down-to-earth people.

Lena and Brad had one daughter, Rachel, age six, who was Lena's twin. Rachel was a very shy and quiet little girl. Her room was a big beautiful room full of beautiful things. Lena said Rachel would be their only child because she knew right away that she did not want to give birth again, it had been difficult for her. "I don't know why any woman would do that again, it was horrifying." Obviously she had had a difficult pregnancy and childbirth.

Tasha was a childhood friend of Lena's who had lived in Oregon and worked in a greenhouse there, never married. Tasha was short and pretty with dark hair and a huge friendly smile. She, like Lena, was very sweet. Tasha had been in a car accident which made it impossible for her to work, so she returned to Colorado. She would be at the residence for about two years before she would move out and marry. In the meantime, she made the most beautiful necklaces and bracelets, and yes, this gal bought one to help her out! I picked the African teardrop necklace, a necklace of many beautiful colors and each piece in the shape of a teardrop. The one necklace that I still wear to this day, and every time I wear it, people tell me how beautiful it is. Thank you, Tasha!

Cleaning Lena's house was fun because it was really never that dirty, and it was big and beautiful, big rooms are easy to move around in. Lena had started design school before she met Brad, she never finished, but I thought she had a natural gift and didn't need any schooling for it. Lena had a knack at decorating. She could walk into a room and decorate the entire place in her mind. I now have that knack, thanks to all the designers and natural decorators that I worked for. I learned it all from them.

At this time, Brad was having a difficult time climbing the ladder in the school district he was in, and surrounding districts had the same philosophy—they didn't hire people in their early thirties to run schools. And so, the family would move north of Denver, into another district where Brad was able to obtain a much-better-paying job, and soon, he would get his PhD and be running a school there.

Lena would decorate the new home and make it beautiful. It was a sprawling ranch-style home with a full basement in a beautiful new neighborhood where they built the homes around the existing trees, so it was just very plush-looking for a new-build neighborhood outside of the Denver area; after all, Denver sits in the high desert.

Most new neighborhoods around Denver have a five-foot sprig of a tree in the front yard and that's it. In the new neighborhoods, everybody sits at their window looking in everyone else's windows because the houses are built so close together, and there are no trees. And if you want to plant a tree, forget it, unless you have the permission of the HOA (homeowner's association), and good luck with that one. In most neighborhoods, you even have to paint your home within the guidelines, and that is about four colors to choose from.

Every upgrade you can imagine was in this home: Italian glass tiles on the walls of the laundry room that looked like the water in Mexico, just beautiful, and travertine tiles on the bathroom floors, granite countertops, the largest kitchen island, or should I say continent, I had ever seen, along with a humongous soaking tub in their master bathroom!

I had walked through the same model home built by the same builder in a neighborhood right outside of Denver, but this home was like walking into a magazine.

How did Lena and Brad afford all of these upgrades? Well, by this time, Lena was working for the builder in the area in their showroom, helping people pick out what they wanted in the new homes being built just for them. Lena did very well at this job because she had great taste and could talk anybody into upgrades, she was a good saleslady.

The family adopted a Great Dane, and in the years to come, Lena would work closely with the Great Dane Adoption Center. The Great Dane was beautiful; Oliver was his name. Oliver was so big that he would take up their entire king-size bed. All the furniture was covered with sheets for the hair shedding of Oliver. Lena was allergic to Oliver and took allergy meds to have him. Oliver was loved tremendously by this family. What do Great Danes do? They are very loving and gentle dogs that pretty much just like a walk two times a day, and then they just lie around. They're really cool, and if they didn't shed so much, I would have one, and then of course, I like room in my bed.

Lena was the type of woman that would spend $500 or more on a pair of high heels and prepare dinner naked in those high heels so that when Brad came home, he would not be angry about the shoes she bought. Lena would even have an aphrodisiac cookbook out on the kitchen island to prepare meals.

When Lena attended a going-away luncheon before leaving her old neighborhood, she talked about the sex she and Brad had and bragged about how great it was. That's just how she was. One of the gals I cleaned for in her old neighborhood who attended the luncheon, Ellen, would later say, "It was embarrassing to eat with her, I mean you can take the girl out of the trailer park, but you can't take the trailer park out of the girl."

"Oh my God what comes out of her mouth! She thinks it's okay to talk about sex. Well, some of us don't get to have great sex!" Jealous, obviously.

I thought that was a horrid thing for someone who considered themselves a friend of Lena's to say, but the friend did look like a boy and was always unhappy, I think, obviously jealous of Lena and her beauty.

In the uppity neighborhoods that I worked in, there was always jealously toward the woman who looked like a model yet had the biggest heart of anyone else. Jealousy is ugly. Why can't people just be happy for other people? The world would be a much better place, let me tell ya! And if we were all the same, wouldn't it just be so boring a world?

Brad and Lena had me over for dinners, fixing me up with men that were never my type, always in the teaching field. They were so nice to try, and they had such good intentions. You know, when you're single and have been for a while, everyone wants to fix you up.

"We need to find a guy for you," they would all say. As if I would fade away and die without a guy!

I am positive that all single women get so bored hearing those words from almost every person they know. My times alone, when I had no boyfriend, sometimes for a few years, well, I grew and I loved that time of my life. It's like being eighteen again, and you can do whatever you like anytime you like. Why do married people think that women have to be in a relationship? Do they think we all have to have a man?

A guy I met at one of their dinners was really nice, not good-looking or well built at all, intelligent, recently divorced, and desperate to find someone to spend time with. Lena had told me earlier that he had a big house in Highlands Ranch. Everything is about who has what in Colorado, or at least the Greater Denver area. Or perhaps she just wanted me taken care of, not working so hard anymore. I don't know. The big house, well, it's not important to all of us, certainly not after we raise our kids.

I don't think the three of us knew most of the big words this guy used at dinner that evening, and Brad and I were both in college, he getting his PhD. Lena had even made the statement that she and Brad were average smart. This man was dumbfounded that none of us received the newspaper every day.

I don't recall why I bothered, perhaps I just wanted dinner out in the company of a gentlemen, but I had a second date with him in a beautiful restaurant where I had the pleasure of listening to him talk about what went wrong with his marriage for four extremely boring, long, tortuous hours.

Turned out his ex-wife had now become a lesbian and left the marriage for a woman she was having an affair with. I had heard this story from men more than once. These men just can't figure out why it happened. It's like their manhood is robbed from them after this experience, they don't get past it easily.

Personally I believe people are born gay, and some try to fight it and go on to marry and have children, and then one day, they just can't play that part any longer, so they divorce. Now these men, they are nice enough, but they just can't get unstuck, they're so pissed off, they just can't get over it. I mean really, our first date alone together, and I have to be a counselor for four long hours. Believe me, the nice dinner was not worth the torture, even though I felt such empathy for him. He was in no way over it or ready for a real relationship yet. I never answered the phone again when he called, I just couldn't.

Another associate Brad fixed me up with said to me, "Brad asked me if I had a problem with going out with a cleaning chic." I could not believe Brad portrayed me in that way.

Now this guy was frumpy, drove a beaten-up older car, and had me follow him all over Denver to the restaurant we were going to. I never went on a second date with that fella again either, and I looked at Brad in a whole different light after that. I mean, really? I was running my own business, going to college FT, and quite an independent hardworking woman.

What do men want? I thought to myself.

I walked away from that one date thinking that I really didn't give two shits what any man wants. Love yourself first. And this was a blind date; I mean, I would not have looked at this frumpy guy twice. Really, Brad!

I told Lena that I really didn't want to be fixed up any longer, but I never told her what the man said to me, and I never looked at Brad as the same man I thought he was. Before that, I always respected Brad, but now he just had a mask on to me.

Brad lost his job after a few years, and so they could not afford my service any longer. I sent Christmas cards their way but never heard back. Lena worked in a furniture store for some time, and I had lost touch with them.

I heard through the grapevine that Brad was again running another school and that Lena was working independently as a designer to rich women, she had no limit on the budgets to remodel their homes. That their beautiful daughter was gay, and that they were very accepting of her lifestyle. They had lost friends due to the fact that their daughter would take them to her room in their basement and try to make out with them. All this gossip came from Ellen whom Lena thought to be her dear friend. Such a sad thing.

They had spent several years trying to adopt a little girl from India, Brad had made many trips there, but the adoption fell through for whatever reason. This broke my heart to hear.

These were kindhearted people who meant to do good in the world. They too have fallen into the world of making tons of money. They will fly to San Francisco to eat dinner. Not one person from the old neighborhood that I keep in touch with ever hears from them. I wish them well because Lena is a sweetheart.

Blair

BLAIR WAS REFERRED TO me by her neighbor two doors
down. They didn't speak much, and that's a whole other story
I will tell you about later. Blair, the bold wholesome tall blond,
who, without a doubt, was the boss of her home. It took me about
five minutes to realize that she was the boss because her smaller husband, John, was hushed each and every time he tried to get a word
in edgewise.

Blair was going back to teaching grade school in a job share program and thought she would be needing some help around the house.
The job share program allowed teachers to share a classroom, each
working only two or three days a week, every other week. While in
this program, Blair intended on obtaining a few certifications which
would allow her to make more money teaching. She also had a master's degree; we all know that never hurts. She intended on acquiring
many certifications over the years with the intention of retiring at
$65,000 a year—not bad. Blair was quite smart, she reminded me of
my daughter.

John was about a foot shorter than Blair, a small man's build.
Not a bad-looking man. John worked out of the home and was always
there when I cleaned. I was never informed of what John did for a living. I was always under the impression that he sold some kind of gear
to sporting goods stores since his office had sporting paraphernalia
everywhere you looked. He would brag about their stock in Target
and how smart he was to buy into it. John's office was right off of the
laundry room and extremely small, hard to clean because you could

barely move around in that room, and all that dirt and dust came in from the laundry room.

They had three kids. The oldest a son, Tommy, an all-American blond-haired boy, a daughter, Madeline, who resembled a princess, and then David, who was behind in every way and who they would soon get tested and find out that he has ADHD (attention deficit hyperactivity disorder) and seemed slightly mentally disabled. John would later tell me that they had had the perfect family until the third child was born and messed everything up. I knew at that moment that John was not a real nice person, and I would never feel comfortable around him again.

In my world, every child is a blessing, and if there are problems, then we are to help them through life and learn many lessons on the journey. Children are a gift from God—every child—and gifts come in many forms. John used this as an excuse to smoke marijuana. He would say, "Who can blame me, look what I deal with on a daily basis?"

This was a very sad and weak man I was listening to.

The home was decorated traditional. The landing on the stairway adorned a large picture of Blair, at least three feet by six feet—just her, not John—in her wedding gown, standing dead center on a beautiful stairway that was obviously in a grand-event center or high-class clubhouse, somewhere back in Oklahoma where they were both raised. You could see the picture from the living room and the kitchen. As soon as I saw that portrait, it reinforced my opinion of who the boss was of this home.

There was nothing special about the home, it was one of the smaller homes in the neighborhood. The home was dark in every way—dark walls, dark cabinets, dark drapes, dark countertops, you name it, it was all dark. The kind of house that made your mood drop while you were in it, quite depressing.

This house was on my every-other-week schedule, and it didn't pay top dollar because Blair was so tight with money. I took on the house because it was right around the corner from my house, so I literally had no drive time.

Now right off the bat with Blair, I was treated as though I was a smaller person than her, meaning that I was the cleaning lady, not to be talked to unless addressed by her, and then it was a very short and choppy conversation. Well, not really a conversation but short orders. I would normally not pick up a client with this attitude, but I would let this go because Blair was usually not home when I cleaned.

John, on the other hand, went out of his way to be friendly. He would meet me at the front door, help me unload my supplies, and ask me if I would like coffee. This was polite and kind at first, but led to him wanting to help me clean, offer to help change the sheets on their bed, which was something I did in no other home, but Blair insisted on it. There were days when John would say, "Let's go golfing, Blair will never know." I would decline of course, thinking he was just having one of those days where he wanted to do something his wife would hate. She was the boss.

John would tell me that all his wife ever did was boss him around and make him remodel the five-year-old house, like putting in new tiles or hardwood floors, wanting walls torn out, a new kitchen, adding a new room where the foyer was to add an extra bedroom above. It was one of those relationships where John was treated like an employee or something similar; she just gave him orders. I never witnessed any kind of affectionate words or gestures between Blair and John. One day he told me I looked like an older Jenny McCarthy. "In that sexy way," he said. I was always relieved when I knew he would not be there for whatever reason when I cleaned.

Within one year of me cleaning, John would hire the neighbor across the street to be his assistant. He said things were picking up in his business, and he really needed someone to run errands for him around town so that he could work in the office all day. Now this neighbor gal was a petite pretty dark-haired woman, always happy and giggling as she made her way into John's office. She was a mother and married. I never knew her personally or professionally, I only saw her come in through the garage, passing through the laundry room, and swooping right into the office, slamming the door behind her. Now when the office door shut, let me tell you, there were sounds that came from that room that you just wouldn't believe was happening while I was in the house.

Those two were obviously having sex while I was cleaning, and they were not quiet about it one little bit. I thought, *Are you kidding me, really, is this really happening?* John had found someone willing to be naughty with him, and he was rebelling against his wife. So now here I am, wondering, *What the heck?* I just did my work and minded my own business and felt sorry for Blair because she obviously had no clue whatsoever, I wasn't the one who was going to tell her what was going on behind her back in her own home. The result would be me getting fired.

There would be many times where Blair would leave me cash for my pay. Then the day came when John asked me if I had enough money to get by. "How many clients do you have now, Angel?" "Don't you do two houses every day?" Questions like that. I would count my cash and go about my business, cleaning, leaving the cash in my Day-Timer, which I always carried with me.

I have lived out of a Day-Timer for about thirty years now, since my days working at Continental Airlines as a reservation sales agent, where my schedule would change almost daily and vice versa with my cleaning business in later years. So this one day, when John asked so many questions about my income, he helped himself to $10 of my money, and then he left the house. I had previously thought that my Day-Timer had been disturbed while I was in this particular house, but I excused it from my mind. There were times I would accumulate cash and checks all week without going to the bank. What a lowlife John was and, no doubt, still is to this day. I never told Blair about the affair or John helping himself to my money, she just was never approachable for any kind of conversation, except to hand out orders. I always felt I was being put in my place. Blair's mother was divorced from her father, who had affairs throughout their marriage. I thought Blair had married the same type of man as her father.

Blair's father had married a girl in Okinawa forty years younger than himself within the past year. Her father visited once with his new wife, and it was rather shocking how young she was because it was like watching a grandpa with his young granddaughter. Blair's father was a retired engineer and had plenty of money. Of course, John chased the new young wife all over the house during that visit, and when he looked at her, you could almost see the saliva running down his chin, it was that bad! Blair was appalled that her father married such a young girl and was concerned that her father would change his will and leave all his money to this new young wife.

I quit cleaning after I had realized John was taking my money, and it was just too hard to see what he was doing behind Blair's back with the neighbor. I saw Blair, John, and the kids at my neighborhood pool a year after I quit cleaning their home. I recall her snubbing me and looking at me like I didn't belong there. Funny, I thought, because my neighborhood was more upscale than theirs. Some people never change!

I often wonder if this couple is still together or if Blair ever had a clue who she was married to.

Christy

C HRISTY AND I MET on a Saturday afternoon while cleaning the townhome neighborhood that I had bought into. It was a beautiful fall day, and several homeowners gathered to plant bushes and do the yard work around our townhomes.

Unlike the previous townhome I had leased, there were no services for the grounds here, so there we all were, doing it ourselves, pride in ownership. Christy was dressed like a farmer's wife who had just stepped out of the barn, stained worn-out sweatshirt and torn jeans. Christy was short, wore no makeup, under 4'5" tall, and obese, with thinning brunette hair. My first impression was that Christy was a tenant, and like so many of the other tenants, no doubt, had little money. Christy was not friendly at first, but as we began to get to know each other, working throughout the day, she told me she had bought her mother a townhome in the neighborhood.

Christy was a member of the HOA board and wanted to know if I would like to join in. Of course I accepted because I like to be involved in the community in which I live. The board was pretty much nonexistent, and something had to be done. The buildings needed new roofs and paint, the sidewalks were coming up in places, and the fencing needed to be replaced. My previous townhome neighborhood was upscale, and I had bought into this townhome in order to fix it up and flip the home, and back then, well, it was all this gal could afford.

Christy had had a service clean her home prior, and she said that their people had stolen her one-carat diamond earrings, and she just did not trust anyone to go in her home again unless she knew them personally. So one thing led to another, and the next thing you know, I was driving to Christy's home to give her an estimate on cleaning.

We had already had a HOA meeting by this time, and Christy was a real earthmover at this meeting. It was apparent things were finally going to get done. She wanted to gain equity in her property like myself. You know how people give you a first impression, and you get to know them a little, and you form a picture of their life in your mind? Well, this gal had Christy all wrong, I could not have been more off track about how I supposed her life was.

Driving into the private airstrip neighborhood in Louisville, Colorado, I could see that there were not too many homes, and that they had at least two acres each, which is rare in Colorado unless you have money, and I mean a lot of money. I could not believe the home I pulled up in front of after passing a few small and older homes.

Christy's home was an adobe-style home, a four-plane hangar built onto the home with an airstrip behind it. At first, I thought I must be at the wrong residence, but nope, it was her house. The front yard was well-groomed with tall grasses and desert flowers, a massive horse sculpture in the center. The entrance to the porch was grand with an enormous custom-made double door. I realized then that Christy had told me they came to Colorado from New Mexico, so perhaps that is why the adobe style felt like home to her. You don't see many adobe style homes in Colorado, at least not the metro area.

Christy greeted me at the door and looked pretty much the same as she always had—frumpy. Just goes to show, some people don't dress like they have money, don't go on about the wealth they have, and just want to blend in with everyone else. Christy didn't come from money and was clearly taking care of her aging mother by buying her a townhome. I thought it was admirable of her.

Christy, her husband, and two friends had come to Colorado from New Mexico. They all were camping in a campground, ate beans, slept in tents, and then a huge hailstorm hit Colorado. They supplied siding to residents swiftly and began their own siding business. It didn't take long before they had built a huge business in the Denver area and became enormously wealthy.

The home was a sprawling ranch-style home with an addition built above the garage. There was a long fifteen-foot-wide open hallway that led back to the three bedrooms, three bathrooms, a laundry room, and, oh yes, the hangar. Not many people have an airplane hangar built onto their home. Along the wall of the hallway were Bev Doolittle paintings with lights over them, like you would see in a museum or art gallery. I was amazed.

Christy's bedroom was the size of three master bedrooms in any other home, and so was her bathroom. Her shower was as big as my entire bathroom. There were French doors that led from the bedroom into an enclosed hot tub room with a view of the entire front range. Christy said, "The floors are all heated because we have so far to walk from the kitchen to our bedroom, and with the tiles, well, we didn't want our feet to get cold." My, my, could I please be that spoiled someday!

The living room and dining room were open, with windows along the west side of the house taking in that grand mountain view. The dining room had a custom-made table that sat twenty-eight people. The table was beautiful. The patio was long and wide and ran around the entire back of the home meeting up with the hot tub room.

Christy's kitchen island was indeed a continent. The island had small refrigerators built into it, along with a microwave and wine fridge. The kitchen had granite countertops and a beautiful huge refrigerator that you would never know was there because it was covered with cabinet fronts. The cabinets were Southwest-style, matching the entire interior of the home.

This was clearly a home like I had never seen before, but wait, it didn't end there. Off the kitchen was yet another laundry room. Christy stated, "We have to have two laundry rooms because the other is just mainly for my husband to use for his greasy clothes that he wears while working on his airplane and helicopter." Christy's husband, Tony, was building a replica of a World War II helicopter. The hangar was like walking into a large warehouse, shelves going up all the walls, planes, and Corvettes—yes, he collected both. I was amazed.

There was a large and beautiful office off the living room that adorned elegant office furniture, again large windows, only looking off to the east, more Doolittle paintings; somehow they looked larger than the ones in the great hallway. As you entered from the garage, you were greeted by a gym—a full gym with mirrored walls and a tanning bed to boot! Christy said, "Now anytime you want to stay after and work out, you are more than welcome because someone needs to use it, we certainly never do." I belonged to a gym so that was never happening, and I mean really, where was the pool? LOL.

A small nook office was right around the corner from the kitchen. Beside the nook were steps that went upstairs to what I knew just had to be a great room with couches and a television. *Perhaps a half bath*, I thought to myself. As I reached the top of the stairs, I saw a large game room with pool table, foosball table, ping-pong table, and air hockey, along with numerous pinball machines, and off to the side, a full kitchen. The entire area was decorated like a '50s diner, so cute!

Off the game room was a bedroom with a full bathroom decorated and designed to fit in with the game room, it was a continuous '50s theme. It was something to see. Off to the back of the game room, I entered a movie room that was like walking into an airplane, and I'm not kidding, complete with airplane seats and a big movie screen, the biggest I had seen to date. The walls were the panels of the inside of an actual airplane. It was unbelievable. I kept thinking to myself, *These people are fun!*

So all in all, this house was the mother of all houses I had ever been in, and believe me, I have been in some beautiful homes. My late uncle Jim built custom homes, and I was dating a man at the time who built custom homes. I thought I had seen it all before I saw this house, I was pleasantly wrong.

I admired Christy because she did not flaunt her wealth. I had other clients at the time who would wear only designer clothes and handbags and drive Mercedes Benz cars, yet they lived in $400,000 homes. This particular home had to be in the range of $3,000,000. This house would not be difficult to clean because it seemed to be pretty organized and relatively clean, decorated sparsely, but there was just a lot of ground to cover.

Christy had one son, Riley, and she said he was never around much. Riley had just graduated high school, had a job in retail, and partied quite a bit after work, sleeping in late, according to Christy. Riley is a whole story himself.

Soon I began cleaning Christy's house, and I would learn much more than I needed to know. Christy did not work, but her husband, Tony, wanted her to work because she suffered from depression. Christy rarely left the home. Christy said that Tony felt she needed to have a purpose outside of the home, but she did not care to be around people. Christy did not like crowds of people, only having one close friend, as wealthy as themselves. She felt people judged her for the wealth after seeing their home. So there were never people around. This house was so fabulous but, at the same time, fabulously lonely.

Her husband did not let up on her getting out of the house, and soon Christy began real estate school. Christy quickly found out that being a Realtor would be more than she wanted to do with the long hours on the weekends for open houses and meeting with clients on weeknights. Christy told me that she did not want to be a Realtor, but what could she do, her husband wanted her to get busy doing something. Their son, Riley, had graduated high school, and she hadn't done much but volunteer for the school system and run errands for her husband until now.

So onward she plunged into becoming a Realtor. She was highly intelligent, and so she passed the tests and got her real estate license but didn't really care to work for a broker. Now under Colorado law, you have to work under a broker for three years at that time. Christy began complaining that it was all too much for her, that she didn't feel comfortable outside of her home, she was content never leaving the house except to grocery shop.

Christy had a large party at her home after she graduated, inviting all the Realtors from the office she worked out of and a few others, around five hundred people came. The party was all Tony's idea. I bartended for the evening. Everyone was amazed at the house by its grandeur and beauty. The party was fun, the people mingled well and were polite, but you could clearly see that Christy was quite uncomfortable. At one point, she came to me and said, "I can't wait until this is over, I hate this, now they know where I live." Tony got quite drunk, and when the night came to an end, he walked me to my car, giving me $300 for bartending and helping set up for the party. He also made a pass at me, but he was drunk, so I excused this. Tony rarely drank, so the alcohol hit him hard. Christy herself never drank alcohol except perhaps one glass of wine while out on an occasional dinner.

Christy gave up on being a Realtor within three months. Soon there would be many days Christy would greet me at the front door with mascara rolling down her cheeks, in her pajamas, hair a complete mess. There were days when her mother would meet me at the door, stating, "Christy is in her bedroom now for two days, she is having a difficult time, please don't go in there."

Christy, I would learn, was on lithium, a drug used to stabilize someone's moods. It began to take me six hours to clean this house instead of the regular four hours due to having Christy follow me all over the house, telling me all of her problems. On one of these days, with mascara running down her cheeks, she would be crying uncontrollably, she began telling me about how an uncle had molested her as a child. Her childhood was not good, and she resented her mother for everything that had gone wrong with it. She told me that people in general were never to be trusted. I suppose this is why she built such a large home with all these conveniences, so she never really had to leave. This home sheltered her from the world. Christy also shared with me that she stayed heavy so that any man would not try to assault her. She actually had a list on her refrigerator of ways to keep men away from her because they might attack.

Christy was cordial to her mother, but it was painfully clear that her mother was a burden on her. Christy and her husband paid all of her mother's bills because her mother's only income was Social Security. Christy said that her parents never had much of anything, and her father did not plan for the future at all, suddenly dying of a heart attack. Christy always seemed to be embarrassed about how her parents had done life. She could not accept that people do the best they can with what they know at the time. And besides, aren't we all supposed to do better than our parents? I didn't understand the grudge she held against her mother. Perhaps she blamed her for the molestation.

Soon it was difficult for Christy's mother to move around in her townhome with the steps, and Christy would buy her a new one-bedroom apartment. The mother did not like the apartment and did not understand why they did not move her into their home with them; she made it clear to me that she was hurt by this. Christy had confided in me that she did not want her mother under the same roof with her and that she had to spend enough time with her as it was, stating, "You just don't see how she really is, Angel."

Now understand, I am not walking around the house socializing and giving my opinion on this issue, but these ladies are voicing all of their feelings to me instead of talking to each other. Let me tell you, this happens to me time and time again, from house to house. I will pick up a house, then the mother's house, and they do nothing but talk about each other to me and how they can't stand this or that about the other. It's sad really.

And here again, I was playing the part of a therapist because that is what therapists spend the majority of their time doing, listening, giving words of advice now and then, hoping they pick up the advice and use it. Now Christy's mom seemed pretty sweet to me. I would say she was a normal elderly woman, sweet grandma type, but I guess we never really know how people are. People carry their childhoods around with them, and sometimes they like to punish those from their childhood, especially those that raised them.

Christmas at Christy's house was something to watch. The fifteen-foot tree would go up completely covered with hand-carved ornaments from the Navajo Indians in New Mexico, it was a sight to see. Extravagant gifts would be bought. The one gift that stood out to me were the tickets to jump out of an airplane that Christy bought for her husband and son, $250 each ticket. Those tickets were never used because neither could lose enough weight within the year before they expired to make the jump. Christy's husband had been on her to help him lose weight. And their son, well, he was very obese.

This was when Christy made up her mind to lose weight and put the guys on a diet as well. Riley never lost any weight, but Christy and Tony did. Christy looked good. She did it all without exercise but by completely changing her diet. I saw a happier Christy begin to emerge, with more energy, and the depression seemed to be gone. She even said to me, "Tony and I are having sex again." Before she had complained that he never touched her or was affectionate to her in any way, not even a kiss. I never knew if it was the weight loss that brought on the change or perhaps a change in her medications. I used to say to her, "My god, you have all this money, a beautiful home, a husband who works hard, and all you do is sit here and watch soap operas, why don't you get out and start living?" And so, she did after time passed, she slowly but surely did start living.

Gifts for birthdays were such that Christy would find a collector Corvette for her husband and have it shipped in from another state. Tony would fly Christy somewhere for dinner on their anniversary. River boat trips would be taken where they would actually have a butler for their room on the boat. Christy didn't like the butler deal. She said, "I couldn't stand the way he would just stand beside our dinner table or deck, waiting for us to tell him to get us something." There would be trips to exotic islands to deep-sea dive. Several more Corvettes were purchased, and they joined a Corvette club. The club members would take long road trips in a competition to find hidden treasure; they all dressed in '50s style. What was it with the '50s? They both loved it.

I felt it was like watching the life of a movie star. It seemed as though Christy began to enjoy the money and was more at ease with living a better lifestyle. Christy had always worried about people knowing where she lived and how wealthy they were. She didn't want to be looked at differently, but not anymore. Perhaps she found her group of people.

There was one time where a high school friend was coming to visit Denver with her husband and wanted to see Christy. Christy told me, "I am afraid of how they will treat me after they see where we live." I told her if it is a true friend, then it should not matter what you have or where you live. Christy never really flaunted their wealth by the way she dressed or presented herself to other people. She didn't even buy herself extravagant gifts but did for her husband.

Christy's son, Riley, was a short and obese young man. Not good-looking whatsoever and spent most of his time snowmobiling and hunting. Riley would go off snowmobiling for weeks on end, and the same with hunting. Riley never seemed mature for his age. Christy had told me he was accused of touching a little girl around age seven inappropriately, and that they had moved him from the school he was in at the time. There had been a court hearing with social services involved, and it had been an awful ordeal.

It was obvious that they were very protective of him and that he did not socialize much, like his mother. Christy was constantly coaching Riley that he could do anything he wanted in life, but that he just had to work harder and apply himself. From what I could see, Riley worked hard at playing and eating, that's it.

Riley was going off to the School of Mines in Golden Colorado for his freshman year. The School of Mines is expensive and hard to get into. Riley had complained to me, saying, "Erie school's system has taught me nothing, and my parents know it, and now they want me to go to this school. I'm never going to make it."

The year went on, and Riley began drinking his way through his freshman year, like so many kids do. Riley wrecked his new truck his father had bought him; he was drinking and driving and ran it into a ditch, hitting a tree. Riley called his dad who called a friend to tow him out, delivering Riley and the truck home. Police never knew a thing because it all happened on a country road. Now instead of punishing this kid, the parents went out and bought him another new truck. Go figure! I wonder why this kid never bothered applying himself to anything, I mean, really!

Of course, Riley flunked out of School of Mines his first year, and somehow his parents were able to persuade the school to take him back another year. Obviously money talks volumes. Riley again flunked out his second year. And so, Riley was then enrolled into Metro State College. Riley is no dummy and knows well that he will inherit everything his parents have built up over the years and really puts no effort at all into improving himself or building a life for himself outside of living with Mommy and Daddy.

Riley is the kind of guy that once told me, "You know the guy you're dating, his son thinks you're a gold digger, you have no money, and his dad is loaded."

I replied, "How do you know what his son thinks, Riley?"

Riley replied, "Because that has to be why you're dating him. I have to be really careful who I date because I am going to be rich one day."

End of story on Riley. He never graduated from college. He lives on his own, or no doubt, in a house that his parents bought for him. He works in the sales department of the siding company that his father built.

I quit cleaning for Christy after I moved back into town. The trip was just too far, the drama was so heavy, it was not a good place to work.

Carolynn

I MET CAROLYNN AT A divorce group, the Fisher Group, a group recommended to me by my divorce counselor. Fisher Group was all about rebuilding your life after loss or divorce. As a group, we followed a workbook throughout a six-week period. The group was led by a local psychologist, Katie Durham, who began showing the initial signs of Alzheimer's within two years of our initial meeting. The last time I saw Katie was about six years ago on the Pearl Street Mall in Boulder, Colorado. Katie had a sun hat on that was rather crooked on her head. She was being led around by the hand of her sweet daughter, it was apparent that she had become totally dependent on her daughter but so touching to me that she was there with her.

The cost of joining Fisher Group was a mere $350 at that time. The course taught me a lot about being single, especially how healthy it is to grow in different directions and learn how you are going to live life as a single person, a happy single person. I had already come to the realization that I felt as if I were eighteen again and able to do whatever I wanted with my life after raising my kids and divorcing.

The main purpose I joined the group was to meet people like myself and form friendships. It was a tough group for me in the beginning because I soon realized all the people around me were severely injured mentally and heart wise, all due to divorce. I was the only person in the group that had been to a divorce counselor and for eighteen months. It was obvious that I had the tools for my recovery work from divorce. I mean, they all looked like me and talked like me back when I first started seeing my divorce counselor. I would soon be in the position of helper, which is where I usually end up. Giving anyone who asked my words of advice that my counselor had given me. Anything to help someone, hoping they would recall it later on and put it to good use in their lives. People, especially the women, cried a ton of the time, they were clearly in pain.

Of course, the group was crowded with women and very few men, as most single situations that I had been a part of, like my book clubs and singles get-togethers. Many friendships were formed from this group. Now Carolynn, she was the much-older woman, today age eighty-four; when we first met, she was sixty-six. Carolynn was a short woman, about five feet tall, and looked like a farm girl to me, plaid button-up the front top, no makeup, long thinning stringy hair that went down the middle of her back, very little jewelry, clothes usually covered in cat hair, and painfully quiet except to voice her hatred of men. Over the coming years, she never changed her look.

I noticed right away that Carolynn, age sixty-six, did not sport one line on her entire face; I found that odd. Carol warmed up to me as most people do. I soon realized that she lived near me, was an older hippie that smoked marijuana, and did oil paintings of the universe, mountains, and woods while naked. Carolynn claimed that smoking pot while painting opened up her senses and made her art more interesting, and this person, I had thought was a farm girl! Well, she kind of is a farm girl because everything she eats is organic—oh and of course, the marijuana is organic. What she is, well, Carolynn is an older hippie gal.

Carolynn has a daughter, Nicki (that's a whole chapter in itself), and a son, Dave. Carolynn lived in a six-thousand-square-foot house and was in need of cleanings because her house was so large, and she wanted to put the home on the market within a year. The house and her new Tundra truck was paid off by Carolynn's ex-husband, who was fifteen years younger than she. Carolynn received a large sum of money from her ex, alimony to live on each month, and she did not work. Carolynn literally had no bills to pay. Carolynn would complain to me that her soon-to-be ex-husband would force her to have dinner with him in a fancy lobster restaurant in downtown Denver to give her the monthly alimony money, otherwise she wouldn't get the money.

I could not believe she complained about having to go to an expensive restaurant to dinner to get mailbox money! When I think back on this, I believe she wanted other women to be jealous, the exchange of money may have never happened this way at all, and I think it could be an untruth. Why? Because I have since caught Carolynn in lie after lie, and each lie was to impress someone by making herself look better in some way or another. She was trying her best to live a false life.

Carolynn's ex was ten years younger than her, a successful man who worked himself up the ladder at the Lutheran Hospital in the maintenance department. He had no formal education. He eventually made a six-figure income there and had an affair with his younger assistant, younger than him by twelve years. Carolynn had put a GPS detector on her husband's truck to track his whereabouts when they were not together. Carolynn did this because her husband was always around the corner somewhere, talking or texting on his cell phone. The final blow in the marriage was when she found him and his assistant in the parking garage of the hospital, making love in his truck. Her husband eventually got his assistant pregnant, and so the divorce was inevitable, but believe me, he paid dearly. Carolynn never had to work because he paid for everything she owned.

Carolynn has been married six times—yes, six times—and prides herself in the fact that she has worked very little in her life, gaining financially from each divorce. Carolynn would say, "When they don't treat you right, well, they have to pay for it." Before meeting women in this divorce group, I had no idea that you could profit from a divorce, it just wasn't in my life before I met these women. I thought that was only in the movies.

The majority of the women in the group did not work and would never have to work a day in their lives again—unless they wanted to work—because of their divorces and the profits they made out of their divorces. Their homes were paid off, their vehicles paid off, and they all received large amounts of money every month in which to maintain their former lifestyle. It blew my mind.

I was the cleaning chic that ran my own business. I didn't want to strip my husband of anything when we divorced, I would never behave like that in front of my kids, after all, he was their dad, and at the time I had made more money than he did. I mean, As I said, this only happened in the movies, I never realized this happened in real life, not until now.

Carolynn revealed everything in the small group, never in the large group. In fact, Carolynn was quite uncomfortable in large groups of people, and it was obvious. Carolynn would stay in the back of the room, never speak a word, never stay after the meetings and have desert and coffee, but shuffle right out the door as fast as she could. I later concluded that Carolynn spoke up in the small groups we were in because they were generally made up of women, most of the men would break off into their own group.

Carolynn was the bitter woman in our group, most women in the group cried and couldn't talk much at all. I was the one that said, "I am woman, hear me roar, I don't need a man right now." Remember, I was fortunate, I was the one that had seen a divorce counselor. I was ready to make new friends and explore life on my own. I have often seen that people who don't go to counseling for whatever circumstances they are going through in their life that is life changing or traumatic, do not fare so well. I would recommend anyone going through a divorce to seek counsel and not date for at least two years because it is important to heal and to find out who you are again, by yourself, rediscovering yourself, as a single individual.

A divorce is like a death; you need a grieving period. I didn't have any clue at the time on dating. When I was young, I dated who my three brothers told me I could. And now, well, now there is online dating!

Now having started out as a friend to Carolynn and moving on to cleaning her home, I learned quite a bit more about Carolynn and her life. Carolynn had been molested by a family member as a child, at age six, and it had left her with bad feelings about having sexual relationships with men. Later on, Carolynn became promiscuous and was pregnant at age fourteen. Because of the time period and how people felt about young pregnancy back then, Carolynn was sent away to have the baby, which was put up for adoption.

Carolynn would later find the child who had become an adult. This all happened six years after we met. So many people want to form a relationship with their bio mother after adoption, but not Carolynn's son. Carolynn said it was all right with her and that she accepted his decision not to meet her, but you could see that she was devastated. I watched her carry a deep pain around with her regarding this rejection, it was sad.

As I would listen to Carolynn talk about her past marriages, she would tell me things like, "He wanted to have sex in the shower, that's disgusting and degrading," or, "He wanted to have oral sex, and I find that sickening." Not normal behavior from any woman I had ever met before. I thought perhaps she felt this way about sex because she had been molested as a child.

One of our friends from the group had fixed Carolynn up on a double date and told me she was shocked at how Carolynn presented herself. Carolynn went to the date in wrinkled clothes with cat hair all over them, dirty greasy hair, and no makeup at all. The friend told me that Carolynn was completely rude to the gentlemen throughout the entire date. I felt that was her way of saying she just wasn't interested. I knew Carolynn would never be in a relationship for a long period of time, if at all, because she never had counseling for being molested, not to mention the fact that nobody in her family believed the molestation had ever happened. She never got counseling for any of her divorces, she didn't believe in it. Carolynn lived her life like a scared person, paranoid of everything, and that grew more intense over the years. Perhaps the paranoia came from smoking marijuana, I don't know.

To this day, fifteen years later, Carolynn has not been on more than a dozen dates with men. Carolynn will tell me after each and every first or second date, "He's a pig like all the others, he wanted to kiss me on the date. I'm just not interested," or, "They all want the same thing—sex—that's all men are after." Carolynn and I had lunch one afternoon, and the man I was seeing stopped by to say hi. After he left, Carolynn told me that she could tell he was a real bad guy.

I recall him spending about ten minutes with us. She could sum up her opinion swiftly without giving anyone a chance.

Carolynn had invited herself to go to dance classes with me that I was taking in Boulder, and was always late getting to my house to ride along. I find it rude to be late, and it embarrassed me to show up to class late. Carolynn is snappy, short, and negative to everyone she meets. Carolynn seems too damaged to interact with people, and she told me she was extremely uncomfortable around people. I soon discovered that she could not be a part of my social life, and our friend Robin followed suit. But we kept in touch over the phone. She was so sad, so lonely.

Some people mask their pain with drugs and alcohol, Carolynn used marijuana to do this and had been using it her entire life on a daily basis, she even supplied her granddaughter, Tina, with marijuana, which came as a complete shock to me.

Carolynn's granddaughter is a bartender, a lesbian who was in a relationship with an abusive woman. Tina had even grown a mustache at one point. I had stopped in the bar/restaurant she worked at on my way to a concert with a date, and Tina appeared with the mustache. I almost fell off my barstool, I was shocked. She had also cut her hair short and was wearing a muscle shirt and men's jeans. My date later said, "What was that, a guy or a chic?" Now I will tell you that Tina was a very gentle soul that would always greet me with a smile and a hug. I felt empathy for her and her world knowing how hard a life as a lesbian must be, I can only imagine. I have seen lesbians go through many relationships, trying to find the right person to spend their lives with. I have a cousin who is lesbian, and I know that her life has been difficult romantically.

I would clean Carolynn's house once each month, and she would show me all of her paintings. Carolynn had a gallery in the basement of her home but, over the years, could not sell any paintings. Carolynn's home was massive and needed a ton of upgrades in order to sell it within a few years. The home was adorned with Southwestern decor and expensive pottery. Some of her pottery pieces would later sell for $3,000 each. The rooms in the home were large, especially the master bedroom, which also had an atrium built on it leading to the bathroom. The atrium supplied light for her to paint and for the plants in the room.

The home was an open floor plan with large dark beams running across the ceilings that drew your eye upward. The living room had an enormous fireplace that rose to the ceiling, all the windows throughout the home were large, letting tons of light in throughout.

The kitchen had older appliances and no granite countertops, which Carolynn was told she would have to upgrade in order for the house to sell; she never did. The home sat on a pretty wooded lot, about a half acre, overlooking the mountains. The three-car garage was filled with things to sell, tons of things! I'm talking furniture, lamps, artwork, dishes, silverware (real silver) in wooden boxes, jewelry—you name it, Carolynn had it.

The basement had a mother-in-law apartment where Carolynn had housed her mother up until her death two years earlier. Carolynn blamed her husband's cheating on her due to the time she spent caring for her ill mother, even though she admitted to not wanting to have sex with him for at least six years prior to the divorce. Carolynn had been caretaker to her mother, spoke of her often, and missed her dearly. There were moments when she would be speaking of her mother that I actually thought she wanted to die just to be with her again.

Carolynn's son now lived in her basement with his two children. He worked nights at the hospital in the maintenance department, a job Carolynn's ex had placed him in. When you were at Carolynn's house, you had to walk softly because her son was usually in the basement sleeping. He worked the night shift.

The cleaning work at the home led to helping Carolynn sort out things and putting them in her garage until she sold them at garage sales or on eBay. Carolynn had tons of antiques and jewelry, and she knew their value quite well. One of Carolynn's husbands had set her up in an antique store while they were married, and another, a nail salon. One of Carolynn's earlier hobbies was to bid on storage units and sell everything inside the units on eBay. She had had quite a bit of luck on some of the units, finding cash in boxes and jewelry safety-pinned inside of clothing. On one unit, she found $4,000-

cash and had figured burglars had, no doubt, stashed some of their goods in this particular unit.

Carolynn's house sold after one year of being on the market. She had $500,000 cash to go buy another smaller home. Carolynn found a ranch-style home with lots of light coming in for her to paint her oil paintings. She soon had lighting put in the ceiling and walls of the basement for her gallery. Carolynn still did not need to work and, within a few years, would do a reverse mortgage so that she would receive a check to be in her home each month; her extra money had run out. I thought, *Well, yes, I can see that money running out.* The ex-husband had quit paying her because he was only court ordered to pay her for a set amount of years after the divorce, and she was living on the money from the sale of the previous house. By this time, her ex was supporting the new daughter that he had had with his assistant, the younger woman, whom he never married. Carolynn would brag about how well they got along and that he would stop by on occasion to get high with her and reminisce about old times.

Now by this time, Carolynn was nine years older and still no sign of a wrinkle on her face. Now don't get me wrong, she had signs of aging everywhere else, like on her neck, chest, arms, legs, and hands, but not the face. To this day, Carolynn denies having fillers or surgery on her face, and she still has not one wrinkle, claiming she has good genes. I believe a ton of her money went to keep her face looking young, like so many of my past gal friends and clients in Colorado. This is just another reason why Colorado is being called little LA. One does not have to look far to see women who have lips like blowfish or deformed-looking lips that they have a problem drinking fluid with or talking with, faces so pulled back that they look like lizards (that's just what they look like to me) and absolutely no wrinkles at all. It's a thing there now. My beautiful granddaughter would say to me, "Please don't ever do any of that to your face, Nini, I love you just the way you are." Grandchildren are little gifts we receive here on earth, sent from heaven.

I could no longer go to Carolynn's home as a friend or a cleaner/ organizer because she had three cats in her smaller home, and cat hair just flew through the air all the time; I'm allergic, and it just was not worth popping an allergy pill. Carolynn had become very weird after this move.

People from the divorce group were not interested in being her friend, and she had told me someone was trying to kill her cats when they were outside. There would be reports of footprints in the snow leading to her windows, strange notes being left at her door, stating that the cats would be killed if not kept in the yard, notes that Carolynn could never produce. Soon Carolynn would put chicken-wire fencing all around her backyard across the top of her six-foot fence so that the cats could not get out. This did not work for long, and so she ended up building something resembling a dog walk in the yard. She told me she was now closing all the blinds during the day for fear that someone was watching her. Now remember this was a woman that thrived on sunlight coming into her home so that she could paint.

There was the day Carolynn called me crying, begging me to go and visit, that she was not wanting to live any longer, and being the natural helper that I am, I popped an allergy pill and went to cheer her up. My ex-mother-in-law had once told me her friend had called her, stating she did not want to live anymore. My mother-in-law did not take it seriously, and so the friend took her own life that very day. I was not about to let that happen to me or my friend.

I was greeted by Carolynn at the door with her crying and telling me life was just too hard, that nobody cared about her, that she was not moving forward, and that she felt helpless. Carolynn was shaking, looked as though she had not bathed for weeks, and was hysterical.

This would be yet another conversation where I would build her up, as any good friend would do, telling her she was doing just fine, that everything takes time to heal from, that perhaps private counseling would be good for a bit, and that she probably needed to at least get out of the house and volunteer somewhere or take on a part-time job in order to be functional and have more of a purpose. Oh yes, and that some sunshine wouldn't hurt.

I received the same response as always, "I'm too old to work or volunteer now, I don't like to be around people, they're always staring at me." During this visit, there was a bag of marijuana on her coffee table, which stunk up the entire room. Now how do you tell a woman who has isolated herself by smoking pot her entire life that she may need to taper it down? Well, you don't. Paranoia comes with smoking marijuana, I don't care what anyone says, it just does. I have witnessed it many times from people I know. I had tried it when I was young with my sister-in-law, Annie, who broke a lamp, and I stood at the window, waiting for the police to come take us to jail, paranoid.

Carolynn had social problems, no education, and just consumed too much marijuana every day. The story with Carolynn does not end here. I had little contact with Carolynn from this point on, except via telephone. Carolynn became very "spiritual," as she called it. She began reading Eckhart Tolle books and listening to his CDs. She would tell me, "This life is just an illusion, it's not real." Even telling me that my son, who was away at war, needed to be told that it was just an illusion that he was living. Yeah, right! Then she decided she would begin a business in which she counseled people to help them deal with this illusion called life.

And yes, it usually is a person who has been very damaged throughout their lives that want to help counsel others, and that's fine, if you are qualified. Trouble was, Carolynn just was not qualified, and I warned her of how she could actually do harm to others. I was in college at the time, learning to become a counselor, and I told her of liability issues. This all went right over her head of course, and so she pursued her venture. Needless to say, not one soul was interested in her counseling, nor did she have any idea how to market a business. There was a young man who kept going to Carolynn's house to be counseled, but I had my suspicions that it was mainly to smoke marijuana with a lonely older woman who gladly supplied it to him. That all ended abruptly.

Within a few short months, another situation took over Carolynn's life. Carolynn's daughter, Trina, would suffer the loss of her husband, Jake, who had died in a terrible skiing accident. Carolynn would move her daughter in to her home after selling the daughter's house, and it got pretty crazy—well, extremely crazy—from that point on.

Trina and her husband, Jake, had married quite young—early twenties—and within one month of their marriage, Jake had been in a car accident, an accident which paralyzed him from the waist down. Trina loved Jake with all her heart and stayed with him, taking care of him throughout their lives together. Taking care of Jake was not an easy task, as she bathed him, cleaned out his rectum, and lifted him often. Trina is not a large woman but actually a very small petite woman, being four feet five inches tall, pretty long thick hair, and clean-looking gal; you could tell she took pride in how she looked. Trina is also quiet like her mother, in the way that she does not like being around people, only her mother and her daughter.

Trina and Jake had bought a ranch-style home with wheelchair access and modeled the home around his ability to maneuver his wheelchair. The home had no upgrades, was very sparse, and practical with a large yard. Trina and Jake spent their days in their yard planting trees, flowers, and shrubs, even putting in a large water feature. It was as beautiful as a grand park, and they took a lot of pride in their yard. The only bad thing was the fire department was right next-door and all the sirens that would go off frequently. But all in all, life was good for Trina and Jake.

Trina had confided in her mother that sex was nonexistent and what sex they did have was limited, but that didn't matter, they loved each other and believed they were soul mates. Life would go on, Jake was completely disabled, earning no income outside of his disability check, and Trina would go to school in order to become a nail technician in Carolynn's nail salon, later moving her work into the home as Carolynn's salon closed down. Jake was an avid skier by using assisted skiing equipment. With adaptive skiing, Jake was on the slopes often and had even starred in a video about adaptive skiing. Trina never skied but often joined Jake at the slopes, waiting for him at the bottom. Soon Trina would be in an auto accident—not of her causing—that left her unable to do nails with her neck injury. After this, money became very tight. Trina acquired an attorney to sue and got a very small settlement, $10,000. In the next few years, they would realize that she was having memory problems and headaches that would disable her for days. Life became impossible for Trina.

A few years passed, there was never a doubt in my mind that Carolynn had been helping them out financially. Then the impossible happened. Jake had gone up to the slopes alone one morning, as he had on so many occasions, and had hit a tree while skiing; he was killed on impact. Trina's life with her soul mate was suddenly over. Jake's disability check ended with his death, and there would be no more check coming in. There was no life insurance. Trina was unable to work herself and had to face the fact that she would have to sell her home that she had lived in for over thirty years. The home was difficult to sell because it had not been well maintained except for the beautiful yard, and then there was the fire department right next-door. Carolynn and Trina worked at cleaning out the home and cleaning it up for a year before it sold. Trina would then move in with Carolynn and be completely controlled by her mother.

As it turned out, Carolynn and Trina's relationship had always been strained because Trina had been molested by one of Carolynn's husband's as a small child. This abuse went on for about four years. Trina had a certain resentment toward her mother for not being able to protect her. Carolynn had told me several times over the years that she didn't always feel welcome at Trina's home when she visited. That Trina would be hostile toward her because of the molestation when she was a young girl, and that she felt her mother knew about it and didn't protect her.

Trina and Carolynn would have many fights after they cohabitated. From what Carolynn was telling me over the phone, it was difficult to live together, and Trina was trying to grieve, and another cat was added to the mix in the small house. I had offered to help Trina grieve as I was a grief counselor at my church for three years, had done my internship at Mothers Against Drunk Driving (MADD).

Carolynn coveted her daughter and would not allow me to be in touch with her. It would be several years before I would even be able to speak to Trina on the telephone. It's been five years since Jake passed, and Trina is unable to work or go on a date.

Trina is now sixty-one years of age and has no intention of ever being with another man, stating, "I can't trust anyone, they're all after one thing." She believes Jake talks to her through signs, like rocks on top of fence posts that she sees while out riding her bicycle. Trina believes that Jake places the rocks there before her arrival to let her know he is still with her and that she is not alone. Trina has tried working jobs as a receptionist at a gym and hostess at a winery but always concludes that her neck hurts too much to work, she forgets things and cannot juggle tasks, and that people are always staring at her and talking about her. Trina smokes marijuana with her mother on a daily basis. Carolynn and Trina do not decorate or celebrate with family or friends on the holidays, nor do they go out much. The last time I saw Trina, I thought that she had aged ten years in just a few. Trina was now frumpy and not taking care of her looks any longer.

Trina has never been able to get disability for her injuries and lives off of her mother to this day. She has posted strange things on Facebook, stating, "We should all be aware of the grocery store aisles because it will one day be a slaughter house where we are shot down, and then our blood washed away with fire hoses, that is what grocery stores are designed for," she would write. Trina will quote the Bible on Facebook with warnings that the end is coming very soon and that we had all better be ready and quit living the sinful lives that we all live.

I had called Carolynn several times, offering to be able to talk to Trina about her loss of Jake, give her several books that I have to help people move on after loss, but Carolynn protects Trina from everyone. The one and only time I was able to contact Trina by telephone, she seemed to be off in another world; it was totally weird.

Trina eventually moved on to a townhome that her mother rented for her a few shorts blocks from her, but Carolynn would not be able to maintain her home and her daughter's townhome for more than two years.

Carolynn left her home due to lack of money. Now from what I hear from Carolynn, once you cannot keep your house up to par when you have a reverse mortgage, it's time to leave, the home has to be maintained nicely. Carolynn now lives in Golden Colorado in a mobile home park right across from her daughter's mobile home that Carolynn had bought for her. I don't talk to Carolynn anymore, and I have even quit calling her on her birthday. Neither women seemed to be in touch with reality any longer, and both live in seclusion with each other, only associating with Trina's daughter, Tina. I would not be surprised if both do not even shop at the grocery store any longer but order their food for delivery. I find it extremely sad that Trina is coveted by her mother, fed negative thoughts, and has no desire to go out and live life at only sixty-one years of age, very sad. I think Jake would be sad for his wife also and want her to move on living a full life.

Brie

I MET BRIE AT THE same divorce group that I had met Carolynn, the Fisher Group. Brie was a short, small, thin and aging woman who sported gray roots, brown hair, and wore miniskirts and leather pants like you would see a biker wear. I say Brie was an aging woman because she was only fifty when I met her in the group, yet she appeared much older. My first impression was that she was in her midsixties. I wouldn't say Brie was a pretty woman, or even an attractive woman, but she was kind and generous to all around her, bringing large amounts of food to the group and small gifts for anyone she may see fit that needed a gift, that's just Brie.

Brie is the mother of five daughters and several grandchildren. There sometimes seems to be not enough words in the dictionary to describe Brie, and you will understand what I am talking about as I tell the story of her. Brie did nothing but cry from the time she began the group until about four weeks in, when she decided to start hosting parties, and oh my, what parties this woman would host! Nothing was spared, and we all came to find out that Brie had once been a sort of caterer. She would go into rich people's homes near Boulder, Colorado, and cook all of their meals for three days, throw thirty days' worth of meals in their freezers. We would all find out that this woman cooked like nobody's business, and the food tasted like no other I had ever had. Through Brie, I would learn all the tricks in cooking and what spices I had never discovered before.

Brie's story, regarding her divorce, was that her husband of thirty-eight years had once again cheated on her with her good friend, a friend that Brie had bought many gifts for, gifts like skiing equipment and a cross-country bicycle. Why did Brie buy this woman these particular gifts? Because Brie's husband wanted the woman to join in on their activities together, she was alone because her husband worked all the time. Turns out that Brie had gone to work one morning, returning shortly after leaving her home, only to find her husband and this woman in her bed. Yes, at Brie's home, in her bed! Brie was devastated and stated, "I would have stayed with him." Then he left Brie for the other woman and was now cohabitating with her in a small apartment.

As I got to know Brie, I found out that her ex had left her many times during their marriage and went off and lived with other women several times. This behavior began early in their marriage when she was only fifteen and pregnant with her first daughter. Yet Brie bought elaborate gifts for the woman that her husband had now left her for. I don't get that one and I never will, not with the prior history her husband had with women. But as I said before, there are not enough words in the dictionary to describe Brie.

I would soon be cleaning Brie's manufactured home in an exclusive small neighborhood filled with these types of homes. It was one of the nicer homes on a corner lot next to the clubhouse which sported a large swimming pool. The home had a two-car garage attached, a nice patio out back, and a small porch built onto the front, with a grand mountain view looking off toward Boulder, Colorado. Brie's house was furnished with everything that a show home comes with and quite nice, I thought, for that type of home. This home had been the show home in the neighborhood when they began selling. Brie had sold her home from her divorce and was able to buy this one, complete with all the furnishings.

I would often wonder how Brie could afford my service, and later I would wonder how she could afford any of the things she did and bought, but she did. Brie was that woman that lived the champagne lifestyle on a beer budget. Brie worked as a secretary and grossed $48,000 a year. Someone with this income, and single to boot, usually does not get a cleaning service. We started out as friends, and then she would have me come and clean, usually prior to one of her parties or if her family was coming in from out of town.

Brie was from Pennsylvania, and that is where her family resides, along with two of her daughters.

Now when I met Brie, I was not dating, and she was continually trying to set me up with her brother, who visited on occasion from Pennsylvania, Bill, a man who wore his pants way high on his waist, who appeared much older than he was, like Brie, and was quiet. Much like Brie, Bill was generous and sweet but not my type at all, and I was not even entertaining the idea of dating. On the other hand, Brie was ready to jump right back out there in the dating scene. And how she jumped. Brie was not the type to go at life alone in any way, shape, or form.

A young twenty-four-year-old man, Harvey, was in our Fisher Group, and it was obvious that Brie had taken a liking to this young man. Harvey was a very tall and slender Greek-looking man, quiet to a fault. Harvey's fiancée had left him and broken his heart. Harvey was buying homes little by little to accumulate rental properties, and he would live in his car from time to time if he had to in order to buy another property. I thought he was quite driven. Harvey would attend all of Brie's parties. Now Brie's parties were not your ordinary get-togethers for singles, not even close. No, not the board games with snacks and a few beers or a bottle of wine, oh no, quite the opposite.

Brie's first party was a luau, complete with all the dishes for such a party, coconut bras and grass skirts for the women, there were large plastic bins full of costume wear, and all the decorations for a luau. Oh yes, and there was a roasted pig with sunglasses on and a flower in its mouth. Yes, a full-size roasted pig! These pigs cost upward of $150 delivered. Did Brie ask any of the twenty-six group members to pitch in and pay? Never! The party was complete with salads, potato dishes, and desserts. Oh, and then there was the alcohol—plenty of alcohol—not a few six-packs and a few bottles of wine but hard alcohol!

I would always put out a donation jar and ask everyone to pitch in, but not one person ever did. Brie would later ask me to not put the jar out, that it was embarrassing. I asked Brie, time and time again, how she could afford such parties, and her reply was always the same, "Angel, this is just how I am and how I live, you only live once." And then she would laugh. There were spaghetti dinner parties, early Thanksgiving parties, Valentine's Day parties, and on and on and on.

Before you knew it, the class was half over, and we had a last party night together at Sing Sing. Sing Sing was a piano bar in Denver. What fun this party was. Everyone showed up and drank and sang and laughed all night, except for a handful like myself who did not drink and then drove home on nasty winter nights like this night. I was always the designated driver, alcohol and I don't agree with each other. I had seen alcohol ruin the lives of too many people, like my siblings and ex-husband.

The streets were lined with snowdrifts brought on by plow trucks, and it was still snowing, visibility was extremely low. But we all piled in to have one last time together, partying happily. A few women showed up at this gathering, dressed to the T, wanting to land a man, it was obvious, and more than a few left that night with a man from the group. I myself adorned an oversized sweater and big boots. I was into comfort and warmth for the blizzardy night. Go home with one of those guys? No way! On the other hand, Brie wore a miniskirt with black patent leather boots that went above her knees, and a leather jacket. I thought she would freeze to death making her way to her car after the party.

Brie began to buy our youngest member, Harvey, quite a few drinks, handing the waiter a hundred-dollar bill at one point, and then handing Harvey the same payment. Brie is famous for handing out one-hundred-dollar bills to her daughters, and this has not changed over the years. Harvey soon left, and Brie followed within ten minutes. I thought it to be odd that Brie would leave a party so soon, not odd that she would leave so drunk she could barely walk, however. There were so many parties and so many times that many of our group would beg Brie not to get in her car and drive home, but she would slip through, and out the door she would go. As far as I know, she has never gotten a DUI, but who knows.

The party continued on for at least two more hours, and everyone was just so happy that night. There would be the few that left together, even though the rules forbid it, but after all, the class was finished, so why not, I suppose. Of course, these bonds from that night never lasted, as all were brokenhearted and just looking for someone to get through some time with, one of the reasons we were not to form that kind of relationship in the group.

Fisher Group was formed to help one grow, rebuild, form friendships, but absolutely no hookups at Fisher Group. Some members never got that concept or just didn't care. It seemed most of the men in the group joined for just that reason. Hey, brokenhearted women looking for comfort, and all I have to pay is $350. I couldn't help but think they thought that way. I mean from the moment a man would walk into the meetings for the first time, they were scanning the area and drooling.

It would be a few days before I saw Brie again after that night. She asked me over for dinner, and who could pass up one of her meals? The meal of the night was crab! Brie was in a giggly mood, which soon led to a depressing regretful mood, telling me that she had spent the night with Harvey in one of his flip houses that he was working on. They had had sex, and she got up the next morning and went home with very little words spoken between her and Harvey. Brie said, "Harvey was not very nice to me the morning after, and I just don't understand it, he won't answer his phone when I call, and I have called so many times." I was shocked, he was only twenty-four, my son was twenty at this time, but I guess not too surprised because Brie was the older woman that wore the leather pants and short miniskirts to group meetings, but still she had been that wounded bird that cried through each meeting. *Who is this gal?* I thought to myself.

Brie had told her daughters, and they were all quite proud of her, she boasted. "Mom, you slept with a twenty-four-year-old, that's wonderful, you go girl," they had told her. Brie had said all five of her girls just laughed and laughed that she had bedded a twenty-four-year-old. Harvey never came back to group get-togethers again and never answered Brie's or anybody else's phone calls. Brie, of course, boasted to all the members that she had bedded Harvey. I believe one of the other men in the group told Harvey what was being said, and this was why he never returned, embarrassed perhaps, ashamed? Maybe. I felt Harvey to be quite shy and timid.

Well, now the plot thickened. Brie had obtained herpes from Harvey, and she would tell me, "How dare he do this to me!" She would laugh, then cry, then laugh some more. She had been to the doctor, and she had not slept with anyone else since her divorce, according to her. Now as the next few months passed, Brie would sleep with men on the first dates that she had met on online dating sites. I kept telling her she should think more of herself than how she was treating her body, mind, and soul. Brie always said that she just couldn't help herself, she wanted to be held. I myself had a teddy bear to cuddle up to.

I said, "What about the herpes, Brie? Are you spreading it to these men?" She would tell me over and over again that she did not care what the doctor said, she was sure she did not have it. To this day, she will deny having it and, then in another conversation, say she takes pills to keep herpes under control.

Soon Brie went to Glamour Shots and spent $700 getting her photos taken. The kind of photos where they tape you up all over to suck you in and pull you together in order to give you cleavage. There were shots of her in Harley Davidson gear, shots lying on her back with her legs in the air, adorned in a teddy. Brie said these photos would help her get a husband on the Internet.

I was always thinking to myself, where does all that money come from. And then there was the fact that the photos did not look like Brie at all. There was a makeup artist who did her makeup and a stylist who did her hair. While lying flat with her legs up in the air in one photo, Brie laughed and told me her boobs were taped up so that they looked plump. I had to laugh, I couldn't help it. I said, "Well, Brie, you know at some point you have to take your clothes off and show the real you."

She replied, "Oh hell, they can't see the real you in the dark, Angel." Laughing all the while.

I kept cleaning Brie's home for her, but soon she was not available to see anyone, not even for coffee, and she was never there when I cleaned. All the cleaning was set up by text messages, and she would leave cash for my payment, and oh yes, there was always a candle or some small gift.

Brie did not appear anywhere for over six weeks, and so I knocked on her door one day, wanting to ask her what was going on that made her drop off the face of the earth, no phone calls, no showing up for anything. Well, Brie had met a man. Met a Promise Keeper.

Promise Keepers is a men's ministry that meet all over the country in large convention centers and stadiums. These men are known to be strict Christians and don't sway much, if at all, from the Bible. Now this Promise Keeper, Jon, was at her home this particular day, and I could tell they had just woken up; he was actually in his boxers, here I am, in shock once again. This was a strange way to meet someone for the first time, but that's just Brie.

Jon seemed very sweet, a gentle man, and extremely polite. Jon was quite tall, about 6'3", and built quite well for an older man in his late sixties, silver hair, silver hair on his chest, *gawd!* Jon was quiet, perhaps unsocial, I thought to myself, perhaps embarrassed, I mean he was in his boxers with no shirt on. It was a brief meeting because I just said I had things to do and needed to be on my way. Actually I was quite taken aback and just wanted to get out of there, thinking to myself, *How long is this behavior from Brie going to last?*

Within a few short—and I mean very short—weeks, two to be exact, I would walk up to Brie's and find her and Jon loading up her furniture on his truck. "I am moving to the mountains with Jon, only ninety minutes away, Angel." Well, here came shock again, nothing new there, but this was a big one. "We have to go now, Angel, but I will call you soon." I didn't hear from Brie again for roughly three months.

One day I just received a call. "I have come down the mountain to see you and my daughters." Brie said on the phone that she needed to explain things to me.

So of course, I said, "Come on over, and we can talk. I missed knowing how Brie was doing, and I was curious as to where she lived now. Well, as usual, or what I can say became usual, Brie was right down the street in her car, arriving at my house within minutes with her overnight bag in tow, and yes, gifts.

I want to spend the night with you, is that alright? My daughter is just so upset with me still that I don't want to stay at her house." And of course, Brie came with two to three bottles of wine, a small gift, and food to cook. And so the conversation began with, "I met Jon through a dinner party at a friend's of mine in the mountains. Jon does construction work all over the valley, and he had worked on their home. He's retired air force and built his own home. You and my girls don't understand, I just knew I had to transfer my job and move up there before someone else found him and swept him away, or even worse, his wife may come back."

Yes, Jon, it turned out, was still married. *A Promise Keeper?* I thought. Of course, Brie and Jon could not go to church together, Jon said it just wouldn't look right, even though his wife had left him, so Brie said.

Now Brie explained to me that she could no longer keep up with her bills and that she was close to losing her home when she met Jon. She didn't tell Jon this. Brie said meeting Jon at his home for the second date was horrific, quite nerve-racking indeed. That Jon had pretty much interviewed her about every aspect of her life, and she had lied about quite a few things, even that she attended church on a regular basis, stating, "If I told him I smoke cigarettes or dated on the Internet and drank like I do, then he would never have another thing to do with me. I had to do this, Angel, I just had to." Of course, I didn't know Brie was about to lose her home and could not keep up with all her payments, but it made sense as to how she had all the expensive parties and spent money like it was never-ending.

Brie invited me up to a dinner party she was having in a few weeks and instructed me that Jon is to never know *anything* about her past. I was never to mention the drinking, the miniskirts, or the young man she had slept with. And never ever tell him about the night she confessed to getting drunk and driving into Boulder to slit all four tires on her ex-husband's new truck—oh, never tell that! She had told Jon the story of her divorce, but she left out all the sleeping around, and of course, she was still in denial about the herpes. Now what gal wants a guy to know her past affairs with men, but the herpes?

There would be many more visits from Brie over the next year or so. I never went to the dinner party, and she kept asking me to come up and clean for her. She said she would pay whatever I wanted, but I could not imagine driving ninety minutes into the mountains to clean for her or for anyone else. Not unless it was a multimillion-dollar home that paid at least $300 for a cleaning.

Brie began to label her visits down the mountain girls' night out, yet she was the one getting drunk and passing out at my house consistently. At the time, I thought this is what she did when she came down the mountain and got away from Jon for a few days. I remember each time she would call Jon and tell him not to call her the rest of the evening. Her daughters would come over, and they drank heavily as well.

It became a burden for me to see her, and now I don't know why I ever bothered. There would be stories of how Jon was an ass who was no fun and that he would scold Brie's grandchildren when they visited, not wanting the children to touch anything in the house he built. Soon Brie's daughters would not like visiting at all and quit going up for quite some time, over a year.

Turns out that Brie just moved without telling her daughters either, not until after she moved, and the one daughter had relied on her quite a bit for babysitting, food, and financial help. Brie was quite close to this particular daughter, and this daughter had quite a hate for Jon. Turned out this daughter and her children had met Jon for the first time on Christmas morning with him in his pajamas. Quite strange for her and her family. There was quite a bit of bitterness in all her girls over the entire matter.

There was the unannounced visit where Brie showed up just a few days after having a face-lift. My parents had died tragically, and she said she needed to come see me. My son opened the door, and there stood Brie, all bandaged up and bleeding. I will never forget the look on my son's face. Of course, I ended up taking care of her that night and through the next day. Jon had also had his bags under his eyes lifted, she said, and that he now had a sagging dripping eye.

I had a hard time believing that Jon, the Promise Keeper, would do that, but he indeed did.

Brie was having party after party and inviting me to all, but I never went. Then came the day that she came down and announced that she had told Jon she would leave him unless he married her. Well, he did not. Instead he bought a life insurance policy to ensure her security if anything happened to him. Jon was quite a bit older than Brie, already in his late sixties. Jon had had five prior wives whom he claimed took him for everything, and he was not about to go through that again. The last wife ended up with $300,000. Within eighteen months, Brie would again threaten Jon with leaving, and he would marry her without any friends or family in attendance. They just drove into town that day and got married. This didn't go over well with her daughters. Brie later explained that Jon, being a Promise Keeper, wanted to keep the marriage quiet because of his church family.

There would be a luau that summer celebrating their marriage. I did not go, traffic was backed up going to the mountains—my perfect excuse not to attend—and it just still felt so weird. There were more and more invitations to Brie's parties, but I never went until a party that New Year's Eve. A New Year's Eve party also celebrating Jon's birthday.

So my date and I drove up in a snowstorm for almost two and a half hours, in tow with food, wine, a Christmas gift for the home, and a birthday gift for Jon. It was quite a scary drive, not knowing exactly what the roads were like in that particular area, and the last mile to Brie's house was off the highway up a dirt road alongside a drop-off, a drop-off I would not see until the next day, thank God!

The road to Jon and Brie's house was a dead end. This man had built a home on top of a mountain, at nine thousand feet, with no people around at all. It was clear that he did not like people. Jon and his former wife had lived in a camper while the house was built, by himself and his church's members. He had saved his entire life for this piece of paradise, even renting rooms out in his home he had near Denver.

When we first approached the house, it looked to be extremely small, sitting on the side of a mountain. Once we walked into the home, it was quite shocking to me that Brie had moved from a manufactured home to this. She had "moved on up" in the world, and I mean *up*. This home was one of the most beautiful magnificent mountain homes I had ever seen. The home was a loft style, wide open. The windows facing out where Jon had saved sliding glass doors from jobs Jon had worked on. The entire wall was windows all the way up, I would say, at least thirty-foot-high ceilings, the door to the deck was fifteen feet tall. There were carved statues of cowboys and bears, five-feet-tall statues. There were logs thirty feet tall going through the house to the ceiling.

The kitchen had a large window to look out over the national forest, a view I would not see until the next morning. They called the kitchen island a continent, and that it was. The dining table was ten feet in diameter with a two-foot lazy Susan in the center, adorned with fourteen chairs around it. Jon had built the table himself. The open living room had a long wall adorning a large fireplace in the middle, an open living room, perhaps a great room, with a fifteen-foot-wide bookshelf, a small office nook built in to it. This was at least a thirty-foot wall.

Above was a large loft area with Jon's pictures of his time in the air force, when he was a fighter pilot and also had commanded a base in North Dakota. The steps on the way up were logs cut in half, just breathtaking. This loft sported a TV room with a couch and chairs, tons of hides from various animals hung over the railing. Off the loft were two bedrooms and a full bathroom. One bedroom was decorated with dolls and hats, a Victorian room I would say, much like Brie's bedroom had been when she lived in town. The other bedroom was like a lake house room with boats and fishing things scattered about.

There was a hallway off the grand living room that led to the master bedroom and laundry room. The master bedroom was quite large; I would say 30×30 feet at least. A door went out to the deck where there was a hot tub, complete with television and stereo above and a firepit area. There was another door in the bedroom floor that opened to the basement. The door pulled up, and stairs led down to the storage area, workroom, a greenhouse facing south, and a wood-burning stove that heated the home. There was a door in the corner that led outside where Jon would toss firewood through and stack up for the winter. This was the only source of heat for this large home sitting on the south side of a mountain.

The master bathroom had a bodet and a large jetted tub for two that had three steps up to it, with a large window looking out into the national park. The walk-in closet was the biggest I had ever seen. The mirrors in this bathroom stood on the countertop with no frames, unfinished to me. Of course, me being me, I was designing this house completely differently, modern log home, in my mind in each and every room.

The house came complete with a photo album on display showing the building process from beginning to the end. Jon took great delight in going through the book, telling the story of how he built this beautiful home. My daughter makes me a similar book every year for Christmas, only my book is all about a year in the life of my beautiful grandchildren. My favorite!

It was obvious that Jon took great pride in his home. He told me he had lived in a house in East Denver and rented out bedrooms for years, saving money to build this dream house. It was magnificent, and I could now see how Brie had given up everything to come up here and be in this home which now gave her the prestige she had no doubt longed for her entire life.

My date and I had traveled to this party in a horrific snowstorm, almost turning back twice. We had arrived, had the house tour, mingled, enjoying the company, food, wine, and then suddenly, everything changed. Jon was done talking about his home and announced that it was time for everyone to go home, just like that! Of course, Brie panicked—everyone panicked.

Brie began telling people that Jon was only kidding and that if anyone would like to stay longer that the party was indeed not over until midnight, and all were welcome to stay the night due to the storm; this was followed by Jon informing all, once again, that the party was over and that we all needed to leave. It was as if Jon had two personalities.

He was so happy to talk about his home that he built with his own hands. Passed the photo album around that had day-by-day pictures of the entire building of the home. It was incredible. This house was unbelievably beautiful to me. And Jon was so happy to give the grand tour and tell us every detail that went into the build. Like how long it took him to build the kitchen cabinets out of the beetle kill pine, but then abruptly, tour over. And this never changed over the years. He was not a people person, at all. And here he had married Ms. Socialite.

All the guests became very uncomfortable quickly and started trickling out the door into the ongoing storm that was not letting up any time soon. Brie invited my date and me to spend the night, which we quickly accepted because of the long drive up and the horrific weather, but it was awkward. I think my date was in shock. Jon was visibly angry that we were staying, and he and Brie had already had words about him ending the party so soon. It was eight o'clock, we had been there a little over an hour. Brie suggested we all get into the hot tub and listen to music, enjoy wine and the snow falling down. Jon became angrier and informed her that the hot tub would not be used.

Jon went off to bed at 8:30 p.m. Brie was quite embarrassed and apologized repeatedly. It became more and more obvious to me that Brie had fallen in love with the beautiful house and maybe not so much the man. The man did not appear to be Brie's type in any way. She has always been social and loves having people over to entertain quite often—oh, the parties! This man built a home a mile off the highway, on a dead-end road, at nine thousand feet. Clearly he had had enough of people.

Morning arrived, and Brie begged us to stay longer; we agreed on breakfast. Jon seemed to be friendlier, and soon Brie insisted we ride into the small town where they were married. "Not too far away," she promised, thirty minutes. "We want to show you the chapel, it's just such a quaint little mountain town." Well, this quaint little mountain town, Fairplay, turned out to be well over an hour away, with the roads plowed. We had a few drinks, ate lunch, saw the courthouse, which was closed on New Year's Day, not a chapel at all, and then we drove back to Brie's house. Turns out that Jon was friendly to us, but the catch was that you had to listen to him talk about how he built his house for hours on end, and that is as far as any conversation with Jon ever went.

Two years would pass, and there would be many girls' nights at my house and parties at Brie's house. Brie showed up on my doorstep one Friday afternoon, saying she needed a friend. She said that Jon did not want to have sex any longer, that he had sores on his penis, and he said it hurt. Brie swore she did not have herpes, but it was obvious to me that she had never told Jon that she indeed did have the virus. To this day, she will say she doesn't have the virus, and then the next time she brings the subject up, it's "My herpes is controlled with medication." I truly believe that she lies so often that she can't keep her stories straight.

I thought the marriage was no doubt going to end soon, that Brie's true self had shown up in the marriage, and Jon was not liking what he was seeing. I mean Jon was a Promise Keeper. This guy had plaques all over the home with Bible verses on them.

Brie continued to overspend and had complained to me that Jon had taken a credit card from her because she charged $50,000 on it in one year. Then came the time that Brie decided they were going to sell a health juice and be part of a pyramid, whereas they would have mailbox money the rest of their lives from getting people to sell this juice. That venture cost Jon $20,000 in just one year. Were they now getting mailbox money? No, they only accrued the debt from traveling around the country to attend all the seminars for this product and buying tons of it to pass out to people, encouraging them to sell it.

Jon was a frugal man that had saved for many years to build his home, drove an old truck, and lived with virtually no bills until Brie came along. Brie insisted on having a Jaguar, which she had always dreamed of. The mountain home had no garage, so this was baffling to me that you would have that car with no shelter, driving up and down a mile-long dirt road, really? But let's remember, it's all about how things look for Brie. Well, they showed up at my house one Saturday afternoon to show me the Jaguar that Jon had surprised her with. It was used but quite beautiful. And what came out of Brie's mouth but—"I guess this will do until I can have a new one." I will never forget the look on poor Jon's face.

Brie and Jon began to drink quite heavily in the evenings until Brie would pass out. This happened on each and every visit I made up to the house. I began thinking that the drinking was an everyday thing for her, not just for parties or get-togethers with the girls. Brie was wanting to quit her job, and Jon was telling her no, they could not afford for her to quit working. Brie's boss retired, and a new younger woman took over, and soon Brie lost her job. Jon was not happy with Brie losing her income. What did she say then? "I'm tired, and I just don't want to work anymore, Jon just needs to understand this."

Soon Jon would begin forgetting things, become distorted and confused. All of this came about after a surgery he had. When he woke up from surgery, he could not recognize or remember certain things and people. Brie phoned me and said she had left the room for a moment, and when she returned, he was out of bed and standing in a corner, like a little child being punished. Now when I visited the next day, he knew me. I was greeted with, "Why, there's my angel face." I cried.

Doctors diagnosed Jon with Alzheimer's disease. Brie was in denial, still spending money, and then later borrowing from the life insurance policy to take Jon to a clinic in San Diego, which cost over $20,000 for one week. She began making trips for him to go into an oxygen tank for $200 an hour, in Boulder, and then he began driving himself there. Yes, he drove down through the mountains and into traffic-jammed Boulder, all by his lonesome! One time I called Brie to see how things were going, asking her how Jon was. "Well, he's not here right now, I sent him to the liquor store." I couldn't believe my ears. Was she swimming down the river of denial or hoping he would crash? My gawd!

Jon began getting up nights and stumbling, hitting his head, messing his pants. Brie would have to shower Jon several times a night from the diarrhea. It was taking a toll on her. Jon soon forgot how to eat, and I saw him go from a well-built construction-type man to a thin and rapidly aging man, within just a few short months' time. It was all so sad.

Brie began getting angry with him. One night, while I was up staying with them, I heard her smacking him back in the bedroom. When she came out, I told her she needed help with Jon and to please do so right away. She was angry that he was ill, angry that she had to take care of him. I called her daughter, who lived close to me at the time, and told her how I felt, and she called in a social worker to help Brie get things in order.

Jon would go in and out of nursing homes and soon have a fall, breaking his hip, followed by a heart attack. Brie would sell the Jaguar and Jon's truck, buying a new large Ford Explorer, complete with a hefty payment. Brie was on her own, getting down the mile-long road by herself in the snow from now on. The county would only plow up her road when they felt like it. Once you got to the highway, a mile down, you were fine.

While at the nursing home, Brie would still be handing out $100 bills to her daughter and buying all the nurses' whiskey to drink with her at night, bringing in tins of expensive cookies and gifts for them. Brie was still in denial. All this time that she was spending money, she frantically told me that if Jon would pass away, she didn't know what she would do because his retirement income would end, due to the fact that he was not married when he retired from the service. She was losing it at a high rate of speed, her mind that is.

Near the end, I would spend the night at Brie's house with her daughter Randy, and she would tell me things I never knew about her mother. Randy told me that her father did all the awful things Brie had told me, but that he did these things because her mother had fallen in love with her father's best friend, had an affair, and one day packed up all the girls' suitcases, waiting for her lover to come and pick them up when they were small children; they would start a new life.

The lover never showed up, her husband stayed with her but acted out throughout the marriage. She told me that Brie had made the marriage hard for her father by always living beyond their means. She told me there was another side to the story. She told me that when she was in grade school, she and her sisters would come home, and their mother would be passed out on the living room floor. I had a difficult time even looking at Brie after all of this news. I felt I didn't really know her at all. This daughter seemed to have a certain love/hate relationship with her mother; she was the daughter that received $100 bills right and left from her mother. It was all too much for me to take in.

Jon left us the next day, he passed away in the early afternoon. I would pick Brie up at the nursing home, and she would come home with me, none of her daughters answered her calls. I was all she had at that moment. Perhaps her daughters felt she was never there for them growing up, so why be there for their mother now? I don't know. All I know is that if my husband died, my kids would be right there by my side for me. I felt such empathy for her, yet I was trying to deal with all her daughter had told me. I thought, *Who is this person, really.*

Within two days, Brie would ask me if I would loan her the money to have Jon cremated. I told her no, that I could not do that. Brie was still receiving boxes in the mail from shopping online almost daily during Jon's entire illness. I was shocked yet again. Here she was, constantly spending, yet no money for the cremation of the man that treated her like a queen.

I left for work the next morning, and Brie had asked me to use my laptop; of course I said yes. When I returned home, Brie was out with her daughter. My laptop showed that she had applied for several loans amounting to thousands of dollars, all in Jon's name. I was shocked. How does one apply for loans in the name of a dead man? And who would even think of such a thing! I thought she had no doubt ruined Jon's credit while he was alive, and she was continuing to do so after his death; it mortified me.

After this I had a difficult time having her in my home, taking care of her, I was her friend and grief counselor, but I no longer wanted to be. Within two days, she had made arrangements for Jon's service and been out shopping while I was at work. Brie brought in gifts, groceries, flowers, candles, I couldn't believe it. Brie had gotten money in Jon's name. I tried to excuse it, knowing that she was desperate, and desperate people do things that are not always right. It would continue to trouble me to this day.

Without Jon's retirement check, all that Brie had was the remainder of the life insurance left that she had already borrowed from, $85,000. She went into a deep depression, never leaving the house, drinking continually, shopping daily online, and began telling me she was making passes at the UPS man who delivered to her home. She said, "He will have a retirement, and I am going to snag him." Well, he wasn't interested. It got to the point of where Brie said this man would throw her packages over the fence, into her courtyard, instead of ringing the doorbell. It was kind of funny, she would get all dressed up and sit and wait for this delivery man to ring her doorbell.

Then she met a man at the local restaurant who drove a Jaguar and pursued him, but his four daughters intervened. Brie said it was all right, that he would not get involved any further because she found out that he had no money at all. Brie had actually googled his home online and could see it on Google Earth. She said that it was not impressive, and that he did not own the gun range that she thought he did, instead he managed it.

Brie went through the $85,000 life insurance within a year, then did a reverse mortgage so she would not have a mortgage payment every month. She never went back to work, just pursued as many men as she could, hoping to marry again. In the meanwhile, Brie had another face-lift and neck lift, and then soon had to sell the beautiful mountain home that needed so many repairs. She did well on the sale and paid cash for another home on the Western Slope, five hours away. Brie began remodeling this home right away, invited me to go visit, but I never did. She would now live close to the daughter she had been so close to before she met Jon.

Brie was still pursuing men, even bragging to me on the telephone that she was sleeping with three men at the same time, swearing that she has told them all about the herpes that she now seems to accept she has. What was amazing to me was that she would go to real estate sites and look up the homes by address to see if they were ever for sale. Then she would be able to view their homes and even go from room to room, shocking. She was summing up their worth.

After a year or so, Brie married a man that she had constantly complained to me about. This man had put his hand up her skirt on their first coffee date—yes, I just said that. I told her I wouldn't give him the time of day again, and that he would have been slapped across the face. Well, she went back out with him. This man ran back and forth to his ex-wife, and every time he did, Brie was not permitted to communicate with him. He would tell Brie he was just housesitting for his ex and that he needed "alone time" when he was there. Everyone was shocked when she married him.

I was just recently back in Colorado for a visit, and Brie wanted to drive from the Western Slope to see me. I declined, telling her I was just there a short time to be with family. She wanted to meet at an expensive restaurant; of course she is still having the champagne life on the beer budget. I don't answer the calls from her anymore, we just really never had anything in common at all. I walked away thinking that I had been dealing with a false person who would do anything they had to do to get what they want out of life.

What I will always remember of Brie is the mountain home. How she would have the grandest parties, all the wonderful food and costumes, and shared the home with everyone she knew. It was a beautiful place to go visit for the weekend. She's the party girl. I recently saw a picture of her and the new husband on FB where they were off to a '50s party at the senior center. That's Brie, no doubt, till the day she dies.

Rita

RITA IS BRIE'S DAUGHTER. When I first met Rita, she was a brunette, quite pretty and smart, physically fit, running marathons, had traveled the world, didn't have to work outside of the home. It seemed she had the world at her fingertips. Rita was full of life, or so she made it seem, always bursting with laughter, after a few drinks, that is.

Now I already knew Rita before I began cleaning her townhome through her mother's girls' night out get-togethers. When I met Rita, she was a thirtysomething mother of two boys, married to an air force officer. Rita had met her husband, Don, while in the air force herself. Rita's husband was on a tour in Afghanistan, and they had just relocated back to Denver so that she could be near her sisters and mother while her husband was on tour.

Rita and her husband had lived all over the world because he was a lifer in the air force. Rita was provided a nice home, did not have to work outside the home, and loved to work out and cook. There were always fresh flowers in her kitchen. Rita was quite fun and full of life. The home sported furnishings from their life stationed in Italy and many family photos throughout. I could see from the photos that Rita's husband was quite an attractive man, tall and handsome and very fit. She would say, "Yes, Don is very good-looking, but he is an officer, and officers are assholes."

Rita's two boys seemed full of life like, their mother, but out of control, tons of energy. I would soon learn that Rita drank as much as her mother. When they were all together, they would get drunk, new to my world. The women I have always known would have a few glasses of wine over dinner, not many bottles of wine. Brie's daughters all took after her when it came to drinking, they got drunk. And when we all gathered for Brie's girls' night out, that's exactly what happened; all the daughters and Brie got so drunk that the night would soon become ugly and soaked with filthy language, and yes, right in front of all of their children. It was always the same script. Brie would start bashing her ex, their father, and then the girls would become angry with their mother. It all would go downhill fast from there.

Rita seemed to have the perfect life but was missing her husband and complaining that she didn't know how much longer she wanted to live this lifestyle. Rita had said she dropped out of the air force for her husband so that they could have kids, kids that she never wanted. She would state this many a time throughout the coming months and right in front of her boys. Rita's boys were five and eight years old at this time. The boys sported black curly hair and big brown eyes; one was tall and thin and the other shorter and chubby and were just the cutest kids on the block. These two boys were always out of control whenever I saw them, even at family dinners, running, jumping, slamming into furniture and walls, throwing balls in the house, you name it, they did it. They even hit golf balls in the house.

Rita enrolled herself and the boys into a karate class and soon began talking about her crush on the instructor, Stan. The instructor was not at all like her tall and handsome officer husband. Stan was sixty years old, not attractive at all and about five feet tall. This man was married with children, and his wife was a corporate woman who ran the home and supported his karate studio. It would not be long before Rita had an affair with this karate instructor. He talked Rita into going back to law school. She had begun law school in the air force but dropped out to have a baby. One thing led to another, and you could predict what was coming—her husband would return and find out about this affair. According to her mother, it was not her first affair. I had told Brie that things were going to get bad for Rita, and how could she jeopardize her marriage? And she told me, "That's just how she is, Angel, she is like her dad, nobody can stop her."

Rita's husband would come home from overseas, and the truth would soon come out about the affair. How did the truth come out? Rita's brother-in-law, Tom, told her if she did not tell her husband everything, that he would himself. Tom was married to Rita's sister, Rachel. Rita partied hardy with her sister Rachel and almost caused a divorce between her and Tom. Rachel and Tom had even split up for a time, and this was when Rita and her sister began to party in the bars. I would say that Tom wanted revenge for the damage that he thought Rita caused in his marriage. Within only six months, Tom would move his family to the Western Slope, five hours away, away from the entire family but now close to his family where they now have a better life. Why this drastic move? I believe for a better life and because of Rita's bad influence on his wife.

And so when Don arrived back in the States, it would only be a few short weeks before Rita would fess up to the affair, and that was not all she fessed up to. Years prior, Rita had also had an affair in Texas, when Don was overseas, and so she told him everything, thinking that Tom would tell him soon. Don is a military man, he see's things one way; he never crosses the line. There was no way the marriage would go on. Who could blame him, twice while serving his country overseas, she had cheated on Don. And what kind of man cheats with a married woman whose husband is serving overseas anyhow? Not a good guy, for sure, at least that isn't my opinion of a good fella.

At first Don let Rita stay in the home, stating that he wanted a divorce and that she was not forgiven. Rita pretty much resided in the basement, but as time went on, Don had her removed from their home and divorced her. Rita would move into a very small older townhome not far from their home, with shared custody of the two boys.

It would not be long before Rita was drinking even more heavily on a daily basis. I know this because this was when I began to clean her townhome. Rita had called me and told me she could not keep up with the cleaning and go to law school at the same time, that she had extra money from grants that would cover the cost of cleaning her home.

Frankly I didn't know how long she would remain in law school with all the drinking. Every time I would go clean, there were empty wine bottles everywhere. Rita had taken quite a few steps back in her living conditions. She was not far from her former home, yet it seemed a world away. She moved across the fine line into the not-so-good area of town and into a worn-and-torn old townhome that she and her boys barely had room to move around it. It was dark and dreary, yet Rita kept moving forward one step at a time. The home was just a total disaster.

She was having Stan over whenever the boys were with their dad, and they would leave all of their sex toys out on the night-stand when I went to clean, along with marijuana pipes. It was as if Rita had lost any class that she had previously displayed. I thought it would not be long before she dropped out of law school. I mean how can anyone party like she was and keep up with her studies?

Soon Stan was taking Rita's boys everywhere with him and babysitting them while Rita was in law school. And yes, Rita paid him to babysit her boys. It would not be long before Rita was insisting that Stan leave his wife and move in with her. Stan was not willing to leave his family for Rita and told her they could not see each other any longer. You see Stan had never worked and had been supported by his wife his entire life.

And so, one eventful night, Rita got drunk and drove to Stan's big beautiful house in the upper-class neighborhood and screamed out to him at 2:00 a.m. to come outside and talk to her, or she was telling his wife everything. Well, one thing led to another, and before you knew it, Stan, his wife, and Rita were all out in the front yard, yelling at one another. Rita disclosed the entire affair to Stan's wife, who then ordered him out of their home.

At this point, Rita insisted that Stan move in with her and the boys, but he refused and took refuge at the karate studio, sleeping on a cot. Six months went by, and finally Stan moved in with Rita because his wife shut off all the finances going into the karate studio, thus he had no business to go to any longer, no place in which to sleep. He began to live off of Rita, sitting at home all day, smoking marijuana, telling her what a whore she was while she finished law school and went on to begin her job as public defender.

Somehow Rita had made it through law school, and the partying went on even as Rita was a public defender. It would only be a few short months at this job before Rita got a DUI. This was when she could no longer afford my services because she had to retain an attorney, pay for alcohol classes, and urine analysis specimens every week. She almost lost her job as public defender and was told that if there was another incident, she would be let go. This was all swept under the rug because nobody ever heard a word about the public defender getting a DUI. I was dating a Fox News producer at the time all this went down, and oh man, did he want that story, but I forbade him, telling him I thought Rita had enough problems as it was. I lived in fear of him televising that story for quite a long time afterward, it was a juicy news story!

I would see Rita only a few times after I quit cleaning her townhome at her mother's parties. Rita had gained about sixty pounds, never worked out any longer, let her gray roots take over, and had become very quiet and even teary-eyed at all the parties; she had aged dramatically. Stan, it turned out, was not going to have anything to do with Rita's family. Things were bad, Rita was now supporting a man much older than her that yelled obscenities at her all day, and she barely ever saw her father, mother, or sisters. And this man was bored and bitter for having lost his karate studio that his wife maintained for him for over two decades. And the worst for this man, his children were not speaking to him.

One the other hand, Rita's ex-husband remarried and bought a bigger, more beautiful house, saw his boys more and more, and even threatened to gain full custody. I don't know that he ever did. Rita was still supporting Stan who sat at home all day smoking marijuana, still was not divorced, but trying to come up with the funds to divorce his wife and somehow gain $100,000 from the divorce. This was a mess.

At one point, Rita was riding a transit bus back and forth to work because she could not afford a Breathalyzer for her car and was contemplating renting out her spare bedroom to make her mortgage payment due to the fact that the boyfriend would not work. This is a woman that threw her entire pampered life away and destroyed her family for a man that never amounted to anything, very sad. I always conclude that Rita had low self-esteem because of her upbringing, watching her parents cheat on each other, and excessive use of alcohol.

This story ended with Stan getting killed on a motorcycle several years after, never having married Rita. Within a year, Rita would meet a man fifteen years younger than her, with two toddlers. According to Rita's mother, Brie, she is now happily married to this man, helping him raise his children, and both of her grown sons are now in the air force, spending most of their time with their father and his new wife and kids. Just goes to show that things can work out for people in the long run. But will she be tempted to cheat again? Who knows.

Harry on the Hill

I T WOULD NOT BE long before word got out of my business, especially since I began working for a few Realtors who would call me at the last-minute needing something cleaned. Many Realtors would call me right from the closing table, asking me to clean a home within a day or so. "Just name your price, Angel, whatever you want, we will cut the check right now." Of course, I would always be available because the money was incredibly good. And when word gets out that you are willing to work 24-7, and that you do good work, they all begin to call you. They don't care what you charge, you're always available.

On a pretty warm and bright Sunday morning in August, I received a call from a gal named Bridgette, wanting to know if I was available to clean two apartments within a few hours of the call. Now I had plans of hiking in the mountains this day, but I thought I could get a workout cleaning two apartments and still have the rest of the day to enjoy. I jumped right to it when she told me what she was involved in.

Bridgette was an assistant to a property manager, Harry, from Dallas, Texas. Harry had bought quite a few properties on The Hill in Boulder, Colorado, and rented them out to college students. Harry was tall, handsome, midthirties, clean-looking all-American guy. Harry lived in a house right off the Pearl Street Mall by one single street, in Boulder, right below his rentals on The Hill. I knew the work would be consistent every August with this guy, and if he could afford to live right off the Pearl Street Mall, well, this dude was going to buy more and more properties for college students to rent.

Cleaning houses on The Hill always paid well. Why did these jobs pay so well? When rich kids come into Colorado to go to school, all they do is party, at least that's what goes down on The Hill. The damage to property is horrific, to say the least, and let me tell you, nothing is cleaned for the entire year that the students reside there.

There were times that there was vomit projected onto the ceiling, and it obviously dried there for the entire school year. After cleaning out a house with carpet, you would still have to come back through and literally rake (yes, with a garden rake) the carpet, getting out all of the debris left behind, before you could vacuum or steam clean. The blinds, if there were any, had to be replaced because they would all be broken. Refrigerators and stoves almost always had to be replaced, especially in the houses where the students had a two-year lease. Drains would be clogged up, and faucets would no longer work. Sinks would be ripped off the walls in which they hung, doors would have holes in them from young people punching them or kicking them in.

These rich kids would move in beautiful furnishings, including crystal for the kitchen, pool tables, sectional couches, beautiful lamps and bedroom suits, and big-screen television sets. The attics would be filled with all-new ski equipment and clothing. Students and their parents would fill the entire houses up. And usually when they left, they would leave it all. Harry liked to rent to young women because, "They cause less damage." Harry would say, but I would soon find out that he had underlying motives.

Now each one of these old Victorian houses was divided into two to three apartments, and Harry would rent them out for $1,100 a month per student, three to four students per apartment. Yes, Harry was hauling in the cash. There would be an upstairs apartment with bath and kitchen, a ground floor apartment, also with bath and kitchen, and then a basement apartment with the same.

The parents would arrive to sign the paperwork with their student in tow and all of their belongings to get through the school year; if they didn't bring their belongings, then they would be off shopping. Most parents would be in complete shock of the condition of the houses, very old and beat-up.

Harry would be checking out their daughters each time. I would be standing there, thinking, *Oh, dear god, your daughter is going to be exposed to so many awful things up here on The Hill, and you don't even have a clue*. The Hill was well known for partying all year long. These people were all from out of state, and they had no idea what The Hill was all about.

The Hill is located right above the Pearl Street Mall in Boulder, and all the students could easily navigate down to the bars, shopping, and restaurants because they were within walking distance. Back then you could easily pay $500,000 for a small home with a dirt basement floor and windows that wouldn't open any longer because they had been painted so many times. Now the same small house would go for an easy $750,000. These homes sit right above The Hill. Why on earth would people pay this? And why would they want to live near all the party houses? Because they could walk pretty much anywhere they needed to go. You have to realize that this is all sitting in the beautiful setting beneath the foothills, right above are the Flatiron mountains, quite picturesque.

When students leave in mid-August, Harry flies his brothers in from Dallas, Texas, and they did all the repairs while I did the cleaning. I would hire gals to help me, but they would never last more than two days. I recall hiring a friend and could not believe she showed up in a pearl necklace with acrylic fingernails on. I do the work extremely fast, and I never get any complaints, that is, unless I hire someone to help. Harry always paid me whatever I turned an invoice in for because he said he never had anyone work so fast and do such a good job for him.

So when we worked, we had a turnover of about six hours, if we were lucky. It was crazy work that paid crazy money. The six hours usually included cleaning one big Victorian house split up into three apartments: basement, main floor, and second floor. This also meant that we had to get rid of all the furnishings before we could clean. To this day, I wish I had rented a truck and hired a few guys to help me load up everything from these apartments because we just threw it all in the dumpsters out back. People would come through with trucks, loading it all up during this three-week period. I'm sure this still goes on to this day.

If you like to flip furniture, clothing, skiing equipment, appliances, and electronics, then go to Boulder Colorado, or no doubt any other college that has high tuition, rent yourself a large truck, and find a place to store all the goods, and you will not have to work the entire winter months, I guarantee it. That's how much these rich kids leave behind. I recall a gal leaving one day with her Kate Spade purse, getting into her Mercedes sedan, and just driving down to the next house that Daddy rented—completely furnished. "My daddy doesn't want me to live up on The Hill anymore, he has already furnished my new place, do with all this as you will," she said.

Harry had a total of eight Victorian houses on The Hill, and we would work a total of eight days straight. Harry's assistant, Bridgette, and I got close, and she shared with me that she had divorced because she was in love with Harry, but Harry was not noticing and could not see her as he did the young college girls.

Yes, Harry would take up with one or two of his tenants each school year. These girls were eighteen years of age, very thin, the yoga type, and extremely pretty. If their parents only knew! Now when the parents of these young ladies would drop them off on The Hill with all their earthly belongings, you could see the parents were already in a panic. They didn't like the area or the condition of the houses. But what were they to do? This was Boulder, Colorado, and there would not be another rental in site.

It made me wonder how Harry advertised his properties. When the parents were signing all the paperwork, you could almost tell which gal Harry was going to hook up with for that semester. I found it disgusting myself. I always wanted to scream out to their parents, "Don't leave her here, listen to your gut instinct!"

And so after three summers and never getting anyone to work for me on The Hill longer than two days, I gave it all up, all that money! I often wonder how many more houses Harry bought and how rich he must have become over the years, and oh yes, did any father ever come after him for taking up with their daughters?

Nora

THEN CAME NORA. NORA and I met at a women's book club while reading the book *Why Men Love Bitches*. Now that was quite the group. Nora came into the group with a mutual friend, Robin, who is a whole other chapter. I found Nora quite odd from the moment I first listened to her add to a conversation among six women. She was Princessie like but without the princess look.

Nora was a short medium-build woman in her late forties that wore no makeup, did nothing with her hair at all, the wash-and-dash look, with sprouts of gray everywhere. Nora dressed like she bought everything at a thrift store, and indeed she did! She reminded me of a much older Annie from the Broadway show. I thought it odd that Nora carried herself like a princess yet dressed like a homeless person.

I was not interested in striking up a conversation at all. I inquired with Robin as to where she had met Nora, and she told me they met at Mile High Church in Denver, and that she felt Nora needed to get out more and meet some people, being that she was divorced, lived quite a ways out east, far from town, living with seven cats and three dogs.

Of course, it would not be long before Nora was showing up at all of our single gal get-togethers, and of course, like all people with problems, she gravitated toward me.

It would also not be long before I agreed to go and clean her home in the country once a month. Nora had been depressed for quite some years and let her home go, as far as cleaning was concerned. The house was set back down a five-mile road off the highway. Grass surrounded the house, and a ton of it. Nora spent a lot of time mowing. The house was not large, actually small, with little character. The inside was dark and full of older things, like an elderly person's home. Her house was like her, everything obviously came from a secondhand store. Her husband had never cared about their home. It would be hard to clean because it was small and hard to move around in, with lots of dirt and animal hair, and it appeared to need repairs everywhere I looked. I wondered why she was getting it cleaned instead of paying a handyman.

I agreed to take it on because she only wanted a once-a-month cleaning, and it was a good price. I was not interested in being Nora's friend in any way, just the business I was getting out of it. I admit feeling sorry for her after hearing the story of her life.

Turned out that Nora had a few degrees under her belt. Her specialty was psychology, and according to her, she had run a center in Denver for a few years that helped abused women. Nora seemed quite intelligent but was not willing to work any longer; she said she was just tired. She had divorced her husband, who was a Denver police officer his entire career. Nora said the marriage had become abusive because her husband took up with prostitutes, meaning he had had several affairs with them and, as Nora put it, didn't mind anyone knowing what he was doing. Nora said she was kept out in the country, away from everything and everyone, that she had always felt isolated living there, yet she was not willing to sell and give it all up. She had a grown son, who was also a Denver policeman, and two grandchildren.

Nora was the only child of an abusive father, who beat her mother, and claimed that she had even witnessed her dad murder a woman at age seven or so. This is why Nora had helped abused women, she herself had been abused her entire life. Because of the abuse from her husband, she had begun to dress like an artist, as she put it, with baggy clothes, and thus did nothing with her hair. Nora said she had always wanted to hide her body but never stated why.

I did not clean Nora's house more than twice because it was very dirty; I would say quite filthy. The kitchen cabinets had a black tar substance around the handles on the wood, the toilets were as if they had not been cleaned for years, the dog and cat hair were not measurable, the house smelled of mold. On top of all that, I did not care for Nora's personality.

When I would work at her home, she would always tell me of a better way of doing things than the way I did them. And it was not long that I realized what she was really doing was drilling me on how much I charged for different-sized homes and the frequency in which I cleaned them. Soon Nora was out cleaning homes. She was broke and had all those animals to feed, along with a mortgage to pay. She was so broke her hiking boots were worn out, and she needed new ones. I was with her the day she tried to return her well-weathered boots to REI in Denver, stating that she had only had them for a few months and that the boots had fallen apart. Of course they did not let her exchange them for a new pair. It was quite an embarrassing moment for me, I was embarrassed for her as well. She said, "Listen, Angel, we overpay for everything we buy, so I try to replace items over and over again. Shoes are the only thing I don't buy used." I was mortified.

We began meeting for lunches and dinners, and Nora started talking about our mutual friend, Robin, in a negative way. "Oh, Robin is just perfect, now isn't she! Well, the truth is, Angel, I can't stand her, and I don't know why you are being friends with someone so vain for so long now." I told her that Robin was a very kind and goodhearted soul, just rediscovering herself living life alone like the rest of us divorced women in the group. Nora was intent on bashing our friend and then began bashing me in a roundabout way.

On top of everything else, Nora had found a stranger on Craigslist to live with her. She had advertised for a man that was a nerd, smart, and had a ton of money. "The opposite of my ex-husband," she would say. Nora found him right away, dated for only two weeks before she moved him in. She said she needed the income because she had already gone through her 401(k). Her only concern, what would her son think.

She would say, "He isn't much to look at, and he is quite boring, but he's loaded with money." I would soon meet Nora and Tony for drinks in Denver, and I was quite surprised. Nora was all dressed up, had her hair done, earrings on, and full makeup. Tony was short, had a very red face, like a heavy drinker, wore shorts that went way above the waistline with a belt, and socks with sandals. He was the guy that held her purse while she was in the ladies' room. This guy seemed very nice, gentle and kind, proud to be with Nora. I was happy for her, she found someone to save her, which was what she sought, and who also cared deeply for her.

It would be only a month or so after Nora moved Tony in when I had been telling her about a professor whose house I was cleaning and how sad he was that his wife had left him right after he built a beautiful new house for her. Nora asked me if I would please fix her up with my client, the professor. "Just for fun," she said, "I just want someone to have fun in bed with. Tony isn't fun, all he does is sit at the computer." Nora had already told me that she would break up a marriage if she wanted the guy bad enough, she would just go after him, but that was when she was alone. When she told me that, it made me realize that she could not be trusted around any man I was dating.

I told her I would not set her up with my client, that his heart was broken and that he needed time to get over what his wife had done. I was just shocked that she asked me to do this.

Nora said that Tony was already insulting her. He had told her to please not put her hair up or back because her ears stuck out so far. I told Nora he was just trying to help her with her hair. She was angry with the stranger she moved into her home to save her financially and already looking for an affair; very sad and crazy to me.

With all these things happening all at once, it was just too much for me. Nora was off balance and did not have the morals that I needed a friend to have. It was really hard getting Nora to just go away. Nora would call me two or three times a day, crying on her phone, messages asking me to please remain her friend. I just couldn't be friends with someone so horrid. Robin had noticed things as well, felt used by Nora, and ended their friendship.

Nora had always claimed that she did all the work on herself in therapy that she needed to go on and live a good life, but it was obvious to me that she was acting out in many unhealthy ways. Lo and behold, a message would come on my phone that Nora had married

Tony and that she was happy. I would see them in a restaurant soon after, and she was sporting an enormous diamond ring and had a grin from ear to ear.

I follow Dwayne Dyer, who was a renowned author, teacher, philosopher, and motivational speaker, who has since passed away. I have many of his wonderful books. Before he passed, he was in Denver, and I saw that a new author, Nora B, was going to be there promoting her book, *Wake Up People*. I was shocked. After researching, I found that she had written a book on how to be happy in life and to always do the right thing, be kind by following the Spirit. She is a phony who would cheat on her husband at the drop of a hat, just for fun. She and Tony had moved to the northeast where she also speaks on a radio show—shocking! This horrid, mean, vicious person is talking about the Spirit. Enough said about Nora and the mask she wears daily. Shocking how people can make a profit on complete lies they tell every day. I mean, I bet she has affairs every chance she gets.

Sherry

I RAN AN AD IN the newspaper for a very short time, and this was how I met up with Sherry. It was a bit of a drive to her home as she lived between Longmont and Lyons, Colorado, in Boulder County. It was the country to me back then, even though it was just outside of the small town of Lyons. Lyons sits at the foothills, just before you go up the canyon to Estes Park. It was quite a beautiful drive, with the winding roads and large trees that adorned them. It smelled different in the country, not the oily smell from the city but fragrant and fresh.

Upon first glance, I knew Sherry was a farm gal. There were eggs for sale in front of her house by the road with a little box to put your money in, not something you would ever see anywhere in town or the city. This gal was trustworthy and from another time, I thought to myself. The property sported a large greenhouse in the back which was visible from down the road. Everything was green, and in the front yard was a swing like you would see on a porch, but this swing hung from a large tree. There were large patches of flowers throughout the yard, like little gardens. It all smelled so wonderful, I felt as though I had just entered a completely different world, a more beautiful world than where I roamed. Where I lived at the time, everything was very well-groomed but just with bushes and hedges. No flowers of any kind, a small townhome community built around a lake.

So out of the backyard came a woman. At first glance, I knew this gal was indeed a farm gal. Sherry is a short, stocky, and heavy-set woman who reminded me of a Boulder chic right off the bat. Definition of a Boulder chick would be not too clean or groomed in any way. There is a certain class of people who live in Boulder that don't believe in soap of any kind, washing of the hair, or shaving any of their body parts. Sherry had long dark frizzy hair with gray throughout, no makeup, dirt under her fingernails, dirty feet, and sporting the ever-popular Croc shoes that so many Boulder people wear. If you saw her on the street, you may think she was homeless. Sherry also reminded me of an Indian woman because of her high cheekbones, and there was something about the way she carried herself. Plain and simple, this woman was quite manly, and for a split second, I thought she may have once been a man.

We introduced ourselves and began to walk around her property. How beautiful it was, two larger gardens out back, one with a variety of flowers and one with vegetables, and then the large greenhouse with more vegetables. Sherry grew several kinds of tomatoes and lettuce varieties in about every color you can imagine, and also basil of several different types, such as licorice basil.

I was amazed; along the walk, we tasted a lot of them, and I had been introduced to several new flavors that I had no idea even existed. Sherry was an organic farmer. There was also a small greenhouse in the shape of an octagon that sported a small fish pond, complete with beautiful lily pads and a large goldfish that even lived there throughout the winter months. This small property on, I would say, an acre was quite impressive. There was even a large chicken coop from which she got her eggs. And yes, I was sent home that day with many goodies to eat.

We entered the house through the back. Sherry's house was a split level with a large downstairs living space, laundry room, and bathroom. There was also a crawl space that Sherry started all her seedlings in before transferring them to her outside gardens, complete with heat lamps. The hardwood floors, original to this old home, were quite dirty from people coming in and out from the gardens. I'm talking mud—this was obviously a working home of a farmer.

The kitchen was quite large, as one would expect on a farm, a working kitchen. Off the kitchen was a large sunroom that she utilized as an office and TV room. It was decorated, as much of the house was, with dried flowers and Indian things, like dream catchers.

Turned out that Sherry did the farming out of the love of it but made all her money from IBM, where she worked on the phone, basically telling people all over the world where to dump, or how to dispose of, their chemical garbage. Sherry had this job for almost thirty years, ten of those years working from her home on the phone.

All the floors upstairs were covered with dirt as well. The house sported many cobwebs and was in no way a well-kept or clean home. My price was going to be high. Sherry hired me for every-other-week cleaning. Things went well and did I ever get a workout in that housecleaning! But there were always wonderful gifts of vegetables to be taken home, so it was well worth it. And then there were the days where I would stay, and we would drink wine and eat cheese. And to drive to the country to do a house, well, it was a treat.

Sherry had two sons, one just finishing high school and the other, popping in and out of college. The younger son, Tom, was a delight and quite a big help to Sherry as he contributed to their farming business each and every summer. The older son, Bill, was a problem because he had some sort of mental issues which had Sherry confiding in me while talking on the phone one evening. Sherry had called me, asking for advice because I had raised my kids, and they were both doing so well. I felt such empathy for her in this area because she raised these two boys all alone. Sherry had married an American Indian who was well educated, and after the second boy was born, he deserted the family. Sherry confided in me that she never wanted children, her husband had talked her into it, and then just exited the family. She told me that she had such a great love for her boys and that she could not imagine life without them, but I could see it was a struggle.

Soon there would come a day when her ex-husband would be coming to nearby Greeley, Colorado, to make a speech. Believe it or not, this guy, who deserted his sons and wife, was out in the world telling people how to live life. He was indeed a life coach, go figure. Sherry called me, so upset, crying, and desperately afraid because the ex had contacted her sons and wanted to meet with them. Sherry was afraid that her sons would like him and maybe even blame her somehow for not being with him all through their childhood. I told Sherry she was being silly, she was the one who was there for them through all the cuts, bruises, flus, colds and nightmares, school functions, and everyday life, their constant. She was obviously the one who fed them and kept shelter over their heads their entire lives. I told her not to worry. She said, "But they seem so curious, so excited."

I said, "It won't last, they will resent him because he was never there, you have been their father and mother, don't worry."

The boys rushed to the dinner to meet their father, who they could not even remember. They had only seen pictures of him when he was a young man. They discovered that this man had a whole other family after them. That he had lived his entire life taking care of two other children and those children's mother. Their excitement lasted all of about one week total, I believe the boys were even more proud and more in love with their mighty mother after this meeting. Both boys seemed to respect their mother now, something I had not witnessed before in either. It was amazing to watch, and I also saw a bigger sense of pride in Sherry, it was as if she now carried herself with pride.

Every Thanksgiving, all the farmers in the area got together for what they called an early Thanksgiving, *Friendsgiving* is a familiar word for this dinner. I was invited four years in a row, and man, did I love this dinner. The food would simply blow your mind. All kinds of homemade pies, squashes that were filled with fruits and nuts, and then broiled in the oven, every vegetable you could imagine sported the many tables; there was even homemade wine to be drunk. Everything was homemade and fresh from their farms. I cannot put into words how wonderful farmers can cook!

Everyone would laugh and have long conversations, and after the dinner, we would all take a walk across the way through a field to work off the food. As we all walked, we were looking at the Colorado mountain range in all its beauty. A few of the men would smoke a tobacco pipe while walking, and this brought back found memories of my grandpa D. Each one of these days celebrating an early Thanksgiving was quite wonderful, and even reflecting back on this memory today, my heart fills with love and my mouth waters. Nobody was in a hurry, and everyone lingered over the food, the day was never rushed.

It would not be long before I noticed people were coming in and out of the house and smelling of pot. You know, marijuana. And they were so silly and happy. And it wasn't long before I was getting the look, you know, the look like why-are-you-here-spoiling-the-fun look. It turned out that Sherry had told everyone that they could only smoke the marijuana outside because of my presence. Nice of her to do that, but it made it quite an awkward feeling for myself.

After our second Thanksgiving dinner, Sherry would decide to go off to Texas for the winters. She could work on her computer from anywhere, and she had an old beau in Texas who would let her live in her camper in his driveway. A guy named Tom. Sherry had found Tom on Facebook, you hear that one quite often. Tom had dumped her years prior because she was raising small boys, and he wanted nothing to do with that, took up with another woman, and left Sherry.

Sherry was having trouble being alone without a man in her life, it seemed. She kept telling me that every man she knew was married. I had sent my guy at the time, Phil, out to put new kitchen countertops in for her. Phil was a custom builder, built cabinets and the works, and did quite a fine job. Turned out that every time Phil had to go out and work in Sherry's kitchen, she was all over him. Anyhow that job got finished very quickly, and I then saw Sherry in a whole different way. I mean, we had become friends, and here she was, coming on to my guy. Now in my opinion, that is pretty desperate and very unkind to do to a friend. Besides that, she had been forming a relationship over the phone with the old beau in Texas. Quite the character, Sherry is.

Sherry's youngest son had married a young girl he had met in Boulder, and they were moving in for the winter. This girl was quite pretty but had a great deal of baggage as her mother had killed herself with a gun, and this girl had found her mother shortly after. Quite a lot to deal with there. Sherry was happy her son had found someone, but it was not to last. Sherry's son had hurt his back and was taking painkillers like M&M's, along with drinking. They fought a great deal of the time. These two did strange things like write "I love you" on his bedroom wall with a Sharpie.

When Sherry returned in the spring, she called me back to clean once again. I raised my rate very high on her because I no longer considered her a friend. And now the fun really began, or should I say, interesting. Sherry and her son were now growing medical marijuana in the large greenhouse. I'm talking eight-foot-tall plants with stuff on top of them that looked like sugar to me. I could smell the plants as I would be driving a half-mile down the road, on my way to her house. Sherry's son would leave the marijuana outside on their deck on tables so that it would dry, "Take all you want, Angel," he would say. It was all too nerve-racking for me. Had I been a smoker of marijuana, perhaps maybe this would not have bothered me at all. At this time in Colorado—and I am sure still—people were getting robbed of their marijuana crops and all the cash that went along with it.

I decided that this client had to go. It was not worth the frustration of worrying about someone coming in while I was there cleaning and robbing the place, and besides, we were not friends any longer, at least not in my book. I was not up for getting hurt or even murdered on her property. I said my goodbyes, and we kept in touch through Facebook.

Sherry and her son moved to Durango Colorado, up above the Colorado River, and ran a medical marijuana greenhouse operation. Her son continued to abuse pills and alcohol until his wife left him and soon died. Sherry's son's wife suddenly had internal bleeding and was pronounced dead within twenty-four hours at age twenty, while living with a friend, very sad.

I was in Telluride, Colorado, heading to Pagosa Springs and posting pictures on Facebook along the way. Sherry contacted me and asked me to visit her since Durango was in the vicinity. I did not visit while I was in that part of Colorado. I just did not have it in me to take a new boyfriend into her home to visit. We lost touch after a few months. Once a girlfriend crosses that line, how do you go back to trusting her? You don't. How do you keep the friendship going, or why would you want to? Sherry does not post much on Facebook anymore. She retired and pretty much just does the marijuana-growing. We really never had anything in common except the love of great food. I wish her the best.

Rob and Eva

I WOULD COME TO MEET with Eva at her front door through, again, another client who referred her to me. As I walked up to her door, her home reminded me of my ranch home my ex and I had bought together. Oh, how I love ranch homes. They're always so big, spacious, and wide open inside. Opening the door to greet me was a tiny, tiny older woman—elderly actually—in her late seventies, I would say, at the time.

I could see the beauty in her face as a young woman, she had class. A blue jean blouse with khaki slacks, and oh yes, Sperry loafers. You know the type, they have money, and they all dress the exact same way. Large diamond stud earrings with a large diamond wedding ring, gold bracelets and watch sported both wrists. "Well," she said, "look at you, you don't look like the cleaning lady I had in California."

"Oh," I said, "and what did she look like?"

"Fat and Mexican," she replied.

"Well, okay then," I said with a slight giggle, "would you like to show me around your beautiful home?" I wanted to change that subject pretty rapidly. You know how old people are, they spit out exactly what they are thinking. What might she say next?

"Well," she says, "I have not been able to trust anyone here and my neighbor told me about you, and so I thought I would give you a chance in my home." *A chance*, I thought to myself, *we will see if I give you a chance, honey.* I mean really, everyone is testing me, and I understand that completely, but I have retained the right to pick and choose who I clean for. I don't want a really dirty home on my route,

144

nor do I want to work for a total bitch. There, I'm just putting that out there because believe me, there are women out there, along with men, who want to degrade you for working your ass off all day long. It's in their DNA, especially the wealthier people.

The home was wide open. From the front door, we flowed right into the formal living room and the dining room, around the corner, into the kitchen, was a large island, with a great room for watching TV.

This house was decorated as though they lived in California on an ocean setting. It was indeed beautiful and light. So many elderly people live in dark homes with the blinds shut and the older furniture, ya know. Some even still have plastic covers on the lampshades. Lol. This gal was different. The way a person decorates their home, it tells you a story of their personality right off the bat. This particularly elderly woman was bright and young at heart, and I could tell I was gonna love her already.

It was like a storybook of a fun life well lived. In the great room sat her husband, Rob, whom I fell in love with right away. "Well, hey there, beautiful," he said to me with a smile. He reminded me of my Grandpa D. At Rob's feet lay one of the biggest black Lab dogs I had ever seen, what a puppy dog! And on the couch, a brown boxer. What was not to love about these people! They had an extra guest bedroom with a bath in the hall. Their master bedroom was quite large with a large bath, huge soaking tub, the works. The basement was completely finished, again in the light colors, ocean or beach colors, I would say. Inside the window wells of the basement were scenes from the ocean with cactus planted in the bed. These two elderly people loved living and never wanted it to end, and it showed in their home. Just light, airy, and full of spirit of life.

"We moved here for our daughter," Eva explained to me. She married a man from Mexico, had her two beautiful children, and then he left her, completely abandoned the family with no support sent at all.

"Our daughter needs us every day, mentally and financially," Rob said, "What the hell else reason would we move to this awfully ugly place? We raised our kids in Santa Monica and Pacific Palisades for years, this place was like moving to hell. It's so ugly here, how can you stand it, dear?"

Well, I had lived in California, Long Beach to be exact, for two years as my husband was transferred there. I hated it—no snow on Christmas there, lots of pollution hanging overhead, and way too many people for my psyche. After living in California, I could not wait to get back to Colorado with relatively clean air and no traffic. Course that was thirty years ago, Colorado now has way too many people and lots of pollution, and traffic comes with all that.

We would set up every-other-week cleanings, and things would go quite well at first, then there would be the little arguments about how long it took me to clean. You know, those old people from the earlier generations, they want you to make little money if you are only there a few hours, and then of course, they had the Mexican cleaning chic who would work all day for pennies back in California. I wasn't that gal.

Now these two were quite interesting people. They had a daughter, Annie, in North Carolina who worked for the labor board and was lesbian with a partner. They lived in a gated community that Eva would fly to for visits quite frequently. These two gals would eventually adopt three brothers from a mother in Guatemala who did not practice birth control. I thought it was interesting. They practiced like the older generation would—one stayed home to be a housewife and the other worked. They're still together.

Then there was their son, Nate, who still lived in California. According to Rob, Nate refused to grow up. Nate resided in a pool house of wealthy people in Malibu. He took care of the property while they would be traveling frequently. Nate also volunteered at a South Los Angeles high school helping underprivileged kids, oh yes, and he worked PT in a surf shop. This is what he loved the most, surfing. They would show me pictures of Nate over the years. He was that guy that was his father's twin, yet rebelled at life at every turn. He was completely covered with tattoos. When I say completely covered, I mean it, except for his face, that is. Rob would say over and over again, "That boy is just waiting for me to die so he can live off my hard-earned money the rest of his damn life."

At first Rob and I would be alone while I was there working because Eva would be out running errands and shopping. She got around quite a bit back then. Rob would tell me the story of their life, at each visit, I would get little pieces. What a life these two had had!

Eva had been a Clairol model. She would have her hair done in different colors almost weekly, according to Rob. "Oh, what a beauty she was," he would say with a huge smile on his face. "Well, she ran my optometry office, ya know, did the books and everything for years. She still manages our money." It was cute to listen to him brag about the love of his life. And soon Eva would stumble in through the door with all kinds of shopping bags in hand.

Quite frequently, she would say, "I saw this car today, Rob, I want one."

"Okay, darling, what color would you like?" he would reply. And sure enough, next time I went, there would be a new car.

This woman had that life, you know, the one where you find the man who loves and adores you, and life just gets better and better. These two went out dancing together, and he still dated her—yes, they had date night each and every week. It was so fun to hear all they did. I was jealous. I thought to myself, *Is this how it was when you fell in love back in the '40s?* You know, back when everything was simple. And oh, the pictures of those two when they were young, quite fabulous!

Now Eva had been busy having the three babies and then working in Robbie's ophthalmologist's office. But the story begins with her growing up in Indiana with three brothers, dirt poor. A mother who married over and over again until she found Mr. Right who would raise these four heathens, as she called herself and her brothers. She would later go off to college and meet Rob. That is pretty much her story. Now Rob, on the other hand, is quite a different story, a very interesting story, to say the least.

I would tell Rob over and over again, "Write a book, Rob, write a book!"

"Oh, it's not that exciting," he would say to me with a giggle. Now Rob, he grew up poor as well, grew up on a farm in Iowa and was very close to his grandfather. Rob would go off to the air force. "In order to get college paid for," he would tell me. He was the guy that sat in the bottom of the plane as an observer. He pretty much would look around and tell the pilot up front what was going on. He didn't go into great detail about his service days, except to say that he had quite the fun times with any women he chose to have fun with. He was quite the ladies' man. And in looking at his photos when he was young, well, this guy was about 6'5" tall and built like a body builder, he had the looks of a movie star. He would tell me, "I wasn't looking for 'the one' back then, I was just having fun."

Then when Rob left the service, he went to California to go to college and worked as a mailman while attending college. Who did he deliver mail to? Bob Hope's house was one of them. Oh, did he tell me stories about Bob Hope! "He was never there, Angel, it was always his wife, inviting me in for coffee. You see, Bob Hope ran around with other women throughout his marriage, his wife was very lonely." Now it seemed to me that Rob was drawn in to the lives of the rich, or that is just how he ended up getting that mail route, I'm not sure. But he would spend most of his life living among the rich, as he would become one of them as an eye doctor, an eye doctor to the rich and famous.

"Oh, they would all be waiting in my office, in the lobby, except for Ed Sullivan, he would come in through the backdoor. He liked his privacy." He would go on to golf with famous people and have them in his home for dinner. They would give him tickets to the Oscars. "Oh, we were there, but we were in the back, ya know. Those were the days," he would say, with glee in his eyes. "Our neighbor in Pacific Palisades was Walter Matthau. He would stand in our driveway and watch my son shoot baskets. He was just a normal fella, nothing special there. He let his wife do their entire home in wallpaper with roses, ya know." He would laugh. I had read that somewhere about Walter. Huh, I guess some things you read about movie stars are true.

These two had raised their kids in Santa Monica and Pacific Palisades and then retired in Palm Desert. That's when the call came.

"I need you here, Mom, I can't raise these two kids without your and Dad's help." Well, it was clear as a bell to Eva that they had to move to Colorado in order to help their daughter, but not to Rob. According to Eva, she had to drag him kicking and screaming all the way to Colorado. And when he talked about his grandkids, it was not with a gleam in his eye, not like Eva had. According to Rob, this move had ruined his entire life. They were retired in Palm Desert and living the high life on the golf course. Sunshine every day with warm temperatures year-round. Rob hated everything about Colorado, and he made no bones about telling you how he hated things.

"What is the matter with you f——ing people, actually choosing to live your life in this shithole of a state? And why do they charge so much for these cookie-cutter homes they build? I paid the same for my house in Pacific Palisades two decades ago, and it was a mansion by the sea," he would yell out in anger. Rob still kept in close contact with all his buddies back on the West Coast through Facebook, protesting the entire time about how he was dragged to Colorado to live. I often wondered why he never went back to visit his old friends.

Things were great with these two the first couple of years, then the fun times went down the drain rather rapidly. First of all, Nate moved into the basement and appeared quite depressed, not knowing what to do with the rest of his life. The family that he had lived with had sold their property in Malibu, and he was homeless, with no real money to live on, not in Malibu, that is.

Rob was not happy at all. Again he would say, "He is just waiting for me to die to spend my money." After about six months of moping around the house, living off of Mommy and Daddy Nate would go to school to become a bounty hunter, which he never got employed for. Then after talking about how that just seemed an impossible profession to get into, he would go to work for the oil rigs, buy a beautiful house out in Brighton, just to have to sell it all in a few short years, after hurting his back at work, and come back home to Mommy and Daddy, Mommy always being receptive, but not Daddy.

In the meanwhile, the daughter, Elda, who was local—and I mean right up the street—needed them for car repairs and everything under the sun. She would get their old couches when they bought new; they bought and kept up the repairs on all her cars. What did she do for a living? She was a bank teller, yah, no money there, and no child support coming in for the two kiddos. Rob and Eva paid for all the two kids' gymnastics and soccer. It never seemed to end, according to Rob. Rob complained constantly while Eva was more than happy to do those for her daughter and grandchildren. And then everything changed once again, and this would be the most devastating and biggest change yet.

Eva became ill, very ill, to the point where she was in and out of the hospital and even had to stay over thirty days at one time; she almost died. I went to visit her and had to hold myself up against a wall in the hallway of the hospital after our visit. I mean, this was a tiny, tiny lady in the first place, seeing her like that, well, it was hard on me. She was withering away faster than any flower I had ever seen without water. This was the woman that kept it all together at home, the woman who made me the biggest plate of the most beautiful and delicious cookies at Christmastime, not to mention the beautiful gifts all year round, the woman with all the energy and the kindest heart to boot. There she lay in that hospital bed. I was seeing a change; she wasn't herself anymore.

Eva would never leave the house much at all after this sickness. She would tell me that it was taking too long for her to die. "Is this what happens to a spoiled woman like me, a woman who has had the most beautiful life, we suffer in the end?" she would say.

I brought her a book on being grateful. I still felt she had so much to be grateful for. She thanked me after she read it, to my surprise, because when I gave her the book, she looked at me as though she was insulted. I mean how could I relate to what she was going through in her old age? But there have been times in my life where friends and family needed this book, just a little reminder of what life gives us every day, the smallest of blessings. It is not a good thing to feel sorry for oneself, let me tell you, I know this firsthand.

Let's face it, most people don't give a damn about us, especially after we stop giving a damn, they just get tired of trying to lift us up. If you can give someone a book to help them, someone that loves books in the first place, like Eva, it can make all the difference in the world, and I saw this difference in Eva after she read the book, which, by the way, I was not so sure she would read. It made me feel so good. We had a good connection, she and I. I mean, there were those days when she would insult me just a little bit, ya know, the old lady thing where she is pissed off because she is old, and you are younger, but I always let it fly because I felt her to be a very special lady, and I treasured her.

We all can learn so much from older people, they can nourish our souls if we let them. And this gal, to me, was one of the mightiest women I have yet to know. She still fights hard to live today, it's amazing.

Now everything was up to Rob, driving the grandkids back and forth to school, buying the groceries, you name it, he had to do it all. Now he was happy to do all of this at first, but then it all became a burden. The next thing I knew, Rob had had a stroke in the middle of the night in front of the refrigerator, like so many men do. And off he went into the hospital and then rehab center for a few months. This was not good. Eva went into fits. "What if I lose him, what will I do? I can't lose my Robbie, I have to go first, not Robbie."

Nate was there for a few months to help, but that didn't last long. Back to the oil fields he went, permitting him to move out. And when you work in the oil fields, you are there for sixteen to twenty-one days at a time before you come home, and he never came home. Nate would begin to live with woman after woman, never being able to commit to any one woman for too long. Soon he had enough money saved, thanks to Mommy and Daddy, that he would buy a cabin up in Montana and live off the land. I couldn't help but remember the time that Nate had told me, "I have to stay here for my niece, because if I don't, she will think every man just leaves her like her dad did." Those were Nate's words when he first came to live with his parents. And then off he went up to the big sky country.

Rob, of course, was never the same. He walked with a limp because he hurt his ankle when he took the fall with the stroke. He had had to have surgery, the ankle would never be the same. He could no longer golf, which took a toll on him. He loved golf and continued to go with his buddies, just riding along on the golf cart, and then of course, there was the drinking and eating that went on afterward at the clubhouse. Rob would have cancer removed from his face several times. There were no more parties to go to unless he went alone because Eva would no longer leave the house. It became a world of resentment and lifelessness for Robbie who never wanted to come to this place in the first place.

Right in front of my eyes, it seemed as though the house turned into a nursing home. There was a gal who came to walk the dogs, a gal—me—who came to clean the house, the service who picked up their laundry, the yard people, the list of caretakers went on and on. I couldn't help but wonder if the money was going to one day run out. It was difficult for me to tell them I was moving away. "Who will we get, who can we trust, you can't go, Angel." I miss those two dearly and think of them often.

Jenn and Bob

JENN AND BOB WERE referred to me by their friends Rob and Eva, just down the road from me. "You will be shocked at their home, and believe me, you won't be able to clean it all in one visit, it's ridiculously huge, especially for only two people to live in!" Rob blurted out.

I hadn't noticed this property prior to this visit, and to this day, I don't know why. I now call it the house on the hill. As I drove up the driveway, I couldn't help but notice just the grandeur of it. This driveway being about twenty feet wide, asphalted, and a half-circle coming out the other side. In the middle of the driveway were beautiful pine trees reaching up to the sky at least forty feet. The entire property was surrounded by a white wooden fence. A fence like one would see in Kentucky horse country, just beautiful.

In front of me stood a beautiful sprawling brick ranch home. The front porch covered the entire length of this home. Rocking chairs all the way across. The double doors would knock my socks off each and every time I would go to this home in the coming years, just beautiful.

I rang the doorbell, almost leaving. A tiny elderly woman finally came to the door. This gal wasn't in any hurry in any area of her life, I could tell. Jenn was just like Eva, the classy elderly woman who wore diamonds, gold, had makeup on, the hair done, and khaki pants with a nice crisp white top. This gal, being so tiny that she must have worn a size-4 shoe.

"Well, hey there," she spoke to me in a scruffy voice, one I was not expecting out of such a tiny person. I would later find out that she was quite a pistol. "Well, get on in here so I can get to know you and show you around the property," she said.

As I entered this home, the foyer alone was at least fifteen by twenty feet with a large brass statue of a cowboy sitting atop an old stump off to the side. The house was quite dark right away, with brown paneling here.

Off to the side was a large living room that you could see an open floor plan with the dining room off it. This living room was at least twenty-seven feet long. I mean the couch alone was at least eleven foot long. This room sported a giant-screen television along with four side chairs. A lighter room painted white. Long beautiful flowing drapes that covered the windows running all along the wall of this room, just beautiful.

As we entered into another room right off the foyer, I could see beautiful views out the back through a large picture window. This room had a huge stone fireplace reaching to the ceiling, the stone was green. Right away, I thought to myself, *Upgrades needed here.* This room had a couch and two chairs made of wood frames and cushions on top as one would see on lawn furniture, quite dated. On each end table were more brass sculptures of buffalo, Indians, and horses. These people loved brass. On the wall leading up toward the kitchen were built-in bookcases of dark wood. These bookcases covered at least twenty feet of the wall and rose all the way to the ceiling. On the bookcases were many family photos scattered about in frames. This family was huge. In a group photo, there were probably thirty to thirty-five people. There were more brass figures on the shelves, along with pewter knickknacks.

Off this living room was a small eating area with an old captain's table and chairs. Very dark wood and extremely old. Off the side were oversized sliding glass doors taking you to the patio area. On the patio were two wrought iron dining tables with many chairs, along with a stone grill and pizza oven built in. I thought that there must have been many barbecues out here.

We went back inside to the kitchen, and again, dark cabinets. It was a large kitchen, what I would call a working kitchen. I would soon find out that this property was a farm right in town.

The dining room had the same type of furniture but almost like something one would see in a castle. The chairs had tall backs with lots of carving in them and upholstered, very heavy. The chandelier was a large wooden wheel with lights all around, like something one would see on an old ship perhaps. Everything dark in this house, but the walls were all painted white in these rooms.

Beyond the kitchen was a laundry room that most of us women would die for, and I'm not kidding. Storage, storage, storage, and two freezers. Everything a woman may need was in this room. Along one countertop were potatoes growing roots to soon be planted. Yes, this elderly couple grew potatoes. Unreal. In the center of the room was a large island for crafting and sewing. This laundry room was just magnificent, every woman's dream.

Off the laundry room was a three-car garage which held a refrigerator and two more freezers. I was trying to figure out why two elderly people needed so many freezers. We would venture to the other wing of the house, seeing three large bedrooms and two full baths. All the tile in the bathrooms were a crispy white, the sinks looked like seashells. The master bedroom had two large picture windows looking out on the property.

Along the tour, Jenn was telling me the story of their grand life. They had five children, four sons and one daughter. As we made our way to the basement, down a spiral stairway, about five feet wide, we approached a wine cellar, and yes, it was fully stocked with wine. My god!

Entering the room, past the wine cellar, was another large stone fireplace reaching the ceiling, only this one was natural brown-looking stones. Picture a fireplace in the movies you see at Christmas in Connecticut, like in a big lodge, that big, only you could see through it to another room.

This room had another long red couch with two chairs and end tables. The furniture was clearly from the '60s. Family photos scattered about everywhere and another grand picture window looking out on the property.

There was a full kitchen off this room with a dining table and chairs. The counter across the front of the kitchen held six barstools.

Behind the counter were the stove, oven, refrigerator, and wine cooler. The basement kitchen had everything one would need.

This was a walk-out basement. The sliding glass doors led out to a patio with a firepit and many places to sit along with a hot tub. Just magnificent. I could see stone steps leading down a hill.

This basement had three more bedrooms and a full bath. These bedrooms were not painted white but dark paneling with dark bedspreads and curtains. I can't do dark myself, but some people find it warm. One of the bedrooms was decorated like the Victorian era complete with Victorian dolls. This had been her mother's bedroom when she visited from the Midwest. The mother, having passed away years prior, they decided to leave the room as it was.

On the other side of this basement, past the living room, was a game room with a pool table and a piano. I knew right off the bat that this was still a party house for these two. And so I asked, "Do you entertain often?"

"Oh, my goodness, yes we do, every chance we get."

Now this gal had been spoiled her entire life, being married to a doctor. They had met in college and had their children, planning on her being a stay-at-home mom, which was not unusual at the time. These two were already eighty-two years of age.

We made our way back upstairs and out to the backyard. What a place. There was the new barn. The older barn had burnt to the ground the year before. Jenn's husband, Bob, had been raking and burning leaves that day, and in the middle of the night, the wind blew, reignited the fire, and burned the barn. This new barn was grand. These two boarded horses for some neighbors across the street where the houses were quite close together.

Off the side of the barn was a strawberry garden, and alongside this was a long fence with grape vines, just beautiful. Off to the other side was an iris garden. These two made the most of their property.

As we walked to the north, slightly down a hill, I could see the stone steps coming down from the hot tub area. There we were looking at the most beautiful wildflower garden. Just rows and rows of flowers. "I pick flowers all through the season and take them to nursing homes," Jenn said with a huge smile on her face. "You can come down and pick as many as you want before you leave today." I was in heaven. Imagine just going out in your yard and picking all the flowers you want, scattering them all throughout your home in vases. Wow, just wow!

Off past this flower garden was a vegetable garden, and in this garden stood her husband, with a garden hoe in his hands, a large cloth bag hanging off his side. He had overalls on with long sleeves and a large hat protecting him from the Colorado sun. Then he came running. "Hi, you must be Angel, we are so glad to meet you, we need you. Welcome to my garden, anytime you are here, you take what you need." After a long conversation, I discovered that they hauled over two tons of vegetables a year to the food bank. Amazing.

There were three or four apple trees and two peach trees. I could see their small pond off to the distance. The was a dock that led out to a small rowboat. Around the pond were several benches. "That's where I fish and do most of my thinking," Bob said with a gleam in his eyes. The memories he must have.

Now these two people may have been covered in wrinkles, but they were still active and hardworking. You could paint a picture of the two, and it would make one think of Norman Rockwell.

A price would be agreed upon. It was difficult to come up with a price because these two were offering me free vegetables and flowers any time I wanted, so generous.

There would be many parties over the years to come. It seemed these two belonged to every club there was. The bridge club seemed to be their biggest joy. Oh, the preparation just bringing all the card tables up from the basement. I was in for more than just cleaning in this house. But they were elderly, and they needed me. It still feels nice to be needed or to be able to just help someone when I know they need something. It always feels better to give than receive.

I was the locomotive that ran through homes, and this gal didn't like it one bit. Keep in mind that the older generation thinks we make way too much money for what we do these days. They think you should spend an entire day cleaning their space. That's not me. There would be many arguments about this. There were times I would be on a ladder changing light bulbs, scrubbing down the wrought iron lawn furniture, and the rugs, well, those had to be hung on the clothesline and beaten. Shows their generation, doesn't it?

Jenn would either meet me at the door as the Grinch that stole Christmas, or, "Angel, I made us lunch, please come sit down." I never knew what I was going to get. I could never figure out her bad moods. I did everything I could to please this client. At times, she would meet me at the door and start complaining about how I might be cleaning this time.

I would say, "It doesn't sound as if you are happy with my work. If you'd like, I can turn around and go home right now, you're more than welcome to get someone else to do the job."

Jenn would do an about-face and apologize, telling me, "Oh no, Angel, I don't want anyone else in my house but you." Followed up by, "Oh, I'm so sorry, I'm just a grump today." She would complain about how long it would take me to clean for the money, according to her, not long enough. She would inspect each and everything I cleaned, even lifting lamps to see if I had picked them up and dusted underneath. I always had.

I even gave blood every six months for this gal's blood drive. I will never forget the first time I gave blood. I was signing in at the table, and I heard Jenn yell out, "Oh my goodness, Angel, is that you?" She didn't recognize me at all. It took a minute. "Oh my, Bob, come quick, look it's Angel."

With Bob replying, "Woo-hoo, look at you." They had never seen me dressed nicely as I always wore yoga pants with a black T-shirt, hair pulled back in a pony, and no makeup. That was a funny day. *Well, perhaps she is a person after all,* I thought Jenn must have been thinking.

This gal had had the best life. But she did often tell of the hard years when her husband, the doctor, would run out of the house in the middle of the night to deliver a baby or tend to a sick patient who needed him. She was glad when the day came that her daughter would join the practice after med school. This relieved a ton of Bob's time.

Jenn would tell me that her husband would not let her spend a dime on decorating or new furniture. He believed one should reupholster the old stuff. I could tell she was the gal that would redecorate to her liking the minute he passed away.

There were the trips to Switzerland, Sweden, Egypt, Italy, these two elderly people were so active. They still snow skied but were contemplating selling their mountain home in Breckenridge, perhaps to one of their children. White river rafting? No problem, off they would go.

There had been a time, before my arrival, that the one son and his wife were buying this property. They said it was too large for the parents to manage. A house would be built by the pond for them to retire at. But it didn't happen. Why? Because the daughter-in-law dropped by with an architect with the new plans for this home that Jenn and Bob had built and raised their family in. Oh no, they weren't having that. The home was to remain the same, no money spent. Bob was livid. How dare they want to change a thing. Bob was the most frugal person one may ever meet.

The story is, according to Eva and Rob, my other clients, these two had sold the bottom portion of their land to the city. This would be the portion beyond the barn and grazing field for the horses. Why did they sell it? The city needed a walking path for children to come from the neighborhood across the road to get to the elementary school beyond. What did they sell for? Millions of dollars, money they would never touch in their lifetime. Why have that kind of money and never spend it? It doesn't register with this gal. These two were bound and determined to never go into a nursing facility, they would die at home.

It would be only a few short years before Jenn would have hip surgery, but she recovered rapidly. The skiing had ended, along with all the travel and white river rafting. The river rafting seemed to bother them the most because their son had a river rafting business, and they quite enjoyed all the trips.

The day came when Bob began forgetting things. Jenn said it was nothing, but it was much more than that. I would go to their friend Rob's house to clean, and he would ask me questions like, "How is Bob doing over there, have you noticed anything different about him?"

I would reply with, "No, I think he is just getting older like all of us." Not wanting to start gossip about another client.

Then he would say something like, "He showed up at Rotary Club, and we all wondered how he found his way there and if he should be driving." I would just listen.

Many things began to happen. There was the day Jenn phoned me, asking, "I'm just going to ask you straight up, Angel, Bob's wallet is missing, did you take it?"

I was a little shocked. I answered with, "My goodness, no, try looking in his dresser drawer or behind the dresser." He had always left his wallet on his dresser with his keys and loose change.

She said, "I hadn't thought of that."

And I went on with, "Try the lazy Susan in the corner cabinet, that's where I found my car keys the last time I misplaced them." That got a giggle out of Jenn. She found the wallet behind the dresser. I got an apology later, but I didn't need one, I knew something deeper was going on with Bob.

Over the next several months, I would arrive at the home, and Bob would be up on the roof, getting the humidifier ready, or out in the yard running the chain saw. Jenn was nowhere to be found. Later she would come driving up the driveway, she'd been off somewhere shopping or seeing gal friends. It was concerning. I knew Bob had the beginnings of dementia. I had watched it with my gal friend's husband. It was so familiar to me. Bob would come out to the kitchen while I was cleaning, start up a conversation with me like, "How is your day going?" We would have an entire conversation back and forth, and just a few minutes later, well, Bob would restart the exact conversation all over again. "How is your day going?" It was like a scene from *Groundhog Day*, the movie. Bob would sit on the couch and read in the afternoons regularly, only now he sat there with the book in his hands, just staring off at the wall with a blank look, as if he had gone somewhere else. Just talking about it today brings tears to my eyes.

I couldn't believe Bob was still driving himself around and being left alone. One day I drove up, and Bob was on his tractor out in the field off the barn. I had asked Jenn what was up in the most courteous way possible. I mean it was obvious, when we three were in the same room together, that Bob had dementia. Jenn's reply to me was that her daughter had run tests on her father, and he is just fine, only forgetful. Someone was swimming down the river of denial. I had seen it before. The wife does not want to accept the fact that her husband is fading away. Who could blame her? Not me. I moved to New York State, and we have not kept in touch, but I often wonder how and where Bob is now, and what would Jenn do without her life partner.

Angie

S HE SAW ME FROM across the street loading or unloading my car. I was cleaning her neighbor's house. She ran across the street, asking me to please come and talk to her regarding her home being cleaned. This woman, unbeknownst to me, would become an angel of sorts in my life for the next seventeen years. She would also control my life at times, but I was okay with that.

Angie had workout clothes on, the normal colorful clothes you work out in, clothes you could go shopping in and to the grocery. She was a pretty young mother, blond, blue eyes, and a nice smile. She seemed soft-spoken and kind when she opened her front door and asked me to please come in. Beside her stood an adorable one-and-a-half-year-old Bria, what a doll Bria was! And she had that quiet sweet look like her mommy, blue eyes and almost white hair, like so many toddlers sport, toe heads, we called them when I was growing up. There she stood, sucking on a bottle.

Angie had that look about her, all you moms out there know the look—*I'm tired and I have a ton on my plate, I need your help, please, please save me!*

Now this house was much smaller than the neighbor across the street and furnished quite modestly, but oh how that would change over the coming years.

The foyer, or entrance, smacked you right in the face as you entered the home, extremely small. A nice staircase led to the upstairs. Near the entrance was a room to the right with living room furniture, just the norm, nothing special. Around the corner from that room was a medium-sized dining room, nothing unusual there, then

162

the kitchen. The kitchen was spacious with an island and also had a built-in desk area, otherwise nothing that stood out of the ordinary from any other kitchen in a model home in this subdivision.

Picture the first floor with a staircase in the middle of the entire first floor, that was this house. In this particular neighborhood, there were about six different styles of homes built, and one looked just like the next. The only difference one may notice is the slight change of color of paint from house to house.

Off the kitchen was a family room sporting a Levi couch that was quite worn out and had stains on it, typical for young people paying off student loans and a mom who stayed home to take care of the kiddos.

Then down the hallway was a half bath, an office, and a laundry room, if you could call it a laundry room. Basically the laundry room was the entrance from the garage with a washer and dryer and a few cabinets above for supplies. Watch out if someone came in from the garage while you were standing there, shifting laundry around, and over the years, I would burst through that door, knocking into Angie doing just that. Her neighbor across the street, well, I could get lost in her laundry room. Most women would kill for a large laundry/craft room such as the neighbors. The neighbor, well, they are a whole different chapter.

Upstairs were three bedrooms, the master bedroom quite large. I noticed the white linen curtains right away that piled up on the floor below. *Quite Italian*, I thought to myself. The master bedroom also had a master bath and the kids shared a bathroom down the hall.

Angie also had two small boys. Angie's husband was an attorney on the Pearl Street Mall in Boulder, Colorado. This info spoke volumes to me, an attorney in Boulder and on the Pearl Street Mall no less! I thought, *What are they doing living in this modest house in this neighborhood full of much bigger homes?* The basement was finished with a full bathroom, living room, and workout room. This was a modest home that was very well kept as far as cleaning went.

Angie and I soon agreed on a price with a once-a-week cleaning right off the bat. I was shocked with the modest furnishings that were well worn that she would want a once-a-week cleaning. *Why not buy some new furniture?* I thought.

I would soon meet Angie's husband, Dominic, as he ran through the garage on his way to work. I had pictured him quite differently. More on him later.

Angie was raised mostly by her grandmother on her mother's side in Fort Lupton, Colorado. Angie's father was an alcoholic who had posed for *Playgirl* magazine when he was young. Angie's mother would divorce him early on and took on a cleaning job at the local hospital. Soon Angie's mother, Ranae, met a man in the bar, one day after work, while having drinks with her gal friends. This man, Adam, would raise Angie and her brother; he was a lifesaver. Angie and her brother would never see their biological father again; in fact, her children would never know who her real father was until their college years, when Angie's bio father died.

Angie's mother, Ranae, and her new husband, Adam, would have a baby girl soon, and Angie and her brother would be left with her grandmother most of the time. Angie had said that it was as though they were shoved aside because of the new baby girl. Angie seemed to think of her grandmother as her mother The emotions ran high over the years when she would speak of her grandmother, sometimes with tears running down her face.

I would see Angie with her grandmother many times, escorting her to Walmart or wherever her grandmother needed to go. She was the cutest and most typical of grandmas, just a joy to be around, unlike Angie's mother. Angie loved and adored her grandmother, and it was very hard for her when she passed away only a few years after we met. She would say, "I don't think anyone realizes how hard it is for me to not have my grandmother any longer." Angie never got any help or support from her mother, but her stepfather was always there to take her to lunches, do electrical work in her home, as he owned an electric company, and did odd jobs for her around the house, like hanging large mirrors above the staircase. Soon I would meet the bouncing, lively boys, Leonardo and Tony, who looked exactly like their father. What a sweet family this was, always so happy, like my family was when I was raising my kids.

Almost immediately, Angie would gift to me a book on how to get in shape and lose weight. I knew I was not in the skinniest of shape, but curvy, and my marriage was so bad; perhaps I could lose some weight. Perhaps I had let myself go for a few years, not really caring about how I looked. I was just holding on, in survival mode. We females now know, when you are in fear of anything, stressing out period, your body holds onto fat.

This was when I realized Angie was a helper as well as very generous. Someone just giving me a book, for no reason, never happened before. The book was *Body for Life*, and I dove right in. It had been awhile since I concentrated on myself. When you are in survival mode, it is the last thing you think of, self-care, that is.

You see, I was building a small business in which I could survive. I knew my marriage was over. My husband had just done his third stint in rehab for drug and alcohol abuse, and when I picked him up on his last visit there, he got in my car and lit up a marijuana cigarette. I had to start making big money and fast in order to take care of myself and my son.

Body for Life was great, and it worked well for me. I was taking back control of my life little by little. Someone had reached out to help me for a change, I was touched. It was empowering, and somehow, this young mother knew I needed to be empowered. I felt I had found a friend in Angie, and soon we would be able to talk about anything, and the feeling of being "the help" never existed in this house.

Now this household was run by an attorney still paying off student loans of his and his wife, but within just a few short years, Dominic would make partner at the law firm, and the student loans would be paid off after years of much hard work. New furniture was being brought in, floors redone, nicer cars and trucks were purchased. Angie began redecorating rooms, and guess who got all the old furnishings from each room? You guessed it—me, myself, and I, and my daughter, of course.

Angie always said, "My husband is an attorney, and that is all that he knows, or all that he is good at, just the law." Everything was hired out. I was even paid to sew letters on the boy's letter jackets in high school, sew buttons on, and do all kinds of mending. Angie either did not know how to do any of these things, or she just did not want to. I couldn't imagine her grandmother never teaching her to sew. But then there are grandmothers out there that don't sew. I always forget this. Either way, I was happy to help.

Angie and Dominic put their kids first at all times. Their life were their kids. As the years passed by, I knew this family could move into a much more expensive neighborhood, yet everything was kept low-key.

The recession hit, and the cleanings were reduced to every other week for a short time, and I mean only a few weeks. People were not paying the firm, and things were tough but only for a short while, then the weekly cleanings began again. I thought that Angie's husband was pretty frugal with the money and would have a nest for them to fall back on, but perhaps not the firm.

The law firm grew bigger and bigger, and they even opened an office in Denver. Dominic began traveling quite a bit. He was a partner at a top 10 law firm in the Western United States by now. And how did I know this? One of the neighbors had told me that Dominic made thousands of dollars every hour of every day. I was shocked, because they never lived like he made that kind of money, at least not yet.

There was a time Angie and Dominic attended a dinner at another partner's home in Summerset, a housing development in Niwot, Colorado, with every home having a full view of the front range, up close and personal. Angie was so angry that the other partner had such an amazing home; she had no idea that this neighborhood had existed. In Summerset, the homes are in the million-dollar range and up. She could not believe the other partner's wife had such a beautiful home, and she was quite upset, livid. Dominic managed to calm her down over the coming weeks, explaining to her that everyone has a scale at which they live up to, and that he preferred to be comfortable and not overextended; he wanted his kids to be raised in a normal neighborhood and held back at living the extravagant lifestyle, no doubt, because of how he was raised.

Now at this time, Dominic had paid over a million and a half dollars in personal taxes. Angie was a mess just thinking about what he had to pay in taxes, while I stood there, thinking about what he had to have made in a years' time in order to pay that high of taxes. Angie was extremely naive when it came to money and what was going on in the world. She never watched the news because she said, "Why do I need to know anything about the world, my world is right here." Angie's world consisted of running the kids around, shopping, yoga, and reading as many books on health and fitness as she possibly could. She also kept up on all the movie stars and all that gossip in the magazines. Sometimes I thought she actually thought she would fit into their world, and perhaps she could.

There was just one time that I totally felt taken advantage of in this client's home. I had already packed for a trip to Oklahoma to see my son's graduation from boot camp and to bring him home. Home, he was finally coming home. I was so excited, and everything was wonderful, except for the fact that I knew damn well he would go off to war soon after, still not so sure if he realized that just yet or not. My money was good, the trip was going to be a breeze until—

I was cleaning Angie's kitchen, had my rubber gloves on, and opened the microwave door to take out the plate and clean the inside. That plate slipped right through my fingers, completely covered with bacon grease.

Now I watched that plate fall onto the ceramic stove top just under the microwave. Slowly it fell, and I watched the stove top crack like an earthquake in a thousand different directions. Yes, I completely broke the stove top. Angie got home and immediately went into a rage. "Oh my god, we are going to either have to eat out or grill for weeks until we can get a new one in." I didn't get a word in edgewise about the bacon grease. *Should I tell her?* I thought to myself. *No...one of the kids will get into trouble...they were no longer allowed to use the microwave.*

Angie had said the Europeans had banned all microwaves because they move the molecules around in our food and ruin the nutrition value while cooking. Well, turned out she decided to upgrade to gas for the new stove and guess who paid for it? Now consider a new ceramic stove top would be about three hundred dollars to replace on my end; that stove was near twenty years old. That hurt me a little bit with my trip coming up, but when she upgraded to gas, well, that did some serious damage on my budget. Three hundred dollars soon turned into six hundred dollars on my end; she would pay the rest.

I didn't think this to be fair because I did not think that I would have to give her an upgrade on her existing stove top. Her husband's sister pulled me aside later on and informed me that she thought that it was absolutely disgusting that Angie had done that to me. "All that money they have, and she did that to poor you!" I sucked it up and went about my merry way, feeling betrayed by Angie. But what could I do? I broke the damn thing, and this woman was paying me $650 a month to clean her house. She had always been good to me. We live with what we can, and those who take advantage of us, well, they have to live with that one day themselves. At least that was what I told myself at the time.

Dominic would always tell Angie when she could spend money, and she did! She would not hesitate to spend $1,000 on a floor lamp, a pair of shoes, or a purse. Angie has a taste for designer things and would often tell me that she knew her husband wished she did not have expensive taste. She was the gal that would be the first in the door at Christmastime for the huge Nutcracker from Pier 1—the $200 nutcracker—soon there would be seven or eight of these in front of the fireplace. Each year at Christmastime, a new nutcracker would be added to the collection, just beautiful! This is where I get my nutcracker madness from, but most of my collection of over one hundred come from secondhand stores. Each one I find, well, it reminds me of when I was a little girl, and I would get a new baby doll. I know it's a little strange, but we all have our quirks, right?

On a particular anniversary, Angie received a new diamond ring with an eternity band as well. These diamonds were so huge that I told her to not hang her hand out the window when she stops at red lights, that someone may chop off her hand for the rings. Angie would just grin. It was a beautiful set that Dominic got through a friend in New York City who had a connection at the Diamond Exchange. He probably paid over $50,000 for the ring, I would bet.

The living room would one day sport a photo of Angie in Italy holding her hand up to her face, displaying the ring—yes, that photo adorned a table in the living room. *Odd*, I thought. She would later say, "It's not what you think in that picture…it was a moment."

I never got it, lol. I don't know too many people who would actually wear that ring on a day-to-day basis; some would put their ring in a safe somewhere, with a replacement on their finger. But not Angie.

With Angie it was all about what you had and what designer you bought it from. I would clean her husband's partners' home for a short time, who made fun of Angie for living in their neighborhood for so many years, "not moving on up." "Why on earth do they live there?" this gal would say. I mean really…it is so awful compared to what they could have."

I think they stayed there because Dominic didn't want to live up to his particular scale but be smarter about his money, at least when it came to a house. Anything else Angie wanted, she could have, but not a new house in a better neighborhood, not a million-dollar home.

Angie would offer me her purses after she did not want them any longer, and after receiving a few, I would tell her to begin selling them at an upscale resale store in Boulder, I didn't want them, they were huge. They were the kind of purses you would see modeled in magazines. They looked like luggage to me and weighed down my shoulder.

Angie and Dominic were both raised in small rural towns on the east side of Interstate 25. Dominic was raised with three sisters and worked in his parents' grocery store while growing up. His parents never lived beyond their means and were quite authentic Italians who still traveled to Italy to visit with relatives from time to time. These two made their own sausage and hung it out in the shed to cure. Made their own wine and mozzarella cheese, along with Italian wedding cake. I would meet them down through the years and clean their home as a gift from Angie and Dominic, many times, usually after Christmas. My service was one of their Christmas gifts from Dominic and Angie. They were quite wonderful people. Dominic's mother would always tell me how she worried about her son and how hard he had to work to give Angie all those expensive things. I wondered how this older woman knew the expense of those "things." Perhaps her daughters would talk about Angie's buying habits.

Looking at Dominic, you could tell right away that he was Italian. Dark wavy hair, dark eyes, and catered to his wife immensely. It was nice to watch! I had that same kind of husband throughout my marriage till the end, only he was French. I was put on a pedestal and catered to in every way imaginable.

When I began cleaning for Angie, my marriage had been falling apart for a few years by then. I longed for my husband to return to his old self, that never happened. My fairy tale was over, and I knew it full well. But what fun to witness Angie's fairy tale, it was exciting to watch. I always left her home with a warm feeling inside my heart, at least most visits. You don't come across this kind of love much anymore, at least not to my knowledge in this business.

Angie had put Dominic through law school, having babies and juggling a job at an insurance agency for years, and with no help from any of her or his family. It was hard for me to imagine because I would help my daughter in every way that I could with her new baby. Angie's mother favored her sister and gave her all the attention; it hurt Angie. She even had to pay her sister to come babysit her children from time to time. The mother and sister were complete opposites from Angie. They smoked, ate processed foods, and wore flannel shirts. Angie was a health food person, exercised daily, and loved everything designer.

Angie and Dominic had lived on the south side of Denver, in Parker, Colorado, before moving to Rock Creek, just down the highway from Boulder. Rock Creek was quite the upper-class neighborhood, and you could not touch a house there back then for less than $450,000. That same house today sells for $650,000 or more, I am sure.

Angie was the most generous person I have ever known. Each Christmas and birthday, I would receive $100. I couldn't believe it, I was so grateful for all that I was receiving, but more than that, I loved the friendship, the normalcy of the home, watching these kids grow up. This was one home where the marriage was rock solid, and these two people genuinely loved one another. Out of all the houses I have done over the past seventeen years, I can count on one hand how many couples were really in love. But it was not just love that stood out, it was the pure honesty they had shared with each other. To this day, still such an incredible marriage.

The family began taking vacations to Italy, something they had never done prior, taking vacations. While they were away, I would pet and house sit for them. Harry was the golden retriever that was a complete joy to watch while they were gone. He has since died, and the day Angie told me he passed, I had tears in my eyes. Harry and I had spent a lot of time together. Angie said there would be no more dogs. Housesitting was so much fun because the house was so beautiful to me. Stay ten days and make $1,200—I couldn't say no. Every day was like a vacation away from home until about the fifth day, when all I really wanted to do was take Harry and go to my house. After all, there's no place like home.

The most difficult thing about cleaning for Angie was that she would switch her cleaning days around quite frequently, but I didn't care. We were like friends, and the money was good. Angie would tell me everything about family, friends, and life, and I would do the same with her over the years. She read every book out there on health and would share with me, it was like having my own personal nutritionist. I loved it.

In the middle of our work relationship, I had a horrific family tragedy happen. I had never been close to my family. There was so much dysfunction and abuse from my father against my mother. Then one day, I got the call—my brother had actually shot and killed both of my parents and then taken his own life. This brother had never been normal. I would go and visit my family occasionally over the years, but it was never good, and so I would keep my children away, only visiting from time to time.

I recall on my last visit, I had told my mother that something was very wrong with my brother, a grown man smoking pot and drinking whiskey in her garage while whittling pieces of wood, body covered with tattoos, rotten teeth, at least the teeth that he still had.

I had driven him to Walmart one day, he said, "Turn the radio off, Angel, I need to hear the birds sing." We were going down the highway at 60 mph.

I had said to my mother, "He is not normal, he will hurt somebody someday."

My mother's reply was, "There is nothing wrong with your brother, he would not hurt a fly, be nice, Angel." This visit would be the last time I would see my parents. I packed up our things, finishing our visit at my uncle's home a few miles away. I had always had a strained relationship with my mother, and you didn't cross her when it came to her boys.

It was Angie that called me when I returned from this tragedy and told me, "I have my checkbook here, whatever you want, just name it, it's yours."

I told her I just needed some time off, a few weeks. But this is how Angie is, like an angel here on earth. She told me, "You have been through worse than this, and you know it, you're going to be all right." That kept me going, the words people say to you, you recall them later in life from time to time, and they help you along in your path. Her words made me feel strong, like a survivor, not a victim, and it helped me keep my head up and be proud of who I am, never wanting to think of where I came from. Life went on, the seasons changed, years passed by.

Angie's kids all excelled in sports and at school. The eldest son, Leonardo, played hockey. His dad kept a book in his office, *How to Get Your Son in the NHL*. Leonardo suffered from anxiety, did not like to fly for hockey tournaments, and had night anxiety, keeping him from sleeping on a regular basis. Angie asked me what I thought about medicating him. I was never for it and don't know if this ever happened, but what did I know, my kids never needed medication for anxiety. Leonardo would go on to college and be the normal kid getting into a little bit of trouble from time to time, working in the summers for his grandfather at the electric company, or in his father's law firm. Leonardo took a break after college and worked in a shoe store, opting out of working for a family member. Then after a few years, he went off to law school.

Bria was strong-willed and independent and did not do well in day care, actually being told she could not attend any longer. Bria was only in day care to give Angie a break, time to exercise and shop. This little gal was ahead of the game from the time she was little, independent and strong-willed. My daughter was the same, and so I understood that independence and strong-willed little girl. I never thought it was a bad thing. Bria would later play soccer and get a full scholastic scholarship to a university in Oregon.

Tony excelled at softball and, later in his teens, had thirteen guitars, some of which his grandfather had made for him. While in high school, he would give guitar lessons to kids and make some money. Around tenth grade, he would do as he pleased in the way of staying out all hours of the night, if he so chose. Angie would say that they could not punish him and take away his car because that would inconvenience her. Some people who have money are a little different than the rest of us. Perhaps she and Dominic knew quite well how to raise good independent kids so that they would be productive adults. These parents were quite liberal democrats. I would smell marijuana in the house from time to time, wondering if it were one of the kids smoking it. I don't know, maybe it was Angie and Dominic, you never know. Tony didn't come around much after he began college. Leonardo was always dropping in.

Each child in this family were straight-*A* students, and it was clear that they were way ahead of the game at very young ages. They are all three excelling and doing very well in life. When it came time for Bria, the youngest, to go off to college, Angie said, "It is the most wonderful thing to finally be alone. I don't understand why some parents fall apart during this stage in life." She was not entertaining being an unhappy empty nester whatsoever.

Before I left for New York State to live, Angie had the entire house remodeled, and it was such a beautiful sight to see. New windows, completely new kitchen and bathrooms, new paint inside and out, new light fixtures throughout the home, and I'm talking chandeliers that would blow your mind! The home was then photographed and used in the remodeling company for their advertising. It was so beautiful! I learned how to decorate over the years from Angie, and I decorated my house from many of the many gifts she gave me. I have been gone for two years now, and we still keep in touch. Angie is one of those people who come in to your life for a reason, the reason was that I needed a very special friend, and I am thankful to know her.

Mira

NOW INTO ANGIE'S NEIGHBORHOOD, a street up came a new family, a small family with just one little boy. The entire neighborhood was talking about this new family. After all, the house was almost completely gutted and redone before they could move in. The gals in the neighborhood would say, "Now you tell me who she thinks she is, buying a $550,000 house and thinking that it isn't good enough for her just the way it is?" They all hated this younger mother before she even moved in.

Who was she? The daughter of a famous golfer, that's who she was, and they all knew it. This fella was so rich that he would fly in on his private jet for all the visits to the family. Yeah, that's being pretty rich. I would meet him and his wife very soon. His wife, well, she had had so many face-lifts that she had that lizard look about her, just weird. I think that look comes about from getting fillers in between the eyebrows, it's not pretty. Did that woman ever eat? I think not.

It would not be long before I got a call needing me to go and clean. It was the same deal. I was overwhelmed and needed help. I couldn't figure out why. You see, neither of these two held down a job, I knew this from the neighborhood gossip buzzing around, like thousands of bees, *buzz, buzz, buzz*. Everyone in the neighborhood was talking about this new gal. Perhaps she just wanted her home cleaned because of her status or because it was humongous!

As I approached the front door, I was just trying to take in the grandeur of the home, which was just up the street from Angie's. The homes jumped from medium size to giant just a street away.

Who opened the door? It appeared to be Olivia Newton John, at least I thought I was looking at her twin. I never saw anyone look so much like a movie star, it was wild. Her name was Mira, and she had the sweetest voice, but stern, very stern. Holding on to her leg was Connor, her two-year-old son. What a cutie pie he was, curly red hair and freckles, chubby, just kept looking at me with a big smile on his face.

In front of me was a staircase like you would see in the movies. It was at least ten feet wide! The foyer, well, it was the size of a very large living room. Mira would begin the grand tour of her home, and oh man, was it grand. I had not yet been in a home this large in this particular neighborhood.

Workers were painting the woodwork white, in different rooms and down the hallway. "I just can't live with dark wood," she would say. I think the master bedroom and bath were larger than my entire townhome—yeah, I'm sure on that one. The master bedroom was the size of my entire first floor of my townhome.

Then there was the cross-through fireplace leading to a small living room. This room hosted a small sectional couch and television set, it was unique. Past this sitting area, as I called it, was the master bath.

The master bath, well, a person could live in that one room, that's how large it was. "Of course, this bathroom will need more upgrading in just a few short years," she said, as though it just wouldn't do for very much longer. To me, well, it was a movie star's bathroom. White marble countertops and a huge shower dressed in white marble. The soaking tub was enormous.

The furnishings? Well, I had never seen anything like them. The posts on the four-post bed blew my mind, at least 24" around, and the carvings in the wood were beautiful. All the rooms had views of the Flatiron mountains. There were four more bedrooms, all complete with baths down the hall. The toddler, Connor, was in the furthest bedroom. I never figured that one out. His room, well, it was as nautical as it could get done with all designer furnishings. "We will have to have built-ins done soon for the bay window, Connor will need a place to sit and read."

There was a bedroom for her mother when she came to visit. Embroidered on the pillowcases was the first letter of her mother's name. "My mother wanted that touch so she would feel at home when she is here you know, my mother is quite uppity".

There was a woman putting up grass wallpaper in the dining room, expensive. This room sported a big dining room table, and glass it was. There were wooden elephants scattered around the room. "From one of our trips to Africa," she said. Off this dining room was a formal living room, just as beautiful as it could be.

The kitchen was fantabulous. Some kind of white granite with the color of blood running through it, and a touch of gold, so pretty that it took my breath away. Off the kitchen was yet another living room. Another bedroom with a bath on the main floor, and then the laundry room the size of two of my kitchens, if not larger.

The house just went on and on, complete with a finished walk out basement the size of an apartment, just beautiful everywhere I looked. This basement had a full kitchen, living room, half bath, master suite, and game room. I am surprised I didn't faint from lack of oxygen as I am sure there were several occasions that I quit breathing. This house was something to see.

By the time I left, Connor was my best friend, holding on to my leg. He didn't want me to leave. I would be cleaning in this home every other week. I told her that there would be no possible way I would clean the entire home each visit. She agreed. "That's fine, Angel, there will be many times I will not be here when you come."

It would be on my first visit cleaning that I would meet Tom. Tom was Mira's husband. There he was, Ken the Barbie doll. At least 6'4" tall, dark wavy hair, and slender. What a nice guy Tom is. I felt just the opposite with him as with his wife. Mira, she always seemed out of her element with me, perhaps with everyone. Tom was kind, soft-spoken, and just a normal down-to-earth type of guy. He would say, "Just do what you can, Angel, we know it's a damn mansion."

And lo and behold, there stood Connor with a toy cleaning cart. Yes, Connor was going to follow me all over the house cleaning with me. Are you wondering what happened when I had to clean the mammoth shower in the master bath? I'm laughing right now as

I recall. Yes, Connor was right there in the shower, scrubbing with me. I didn't know what to do or say about all of this, so I just let it go. Little Connor, well, he stole my heart every time I went to this house. And every time I left this house, he was holding on to my leg as I dragged him to the front door; this was after several minutes of telling him that I needed to go home.

There were pictures of me and Connor on the refrigerator. And oh yes, it wasn't rare to see the famous golfer grandpa in his boxer shorts giving Connor horseback rides all over that house. Grandma, she was never around much, just to fly in and snatch up her daughter for a week or so, and off to Napa Valley they would go. Grandpa might have been famous, but he was the real deal.

This house was a very sad house to be in at times. I would see Tom more often than Mira, she was just always gone, either out of state on a trip, shopping, running errands, etc. You get the picture—she was never there much. Soon Connor would have a friend. Mira said to call her that. She was a twenty-something gal who was like a nanny, a daytime nanny. "I just can't be with Connor all day, it's too much for me."

I didn't get it, she had one kid. I recall going to the YMCA to teach aerobic classes with all three of my toddlers in tow when I was younger. How could a mother not be able to tolerate one full day with her only child?

And then along came Vincent. I don't recall even seeing Mira pregnant, it was like she hid it from the world. Now Vincent was a different story than Connor. He had black hair and was quite quiet and shy, unlike my buddy Connor.

One day I arrived, and Tom was at his wits end. "Please come to the kitchen and help me, Angel, please." I heard him call out. Vincent would not eat, Mira was gone for a week with her mother and father, or at least he thought a week, maybe longer. "Please get him to eat for me, you can get Connor to do anything." And of course, I got him to eat. What a beautiful baby boy he was. While I was feeding Vincent, Tom told me that it was really hard when his wife would just take off out of town with her parents and leave him for a week or more, all by himself with the boys. "This is not how I want to raise my boys. I want a more normal life," he would say with a sad pouty look on his face. I felt so badly for this guy.

I came in one day, complaining about it being Monday, the weekend had flown by so fast. Tom told me how hard it was to never have a Monday. "I have nowhere to have to show up. Well, be glad that you're productive and have to be somewhere where you are accountable," he would say to me. Tom was on the father-in-law's payroll, but he didn't seem to ever have to do anything for the paycheck. Tom had a college degree, that was where he met Mira, in college.

"I always wanted to be a weatherman on TV, that would be a great life," Tom would say. Mira, well, she was a trust fund gal, Daddy had her set up very well indeed. Their main purpose was just to live out each day however they liked, no pressure to be anywhere actually. All either had to do was run their household. The perfect life, one might think. Not so much, according to Tom.

Mira had a difficult time making friends, and I believe it was because the entire tribe was jealous of her. Her looks, her lifestyle, the works. I thought it to be cruel the way the neighborhood went on and on about her. They had no idea how she really was. Mira sometimes seemed, to me, like a lost soul. Like she didn't know what to do next or where to do it. I mean really, how does that work out in life, you're raised in boarding schools and then off to college, then you just fit in to your parents' world as an adult suddenly, doing whatever they request of you at a moment's notice. I thought it all must have been hard on Mira. And how do you tell your parents no when they pretty much supply you and your spouse with the money to live on? You probably don't.

Tom would say, "She had a strange upbringing, Angel, she is still learning how to be a mom and run a home." I told him that she sure knew how to decorate a house, what great taste she had. He said, "Please tell her that because she never knew that she did a good job with anything because of her mother."

Now I had met Mira's mom, and this woman looked me up and down like I was a piece of trash, it was awkward to say the least. All the while, Connor was holding on to my leg. I was standing there, wondering how many face-lifts this chic has had, she definitely was not the grandmother type.

I would tell Tom how beautiful and large the house was, that most people dreamed of owning such a home. This home was at least seven thousand square feet. He would answer with, "You have no idea what a nightmare it is to keep up a house this large, the damn thing has four air-conditioning units for God's sake." Tom was hating life.

I only cleaned there for three and a half years. Tom made a stand and moved the family back to Missouri, got a regular job that he had to show up at. "We can have a normal life in Missouri," he said.

"We will never have another Angel again, and that makes me sad," Mira told me. I never heard from them after they moved away, and that made me sad.

Melinda

MELINDA WAS REFERRED TO me by her neighbor in a neighborhood where the houses started out for $350,000 to buy, a nice upscale neighborhood in Broomfield, Colorado. I still think of her to this day, and I wonder how she is, and when I do, I lose my breath, as if I were scared to death for a moment, it's not a good feeling.

Melinda opened the door and seemed quite shy and on the alert, or cautious. Right away I thought to myself, *Why is she wanting her house cleaned? This gal isn't comfortable with having me stand here.*

Melinda was frumpy, hair was wash-and-run type of style with gray, no makeup, and she was dressed in what appeared to be men's sweatpants with a flannel shirt, which could have quite possibly been a man's shirt. She was around forty pounds overweight, and I could not judge what age she was. *Perhaps fifty*, I thought to myself.

As we walked in to the house, I could smell all kinds of different smells, some not so good. The carpet was extremely soiled, and I could hear a small child in the next room. The child was actually a baby, maybe six months, dark-skinned, sitting in what I call a hula coop. You know, the round plastic chair with wheels on it and all kinds of toys for the baby to play with. Only this baby just sat there and made noises, not the normal noises a six-month-old would make. The baby mostly just sat there with a blank stare. Right away, I thought something was wrong with this child. I began to talk to the baby and never got any response, just that stare.

Melinda told me she had another son, her husband's son from a former marriage that was school age and spent a lot of time with her in-laws. This baby I was looking at did not look like his mother at all. I could tell he was Indian, Indian decent. At this point, I began to realize that most of the decor in this home was from India.

Melinda took me around the kitchen, living room, and dining room in the downstairs of the home; the house was a mess. This was not the normal house that I would pick up. The dining table sported a filthy carpet under it, little artwork on the walls, no centerpiece on the table. There was an artificial tree in the corner that had about four years of dust on its leaves.

The countertops in the kitchen were cluttered with bags and canned food. The kitchen table had a braided rug under it with lots of food stuck to it. Everything in the house was dark and dingy. Nothing seemed to fit, it just didn't feel right in this home, something was off, way off. This was not a happy home, or this was not a home that the lady of the house cared much about. Perhaps she was not permitted to care.

As we went upstairs, I could not believe how big the four bedrooms were, two were master suites plus two full bathrooms down the hall leading to two more bedrooms. On the floor of one of the bedrooms, next to a king-size bed, was a mat that Melinda said her in-laws slept on when they were in town. "They're from India, they are uncomfortable in beds," she said.

All the bathrooms were very dirty, mirrors splashed with all kinds of film, and the showers and tubs had not been cleaned in a long while. This was definitely not the kind of house that I wanted to pick up, too much work. I liked to work in beautiful homes full of beautiful things, it made the work fun, more enjoyable, I suppose.

As we went back downstairs Melinda began to tell me that her husband was from India and that his parents would come from India and visit for a five-month period each year, which would at times turn into a seven-month stay. Melinda told me that she was given permission to get the house cleaned at least once a month. I thought to myself, *This house needs a complete overhaul, a two-day job just to get it up to par.*

There was something going on in this house that made me feel empathy for this woman. She seemed so sad, this told me to pick the house up, even though it was so dirty and unorganized. I'm a helper, a fixer, and she needed the help.

The initial cleaning was a tough job, to say the least. I could not make the home look like a show home, as I could in all my other houses. It was important to me that every house would shine before I left. I never got there with this client. The carpets and rugs were too filthy, and the walls were dingy, so much clutter everywhere on the countertops, I just couldn't make it all shine.

It would not be long before Melinda started opening up to me. She and her husband had quite the story. Melinda had a college degree and was a dog catcher for the city before they married. One day, she was sitting in her truck and saw a tall, dark, and handsome man standing on a hill by the hospital with a long white coat on, the coat blowing in the wind. As she told me, her face softened. She thought to herself, *I could never imagine being with a man like that.*

Well, the next thing she knew, and within a few short weeks, she was on a blind date, arranged through a friend, with that man! She couldn't believe she was dating a doctor. A doctor who she felt interviewed her on every date, right down to her credit score, family history, and past history with men.

As it turned out, this man—and I won't mention his name ever—was in an arranged marriage prior. From this marriage, he had this first son. Melinda was told that the first wife had mental issues and that she had abandoned him and his son and that his parents were in the country from India quite often to help him with his son, who, at the time Melinda met him, was three years old.

His parents would take the child to India with them for long periods of time. The ex-wife was in Florida, going to college, and he was making alimony payments of over $3,000 a month to her. The ex-wife had no rights to the son. What stood out to me the most was that Melinda told me that when her mother-in-law was in town, she was the boss of the house. I asked her if she was all right with another woman being in charge of her home like that, and she replied, "It's just how it is in India, and so that is how it is when she is here visit-ing, but I'm working on changing that." I had never heard of such a

183

thing, and quite frankly I knew right away that this had to be a type of mental abuse in the United States.

So here I was looking at an educated woman who did quite well on her own before this man came into her life. I would later find out that Melinda had been in a relationship prior with an abusive man, looks to me like the cycle was repeating itself. Now here I am, the helper, and everybody knows it. I draw people to me like a magnet when they have problems, and at this time, I was in college taking courses for how to help abused women. I couldn't help but think that this woman needed a friend.

I initially took on the job, thinking I would get the house up to par for her but ended up staying for around six years.

There would be times I could not go to clean because the in-laws would be home and the father-in-law did not want me in the house when they were present. Why? I don't know, because in India they had servants who waited on them hand and foot. They would be in town for a few months at a time and then off to Florida to the other son's home for a lengthy stay. I was told while, in Florida, the father-in-law was given the right to abuse his wife, but not in the son's home in Colorado. At this point, I had still not met Melinda's husband or the other son.

Soon Melinda would tell me that all the furniture in the home was her husband's and his ex; she did not bring much into the home of her own and was not really able to decorate as she wished. Her husband told her that they did not have the money to get new furniture. I thought it must be unsettling each and every day to be married and not be able to make your home your own, but instead live among another woman's things.

Soon Melinda told me that she had found the e-mails that went back and forth from the ex-wife to her husband and some letters and that the story she had gotten from her husband did not match with the information she was reading. I felt fear in Melinda every time I was in her home working—fear for her.

She began telling me that she was married to a doctor who specialized in allergies, and that it all looked good from the outside, but it was quite different. I thought to myself, *Honey, this does not look good from the outside*. Perhaps she was thinking of the outside of the enormous home that she now lived in, in the upscale neighborhood. But this beautiful home was not kept up outside either. The front yard was nothing but weeds, the backyard nonexistent of any kind of weed or grass but only dirt. The back sported a small deck that appeared to be falling apart, rotten.

Melinda told me her husband's parent's fled to India with his first son so that his mother had no contact with him for over one year. That it seemed to her that the ex-wife was abused mentally and physically, and later found to be psychotic. Melinda was questioning how honest her husband was, you know, the fella that had interviewed her on each and every date.

She confided in me that it was the three-year-old that she fell in love with first. Her husband was the man who came to the States for his degree and stayed to practice medicine because he could never make the same money in India as a doctor. The neighbor, who was also a doctor and whom I also cleaned for, told me that the minimum that Melinda's husband made a month was around $35,000. I was amazed.

Melinda complained to me all the time that her husband had no money because he had to pay the ex every month. I mean, really? Even after paying the alimony of $3,000 to his ex, he was still bringing in a minimum of $32,000 a month. I knew then that Melinda was not included in the finances, and this shocked me because she said she had owned her own home before and even had a time share, along with a new car, and took trips whenever she could.

Melinda and her family were moving after one year. It seemed the in-laws needed to spend more time in Colorado, and so they bought a six-thousand-square-foot home in an even more expensive neighborhood where the in-laws could pretty much live in the basement but have full use of the entire home. Melinda's husband had finally told his parents that Melinda was in charge of her own home. This would be a good thing, a new home, and she could make it hers, put her stamp on it.

I thought things were looking up. They had bought the new home on a short sale and so had gotten quite the deal on the price.

The home was huge, to say the least. You don't realize how big it is from looking at the front because there is a full walk-out basement. There were no window coverings except for dark wooden blinds. The house had white paint on every wall. The kitchen was amazing with an enormous kitchen island, lots of counter space, and a large eating area with a view on top of being open to the family room. As you looked out back, you were looking at a prior dump—yes, a dump or landfill—for the city that was covered up on this side. I could see methane gas vents coming up out of the ground, a field covered with green weeds and grasses, so it was not hard to look at.

All Melinda's prior neighbors were jealous of the new house she was living in, I told one not to be and asked when they visited. They all said on the weekend, and I told them that during the week, you can see the garbage trucks going back and forth all day long, don't be jealous, instead be happy that they seem to have found what they love.

It would still be another six months before I would meet Melinda's husband or the older son, whom she considered her own. When I finally did meet Melinda's husband, he tried to give me a bottle of wine for cleaning, said he had never seen anyone work so hard and get so much done in a short period of time. I turned down the wine, telling him Melinda paid me enough. I had already summed him up from all the Melinda had told me, I guess I was poisoned against him in a way, so he never had a chance in my book, he was an abusive controlling ass, no more, no less.

The youngest boy still was displaying problems with speech and the ability to play normally. He would take off his diaper at age three and swing it around his bedroom with feces in it, and Melinda would say, "Don't go in that room because there are feces everywhere." The boy would write on all the furniture and walls with permanent marker, and on top of everything else, he was violent. He would pick up a heavy end table, then throw it at least a few feet. I was uncomfortable around him. If Melinda and I were in a conversation, he would let out loud screams and smack her in the face or hit her to get her attention. This child was wearing her down, she was always exhausted.

The oldest son was quite handsome, tall, smart, soft-spoken, and polite. I met him when he was home from school one day. He catered to his little brother and showed him an unconditional love that was sweet to watch. I often wondered how he felt about Melinda. She was always stern with this boy, more so than the younger child who seemed to have no discipline. I knew he loved his mom, you could see it in the way he looked at her, even though she was not his biological mother.

Melinda pretty much never changed over the years. Still frumpy and even walked around with her head down. She always said she knew the girls in her husband's office would no doubt talk about her every time she left there. She said, "They probably wonder why he is with me because I am so overweight, and I am not pretty." She would say, "I know they think he could do better." I would build her up every time she talked like this. She would go to Kentucky with gal friends for a weekend from time to time, I thought that was nice. She would always tell me, when she returned, that her husband seemed to appreciate her for a while after taking care of the boys for a weekend, that he seemed to understand her struggles more.

I would begin to clean her parents' home every few months. Melinda's parents lived about ten miles down the road. This is where I learned more about Melinda.

Melinda's parents were in their late seventies, and they had had her at an older age. They were horse people and lived on their horse farm. Melinda had been a show horse rider of quarter horses throughout her childhood and was raised by these down-to-earth very normal people. The father did not like Melinda's husband and had no problem voicing that to me, with his wife always trying to shut him up.

Melinda's brother would visit from Washington State from time to time and tell me, "You know how every family has a nut? Well, Melinda's son is our little nut." Melinda's boys loved to go to the farm. There would be lambs born in the spring, the horses, and always pigs and chickens running around. It was a beautiful place.

Melinda finally got a new set of leather living room couches and end tables. She was so happy, and then she asked me if I knew anyone who did window coverings, like drapes. She said, "My husband is going to start letting me decorate this house." Melinda asked me if I knew of anyone who could help her with drapes, and so I got her in contact with a gal who did another one of my client's window coverings. This gal came in and measured and brought fabric samples and made several trips to the house only to be told that they did not have the money for the drapes.

Melinda told me, "My husband says he is not spending money on something he does not want, or care for." All the meanwhile, he took many hunting trips and was always buying guns. Soon the walls would be painted with bright orange and green colors, like in India. It was happening all over again—Melinda was not able to make this house her home but her husband's home. There was nothing in the home that was of her taste. *What about her happiness and her comfort zone?* I always thought to myself.

Melinda would display pictures of her son and her together, but the pictures of the oldest son were sparse. I always found that strange, he was such a nice boy. Melinda claimed to love him so much, always said he was her son too, but no pictures put around of him. I've never seen anything like that in anyone else's home. There would be pictures of the youngest son and Melinda scattered across her long vanity in her bathroom and pictures taped to her mirror. I had always thought that this may well be sending an awful message to the older boy. So sad to me.

I would soon be confided in, on a stormy and rainy day, that Melinda was quite fit to be tied. She wanted to do the right thing but could not. I said, "Do the right thing about what?"

She said that the in-laws were only spending time in the United States to gain citizenship in order to have the surgeries that they needed, and she knew it was wrong. She knew of people here that were elderly and could not get surgery. They lied to the government.

Turns out that these two were filthy rich in India and just did not want to pay for surgeries there. Let alone the fact that good doctors were not in India. There was no money to be made there by doctors. They both needed surgeries to replace hips and knees. The in-laws kept flunking the tests to be US citizens, and she was sure they were going to pass this time. That her husband had to pay $2,500 each time they tested, and they then would have to wait another year before testing again.

Social workers came into this enormous home to interview them. And guess what, within a year, the mother-in-law had new knees, compliments of the US government. Amazing! It made me upset. Both of their sons were doctors who made a fortune! I could see why Melinda was upset about the whole deal, but I told her that's on the US and the social workers that interview them.

Melinda couldn't stand it! This is about the time that she began to stand up to her father-in-law and disagree with him on matters, something she was told to never do. Now let me tell you, this man had a strong presence, and I was there a few times when he was in the house by this point. He was about 6'6", and he was just strong-looking and, let me tell you, one gross dude. He would wipe boogers all over the nightstand in the bedroom that they slept in—it was sickening to me—and he would have olive oil in the shower to put on his long hair. One day he asked me, "How are you doing?"

I answered, "I'm fine, thank you."

Then he scolded me, saying, "I asked you a question, now answer me!" After this I told Melinda that I would not be in the house when he was there. Melinda had already shared with me that he actually beat his wife while in the other brother's home in Florida. He had that son's permission to do so. Just insane.

I was busy cleaning one day, listening to my headset, and in quite a good mood. I loved cleaning houses, it was such a good workout for me. I was always so proud of how the houses looked and smelled when I left. My mood would be changed abruptly by Melinda. She began telling me how she had disagreed with her father-in-law on their visit. That he was now back in India, and she was worried that he would send someone over to kill her for disagreeing with him. I suddenly felt sick. I told her, "No, this would never happen, you're just being silly, right?"

She told me, "It is very possible that he would do just that. He could fly someone in from India to kill me, and nobody would ever know the truth of how I died. People come and go from India all the time, Angel, I'm horrified, I can't sleep." Melinda had never argued or disagreed about anything with her father-in-law prior to this.

When I left her house that day, I was really sick from what she had told me, along with the fear I saw in her face. I had to stop my car on the side of the road to throw up. I didn't know what to make of it all. I thought to myself, *Is she trying to tell me to tell someone of her situation or what.* If I did tell someone, what would happen to her then? This incident brought on a migraine that lasted for three days with me. I had already been told several times by Melinda that she wanted a divorce, but that her husband had told her, "Go ahead with a divorce, you will not get either boy nor will you have a home to live in any longer." I had told her to get a good attorney, but she was too afraid, always living in fear.

The situation in this home worsened with the news that their younger son had autism. In India if there is something wrong with a child, the family pretty much denounces them. The in-laws would visit and have nothing to do with this child, never interacting with him in any way. When they were in town, it was as if the boy was invisible to them. Really strange to watch.

Melinda would tell me that her husband would come home, eat dinner, even cooking dinner at times, but then retreat to their bedroom in his lounge chair, watching television or studying all night, no interaction with the family at all. Melinda said he was upset that they had a child together that was mentally ill, and very verbal about the subject.

I was always very delicate with Melinda, in that I would not give her too much advice but just try to listen more. I did tell her at one time that she came from a good family who would be there for her. I always reminded her that she had a degree and was a strong and capable woman who would do fine out in the world. It was the chance that she could lose her son that held her back. This woman did not even grocery shop, her husband did all that.

Melinda would go to the beauty shop only once every six months; it was as if she had no life at all. There were the frequent visits to her parents' home down the road. I think those visits kept her spirits up. Her youngest son loved to go there and see all the animals. Whenever Melinda talked about her parents, her face lit up, she loved them so much.

She still had no control in her home, she didn't dare decorate. She was always so nice to me, giving me extra money every holiday and whenever she thought the house was dirtier. She was given money to live on throughout the month, and that was how she paid me; it was like she had an allowance.

When I told Melinda I would be moving away to New York State, it was very difficult for me, difficult to leave her, not knowing how she would be in life. She wished me well and told me that if I ever wanted to come back, even just for a visit, that I was welcome in her home.

And so I left the house that day looking back in my rearview mirror, thinking about all her prior neighbors in the old neighborhood who were quite jealous of her new big home. I couldn't help but think, if they only knew what a prison it was for Melinda, that new big home. I wish her the best in life and send her strength in my prayers. And when I think of her, I sometimes have a hard time breathing.

Kyra and Manny

WHERE DO I START with Kyra? She called me from a business card I had posted at the grocery store community bulletin board out in Firestone, Colorado. They were building a ton of new houses in Firestone at the time, and I thought I would pick up a few clients. New homes are so much easier to clean.

She would call me on a windy day. I happened to be sitting on my front porch, enjoying the air and the view of the lake. This very deep tormenting loud voice came over the phone. This gal would go on and on about her entire life, how she came to Colorado and where she grew up, interviewing me as well, for over an hour. Clearly she wanted to know me before I went to look at her home, a good indication that perhaps she was afraid to have any person she did not know in her home.

I would fit her in to my schedule, looking at her home within the week. It was a drive, thirty minutes, to a barren spot off of I-25. Not many trees out that way as of yet. Some would call this community a bedroom neighborhood because of the commute to work in Denver, Boulder, Fort Collins, Loveland, or Longmont. Kyra did not live in the new home division, but her home was relatively new, about eight years old.

And so, I was greeted by a taller fat woman, halter top on with her tummy exposed, and a full floor-length summer skirt on. No makeup, hair bleached and undone with manly looking glasses on, which sat crooked upon her nose. Not the woman I had pictured on the telephone at all.

Kyra described her childhood as coming from a rich upbringing in New Jersey, and that they had a family home on Cape Cod, which she shared with five siblings, also having a mountain home in Grand Lake. I was quite shocked by her appearance, but then you never know, do you?

She went on to say, "Oh my, you're so skinny, how did you get so thin?"

I was taken aback and just replied with, "Well, I work hard, I sweat all day." As I entered the home, I smelled a strong scent of air freshener. The walls were covered with dark paint in gold and green. The furnishings in the front living room were Victorian, very old, the couch was small and floral print, all her mother's, who was now deceased. There were antique chests, two-winged back chairs that were in decor of royal blue with stars on the fabric. A large painted picture of the ocean hung over the fireplace, she said her mother-in-law, who lived in Florida, had painted the picture.

This room was adorned with many knickknacks that did not really go well together. Everything seemed to just be thrown together. In fact, there were tons of knickknacks everywhere I looked, along with plastic flowers and vines that were covered with plenty of dust.

The dining room was wide open to the front living room, open floor plan as we ladies call it, and had antique furniture that she was very proud to show off. *Too much furniture for such a small room*, I thought to myself. I was also noticing how much art was on the walls. It was as if every inch of space had to be filled up, all the way from the floor to the ceilings. She bragged of the staircase leading up to the second floor (it was normal, nothing grand), talking about how much money they had put into the wood. As she continued to show me throughout the home, she put a price on everything. They had had this home built. Although she had great pride in her home, as we all do, this home was cheaply built.

The kitchen was large and dark as well with a table that looked like it belonged in a patio room, wrought iron. The walls were covered with pottery from Mexico. The floors were covered in a large square tile that one might see if in Mexico, you know, big brown squares that look like shiny clay.

I could not see the kitchen countertops with all the mess; she apologized, saying that she had not had time to clean up with all the work she had going on. Kyra is a travel agent who had begun her career working in West Palm Beach, Florida, relocated to Colorado for her husband's job, and now works from home.

"Phone ringing constantly, you know!" she screamed out. The cabinets seemed worn and much older than the home itself. The appliances were black, of course. As I looked out the window, I could see a row of pine trees, which were hiding the busy road behind the home, a road that is now like a busy highway after only a few years of the new subdivisions coming in all around her. The deck sported worn-out furniture and a hot tub that was broken and due to be fixed soon, she said. Ten years later, it still sits broken.

The lower living room was four steps down and sported a modern sectional couch with an antique side table. The coffee table was a large trunk with an antique weighing scale in the center. This was a confusing room. There were things all over this room from all of her and her husband, Manny's, travels; nothing went together, it did not flow. This kind of room gives me a headache. In the corner was a large six-foot cat tower for her three cats to climb and sleep on. As my eye wandered around this room, I began to see the cat hair everywhere and smell the litter box, ugh.

Then off of this living room was her office. The entrance, solid-white French doors, was very pretty. This room was completely done in beach furnishings, along with pale-blue paint on the walls, unlike the dark paint in all the other rooms, quite refreshing. There was a photo of her and Muhammad Ali hanging on the wall. I would say she was around sixteen at the time the picture was taken. In this picture, she was very pretty and petite. I now had a different image of her. I said, "Wow, look at you!" Kyra told me she had hurt her ankle in her twenties. Exercising was extremely difficult and pretty much nonexistent for her, all her adult life now. Hence the fat body, you could put a plate of food on her fanny and use it as a table.

In her office was a treadmill covered with boxes of I don't know what. There was a large hutch that you would expect to see in a dining area, covered with—you guessed it—more knickknacks! There were two wicker chairs in front of the desk, in case a client should stop by. These chairs were piled with even more boxes and papers. I don't think any client ever stopped by, thank God. Behind her desk were mounds and mounds of paperwork with trash scattered about on the floor, hence her missing the can, and well, just not emptying it often. This gal was clearly lazy and just sat at her desk all day or in front of the television.

As we went upstairs, it got darker. Her bedroom was full—and I mean full—of beautiful antique furniture. There was a king-size bed with a seven-foot-high headboard, a beautiful antique. The bed had a box on it. I asked what the box was for. "My cat gets in there at night when he has to go potty." I was mortified. There were piles of magazines on the bedside tables, and this room seemed like an old parlor of sorts.

The lampshades had gold ribbons hanging from them. Dresser drawers were open with clothes hanging out, and clothes piled four feet high on top of each dresser. There lay a pile of hair that one of her cats had obviously choked up. Yes, I'm gagging just thinking back about all this. I thought to myself that this room had not been cleaned for years, and how could anyone possibly sleep in it? I mean, how on earth could you relax?

The master bathroom was just as bad. The shower was done in black tile, very dark. I could not see the countertop in the bathroom, same as the kitchen. And see through that shower door? Forget it, honey, that thing needed a chisel. I won't talk about her toilet in there. To this day, the thought of it makes me ill. The soaking tub was a dream come true, except for the plastic plants gathering dust all around. The wooden blinds in the window, well, it was covered with dirt—yes, I said it, dirt, not dust. This happens when you open the window, and you live near open fields, the dirt comes in, and apparently, she never took the time to wipe it off, and yes, more cat hair. Her master closet, well, let's just not go there, and yes, I'm gagging again.

But as I am touring the house, she is just giggling and laughing all the way, putting a price tag on everything in sight. She was comical, much like a cartoon character.

Kyra explained to me that her husband slept in the bedroom down the hall because he rose so early to commute to work. All the while I'm thinking, "No, honey, it has to be the box on your bed that drove him down the hall." Her husband, Manny's, bedroom was done in mismatched furniture with old sea paintings on the walls, doilies on the end tables. I thought this could not be the room of the man of this house, but it was.

The extra bedroom was done in beach furnishings, like her office There was no room to walk around the bed. It was as if she collected things of completely different decor and just threw them all together. There was wicker, there was metal, and there was a piece of furniture that looked as if it were made from plywood. You could not see the bed due to all the clothes thrown atop it.

We talked for quite some time, I mean it took a while with her putting a price tag on everything and telling me exactly where she bought it. Seemed as though she got a deal at every thrift store up and down the front range. We had something in common, I loved the deals myself.

I sat with Kyra and had a small glass of wine. Come on, ladies, I deserved it, this tour was exhausting. We eventually agreed on a price. This chic had to get the best deal on everything, called herself the coupon queen, and she was not about to pay me a penny more than what she had in her mind. I got my big money on the first cleaning, I tripled the quote just to get started. I mean, really? This place was large and absolutely filthy. I mean, bless her heart, she loved her home, but man did she live in it.

Kyra seemed to be lonely and wanted a friend. I couldn't get her off the phone on the first call, and this tour took over an hour and a half. Little did I know that this would continue on each and every visit.

Now at this time, there was no hint to me that this woman smoked in her home, although I wondered why the heavy smell of air freshener my first time in. Nor did I realize that she may drink quite a bit as well. But I would soon experience both.

It would be about the third time in cleaning that Kyra would begin to smoke in her office. We agreed that she would not smoke again while I was there working. The next time in, I noticed around 2:00 p.m., that Kyra was getting hammered, drunk that is. And this woman was not a nice kind of drunk but insulting and downright mean. I learned early on that I needed to change her cleaning to the mornings in order to avoid this behavior. "Mornings, well, that isn't going to work for me," she said. I reminded her that she had told me she awoke early every morning due to her richest clientele being on the East Coast. "Well, I guess we will try it, but afternoons would be better for me."

I replied with, "Well, I am so sorry, but I am fitting in a new client, and she insists on afternoons, you can always get another lady if you need to."

"Oh no," Kyra would say, "I only trust you in my home, and we are friends now, so I will work with you on this."

I would have gladly dropped her as a client because the smoke coming from her office was bad enough, and I was damned if I was going to put up with a mean drunk.

As long as Kyra was not drinking, she was fun to be around. Soon we would begin to go shopping together and have lunches. We both loved Home Goods Store, antique shopping along the front range, and flea markets. Every restaurant we ate at Kyra would have a coupon, and she would calculate a 10-percent tip, this was embarrassing to me. But Kyra was the coupon queen. If she didn't get it cheap, she wasn't getting it.

Her Christmas gifts to me and her entire family were from thrift stores, and she would announce this with each gift. I would just laugh. But they were always cute gifts that went with my decor. Just part of her quirky personality. Imagine a woman, fat with a large backside, dressed in sundresses, exposing her tummy and cleavage whenever possible, and covered with gold jewelry. She was just comical. She thought of herself as a rich Palm Beach lady.

The next summer, she would invite me up to the townhome in Grand Lake. Manny would take us out on the boat. I would get a grand tour of the lake and all the homes that adorned it. It was the grand tour of the homes that were only accessible by boat or snow mobile in the winter months. Such magnificent homes that were built over one hundred years ago, stately. It was quite fun. We would bring the kayaks and drop them in the water. The next morning, we would go into the small town and have breakfast and later drink Bloody Marys on the beach, at the end of the lake. These two loved to party and entertain. Those were fun times, and there would be more to come. I learned to go to bed early because of the drinking, though it was always manageable visits with them.

Kyra and Manny had dinner parties, and I would always bring a date. The bad part was that Kyra would get drunk and chase my date around their pool table in the basement and begin throwing insults her husband's way. Of course, my dates would always say that they would not go back, that she was funny but that they didn't like getting their ass grabbed; yes, that is how bad she was when she drank.

It was clear that my client and friend had a drinking problem, and Manny loved his beer and even had a full bar in his man cave in their basement, yet he never got out of hand while drinking. I was thinking it was good that he had fallen in love with Kyra while she was young and beautiful. They say men have to be able to see you as a young woman first. I don't believe this to be true at all because I have had my share of great loves after the age of forty. But in Manny's case, I thought it was what kept him going.

Kyra confided in me that they had not been intimate in over eight years and that on every vacation, Manny would always walk ahead of her while touring the sites they visited. I could have told her to lose some weight and perhaps not get drunk every night, insulting him and smoking like a sailor, but I didn't want to hurt her feelings, and I don't think Manny wanted to hurt her feelings either.

Manny and Kyra have the most wonderful garden every summer in which they are quite generous in sharing. There are tomatoes, zucchini, butternut squash, cucumbers, and on and on. They always had me over for the best dinners made from all these wonderful vegetables. Yes, these two love—and I mean love—to cook, and man can they cook.

I would soon be asked if Kyra could come to my pool to spend a Saturday. "Please, please, please," she begged me. She had dropped by one day to give me a gift and wanted the tour of the property. She discovered I had the pool.

My townhome was on a small lake with a huge swimming pool overlooking the lake. I always made it a point to be the first in the gate, as I would save my spot overlooking the lake. This property was complete with a full kitchen, locker room, and plenty of shady spots; it was quite fabulous. There were tennis courts, volleyball court, basketball courts, and a private playground, only accessed with my key, all which my grandkids used quite often.

Of course, I could not say no to Kyra because she had been so hospitable to me. The problem was that she showed up in a two-piece swimsuit. Now this was never a problem to me out on the lake, while on the boat, but in my pool, it was different. Now the same day she was coming, so was my beautiful daughter and her three children. I called ahead and warned them of her appearance, but still the look on my grandchildren's faces when they saw her, well, it was priceless!

On this particular day, Kyra appeared to have dark stains going up the back of her bottom swimsuit. She threw a towel around herself. Now I had come across this with her once before when I came to clean. She came out of her house to greet me and turned around with what appeared to be old stain marks up the back of her sweatpants from diarrhea, I would suppose. Yes, ladies, I'm gagging. I told her about her backside, and all she said was, "I know, I can't get the stains out, and who cares, it's just you."

Yes, Kyra has shocked me many times. Kyra is one of those people that loves to brag about how much money she has in her savings account, what she pays for everything, and where she came from in New Jersey, but she does not much care about her appearance unless you are coming to one of her dinner parties or Christmas party. She just doesn't care.

I have come across many clients who work from their home, and they pretty much are the same way, pajamas or sweats on all day but never stains going up their backside. I recall the time she phoned, saying she needed to stash Manny's Christmas gift in my garage and would I help her pick it up at the store. It was a large barbecue grill, and while she was applying for credit to buy it, she was bent over the counter in leggings—yes, I said leggings—with bubblegum stuck to her ass. Everyone in line was pointing and laughing. It was all I could do, so I walked out of the area. I mean what was I to do, tell her in front of all of those people that she had gum stuck to her ass? I'm giggling because had I told her, she would have replied, "F——them all, I have more money than all of them." That's just how she rolled.

Kyra became a needy client and friend, as she would call me countless times when she and Manny were fighting and ask me to please text or call him and tell him this or that. I always declined, and I learned not to answer my phone past 3:00 p.m. because she had already been drinking for several hours by then. Now at the lake house, the drinking never began until around 4:00 p.m. or later. There was the boat and then all the cooking after boating.

I have moved away, and we still keep in touch. I will see her at their family home on Cape Cod this August. Kyra is a travel agent, and she travels at least three times a year. I'm lucky, this year they're going to Cape Cod, they make it there about every other year. I'm still contemplating whether to go or not. How much will they drink? How much will she smoke? I'm married now, will she chase him around the house and grab his ass? I don't know if we will go, but if we do, it will be fun.

Some people come in to your life, and they stay awhile, and I am glad she has come. No matter how long it has been since we have talked, well, it's like we just saw each other the day before. It's always as if we have known each other our entire lives. We still read *House Beautiful* together over the telephone. It will be so much fun because of the restaurants, beach, and antique shops, and yes, this gal will go to bed early. And my guy, well, he's been forewarned. Now I'm laughing.

Robin

I MET ROBIN AT MY divorce group. We quickly became friends, later becoming a client as well. Robin quietly joined the group after divorcing her second husband who had alcohol problems. Robin was petite with blond curly hair that seemed out of control, freckles, a tiny nose, pretty blue eyes. Robin wore little makeup, and her clothes seemed to be from a thrift store, another Boulder type of gal but guarded—extremely guarded—in nature, a lady. She was like myself in the way that she joined the group in order to find single friends, explore life as a single person, and grow from the experience. She was not there to find a boyfriend, like so many others.

I swear most of the men there, and some of the women, paid their $350 all to get hooked up with someone for sex or a relationship; it was so blatantly obvious. We all signed the same contract, we were not to mingle in those ways. It was always refreshing to come across someone who was there for the same reasons as myself, excited about this new single life and how to go about living it.

Robin's story was a lot like mine. Her husband had abused alcohol, and he would not stop. It was the same thing over and over again, and she finally had had enough. Robin had never had children. She came out of the divorce with her home and automobile paid for but was not getting any alimony, like so many others in the group. Robin was a nurse that worked for ten or twelve-hour shifts each week, and when she could, she traveled. She wanted to travel more but needed to be able to afford it.

Robin came to all of the parties that the group had away from the meetings, and she still remained quiet for a long time. You had to get closer to her to really know her. I did not get to know her in group because we would split off into several groups, and she and I were never in the same group together. It would be after the divorce group that we would get to know each other.

Robin began to have gatherings at her home in Louisville, right outside of Boulder, Colorado. Her home was large and older, probably built thirty years prior. It sat right at the end of a hill overlooking the front range. Robin had quite the magnificent view. You could see most of Boulder, there were the mountains and then a pond about a fourth of a mile from her backyard. It was ideal to just take off from her backyard and hike for hours at a time.

The house was decorated with a ton of cats. Like pictures of tigers and lions and statues of them too. Nothing went together in this home, it drove me crazy. There were many plants in the house and all of her furniture appeared to be older, like the clothes she wore. Robin had no pets at her house. The house had wallpaper on most walls, the kitchen was older but large, and there were five bedrooms with two and a half bathrooms. The basement was finished and had a large laundry room. It would be some time before I would clean for Robin.

The first gathering at Robin's house was for a book club. We all read the book *Why Men Love Bitches*. It was a silly book to read. The whole point of it was to treat a man poorly, and he would do anything to keep you happy. One example was to never have more than a hot dog in your refrigerator so that he would always take you out to dinner or buy you groceries. The group came to the conclusion that we didn't care much for most of the book, but we had so much fun reading it and getting together to discuss it, drink wine, and eat.

Robin and I would later get together for concerts, dinners, lunches, snowshoeing in the mountains with groups, and large psychic gatherings. Robin and I were so much alike—we ate clean, worked hard, loved the mountains, hiking, and just the simple things in life. We both had become strong independent women.

It didn't seem to matter that she didn't have children and I did, but she would always ask me how mine were. She was always so caring and considerate to others. I don't think she ever regretted not having children because she said she was terrified she would not be good at mothering, but I think she would have been a wonderful mother. Robin was raised prominently by nannies due to the fact that her wealthy parents traveled most of the time, and she said her mother was never attentive to her needs, but she still loved her mother visiting her often in Florida. Her parents divorced at some point, and her father had remarried. Robin kept in close contact with him. You could tell that she was the apple of her daddy's eye by the way she talked about him; she would visit him often.

It seemed as though, very suddenly, Robin just disappeared from everything. When I was able to get ahold of her, she told me she had chronic fatigue and that she was going to have to give up her nursing job in order to heal. I'm thinking she was down and out for around four months. During this time, her father passed away. I could hear a heavy sadness over the phone when I would talk to Robin. I knew it laid heavily on her heart that her father was gone. Sometimes I thought there was a sadness in her that never went away, perhaps because she didn't have children, the parentless childhood, the two previous marriages, I don't know, but that sadness was always there, lingering over her like a rain cloud.

Robin's father had left her a trust fund to live on. She never said how much money he had given her, but she was planning ahead on starting her own business. She came up with a strategy to pet sit for families while they were on vacation. "I will get my pet fix this way," she said. Robin absolutely loved to travel, so pets were out of the question for her. She had once told me that it would not be fair to the pet to leave them all the time because she traveled so frequently. I think she felt so strongly about this because of her childhood. Her parents left her with the nanny to travel the world.

The first thing she did was to set up a booth at her church in South Denver, Mile High Church, while they were having a festival of sorts. She obtained many clients through her church, and the next thing you know, Robin was staying in homes all over Denver and the mountains, pet sitting and house sitting. It then became hard to get-together with her again because she could only be away from the pets for so long a period at a time. This was her business, and she took it very seriously. I was excited for her, she seemed to get happier and happier and doll herself up quite a bit, like she stepped back into life again. The depression had passed; new things were happening. Robin would be staying in beautiful homes all the time pet/house sitting. It was all so exciting to her, never a dull moment, it was all good.

She began dating on the Internet, and this was when crazy things began to happen. The quiet reserved gal I knew was now completely different. She once told me of a date where the guy took her to his home in the mountains. "There was an embankment full of large holes," she said, "like as if you would put bodies in them, like a tomb." She spoke of how she had goose bumps all over while at his very strange home. In the home, his bed was in the middle of the living room. I told her to not see this guy again, that he seemed scary from what she had told me. The next thing I knew, she had gone up in the mountains with the same fellow for a weekend. When she returned, she told me they stayed at a hotel, and he brought camping equipment and that they never left the room. He cooked their meals in the room the entire weekend. She never saw him again, thankfully.

But then there were the times she would have just left Home Depot to buy paint, stop at a red light, and get acquainted with the guy who pulled up next to her; she would take him home with her. I felt she was living dangerously. She would drive up to Montana and camp alongside the road all by herself with no gun for protection, and she would tell me she could hear trucks driving by, then stopping and going on. It all scared me. I felt she was exploring on the dark side, being too brave. There was a period of time I felt that I may turn on the news, and it would be Robin's body that they had found. I was always telling her to please be careful. I felt she may be acting out from the death of her father. People handle death in different ways, no one is alike in the grieving process.

Then Robin found a guy that she stuck with, at least for a while. He showed up with her at a bar in Arvada, The D Note. We gals would frequent this fun diner restaurant where they always had great bands to dance to. Now this guy, he was disgusting-looking to me, and I could tell there were problems because we all had not seen her since she had gotten in this relationship. Robin always swore she would not disappear into a relationship again, never seeing her gal friends.

This guy was just greasy-looking, greasy hair, clothes looked like they had been worn for weeks at a time, just a shady fellow. Like someone I would imagine seeing on the bad streets of a large city somewhere, just a bad dude. Robin had told me over the phone that he did funny things with money, like he was not legitimate, he had a painting business, and that he did not treat her well.

He would take her to a not-so-nice restaurant for Valentine's Day, and she would call him out on it, then the next day, he would overwhelm her with tons of teddy bears, flowers, and chocolates. She finally ended the relationship after a stormy period of time with him. He stalked her for months, but once the police were involved, he stopped bothering her and just disappeared. I was relieved to see him go.

My parents and brother died, and then I drifted away into my own state of shock. Robin would be one of the first friends to come and visit me. She brought ham with another one of our gal friends. She didn't know what to say to me, I could tell, so she was just her quiet sweet giving self. I so appreciated her coming to sit with me and just be.

Later we kept in touch through phone calls but never really saw each other. I had now been the one to drift away and deal with my own problems of grief, once again. Those times were hard, life became too difficult for me. I went into therapy, and friends were the last thing on my mind. I was trying to keep living, I didn't want to feel grief again, but I had no choice.

It was through therapy that I would find the strength to go on, and my beautiful daughter had told me, "You don't always have to be so strong, Mom." When she said those words to me, I felt as though a ton had been lifted off of my shoulders. I felt as though I could just live one day at a time and not have to make any plans, just to go on living, be in the present moment. It was those words that gave me such relief. You always hope you can say something to a person that they will grow from or take away with them and recovered from later.

My daughter did that for me that day. She did the same thing after her sister died, and she was so young, only thirteen, but she knew what she had to say to me.

This daughter of mine, she is so wise. My beautiful daughter heard me crying in my bedroom, as I did so often. She opened the door and said to me, "Mom, I can't believe you're still doing this, I'm here, Mom, I'm still here." It shocked me out of my grief for her sister and made me realize that I needed to start living again for her and her brother. What a fool I had been. But when your child dies, no matter what age they are, it can kill you. I wish that pain on nobody, not even my worst enemy.

Being in the present moment is so much of a gift because you are not thinking about the past or worrying about the future. This moment you are in, it truly is a gift if you can recognize it on a daily basis. As when my daughter had died, I again had to retrain myself to look at every gift in every moment. I would thank God for my bed, the pillow, the soft sheets, the fact that I could get up and walk to my coffeepot and have hot coffee within minutes, all this before I even opened my eyes. Thank God for my surviving children and my husband. It is still a daily process for me, always looking for the gifts. We are so blessed to live in America, and we have so many luxuries that people in other countries will never have. To live a life of gratitude and being grateful for every little thing is the only way I survive grief; and God, he carries me some days.

Robin and I would meet again in downtown Denver for a lunch. She had just been to a spiritual meeting and was on top of the world, she looked healthy and full of life. I wasn't quite there yet, but I was getting out more.

The next time I heard from Robin, it was news that she had been approached by a guy at her church who she had taught a class with there prior. She was in love, true love. She told me he asked her for coffee after church, and so she went, and they had been inseparable ever since. I was so happy for her. It all came out of the blue. She had no idea he had a crush on her for so long. He had lived with a woman for many years but never married, and he was now on his own. He told her she had been on his mind ever since they taught the class together at church.

Robin was giddy every time I talked to her. "Oh you wouldn't believe the things he does for me and says to me, he is the perfect man, except he will not have sex with me until we have been together longer, and it's killing me." I told her this was a great respectable man she has met.

Well, the next thing you know, I'm calling Robin, asking her when we can get together, and she is having a hard time finding a way to fit me in. Robin had gotten back online to find a friend with benefits until her new beau came around to having sex with her. Oh yes, she found a younger divorced man, with toddlers, who was looking for the same kind of friend, and whenever he called, she came running. I couldn't believe what I was hearing. Here she had found the perfect man, and she was cheating on him behind his back. She said she had every right because her new guy was holding out on her, and she felt that to be cruel. So here she was, living dangerously once again.

At this point, Robin was leasing out her home as an air and breakfast while she would be off pet/house sitting. It was perfect. Her home was being occupied by vacationers, hence she was making double money. She would lock everything up in her basement and garage, and off she would go. She had a Realtor managing her home, and she was pulling in the big bucks. She was always in the mountains in some grand home, sometimes for a month at a time. Then Robin and her new beau realized the Realtor was taking more money in than she was telling Robin, pocketing money for herself. This is where I began cleanings for Robin.

I would go in and clean after each group would leave and get the house ready for the next group. While on one of the days I was cleaning, her new beau, Dan, stopped by to tell me he was now in charge of the air and breakfast business so that things would be easier on Robin, and he could manage the money for her. Here I was looking at this wonderful man, knowing what Robin was doing behind his back, and I couldn't betray my friend and tell him. I couldn't do that to Robin, but I felt like a horrible person.

Robin and I didn't speak for some time. She would just always mail me checks for my service. This went on for two years until finally a group of people had done quite a bit of damage to her home. It was now out of business for repairs done by Dan. She and Dan decided not to pick up that business any longer, but they began traveling together to do pet/house sitting all over the mountains. I wouldn't see Robin again for months on end.

The next phone call was that her beau, Dan, had proposed to her on a beach in Mexico, complete with a video on a screen with shots of their entire romance. He was perfect. She gave up the friend with benefits, and the next thing I knew, I was at their wedding reception in her backyard.

They had had a small family wedding up in the mountains, and the reception was for friends. It was a wonderful time. All the food was made by Robin and Dan, they even made their own beer. Robin wore her wedding gown, and there was a lot of drinking. Only one person was there that we had both known together, everyone else was from the spiritual world she now lived in.

One woman was telling me I should sell everything I own and live in a common home in Boulder or Denver. A home where you get your own bedroom and switch homes every three months. "Everyone has their own chores in the house," she said. "This week I am in charge of making salad dressing."

I was mortified. I saw this woman climb into her old VW van when I was leaving. Everyone I talked with seemed to be the same type of person. I don't know what you would call it really. Robin lived in this sort of spiritual world where there seemed to be a ton of older hippie-type people. Everyone was getting pretty smashed, so I was not there long, I'm not a drinker. Dan was drooling over me, and it made me uncomfortable, to say the least. Robin was living it up and enjoying life I was happy for her but wondered what her new life with Dan was going to be like. They were both drunk when I left, Robin hardly being able to stand. I chalked it up to just getting married. Never seen that before.

After the marriage, I saw Robin only a few times for lunch or coffee. At one point, she gained a ton of weight. I almost didn't recognize her as she walked into the restaurant we met at. On another visit, she was extremely thin. I wondered what was going on with her, but she never opened up. I knew at some point we would not see each other again, even though she had always vowed to not give up her friends if she remarried, which is what her past husband made her do.

I would watch their life on FB, and we would pass a few messages back and forth. Dan gave up his teaching job so they could travel all over the country, pet sitting. At one point, they were in Hawaii. Then the next thing I knew, Dan was a bag guy at the airport, hence, free flying privileges. They had it all figured out.

I never saw Robin again, except at a concert when she walked past me, quite drunk, with Dan helping her along. She didn't see me, and I didn't reach out, it was 4:30 p.m., at an outdoor event concert that started at 7:00 p.m. I was shocked.

I left hoping that Robin was not drinking like that all the time. It made me sad to see her like that. She is now enthralled in her new marriage. I watch them travel the world on Facebook, and we would chat once in a while on the telephone, but now it's just messages on Facebook. She has a wonderful life with what she called the perfect man. It is fun to watch them travel, they have been all over the world now, and Dan is teaching again.

We all get involved in our lives with men that we marry or have relationships with, and our lives go on, and that's okay.

Don and Trixie

T HEN ALONG CAME DON, Don the Man, I would later think of him. Don saw my ad in the Boulder newspaper, *The Daily Camera*, and called me to clean his rental home in Boulder. I frequently ran ads in the late spring and throughout the summer because all the college kids were moving in and out of the area, and believe me, they weren't going to clean their own places. The work in Boulder was plentiful and high-paying.

It was a beautiful spring day, and I was more than happy to go give an estimate on a place in Boulder. All those tulips everywhere you look, so beautiful! Spring in Boulder, I just love it! I already knew the perfect place for lunch, Mateo's, a French organic restaurant on the famous Pearl Street Mall. I would eat outside on the patio where beautiful vines with flowers hung down from the trellis above the tables. Many times, I would go there, enjoying their mushroom soup with a burger, but first I would meet up with Don so that I could enjoy the rest of my afternoon kicking around Boulder. Oh, how I loved the shops and restaurants.

The drive approaching this house was a curvy one, covered with enormous oak trees and lots of shrubs, it was quite beautiful. There is no part of Boulder, Colorado, that isn't beautiful as it is nestled right at the bottom of the foothills. Boulder is an old exaggerated version of a college town that this gal shall forever be in love with. Oh yes, and Colorado University, just such breathtaking architecture on all the buildings.

I met Don in front of his rental home. He drove up on his Harley Davidson motorcycle. Right away, I thought, *Oofta! Cute guy.*

Don is a shorter dark-haired man that was quite handsome with an athletic build. He showed up in a white T-shirt and jeans, typical to Boulder attire. I would have never guessed that this man was a judge and an attorney who had his own law firm on the Pearl Street Mall. I would not know this until a few years had passed, when Angie told me her husband did work with him.

Well, you know, who says a judge or an attorney has to look well-groomed. This guy had that bad-boy look. Don was quite shy and soft-spoken. He seemed drawn to the diamond cross I wore around my neck and would later tell me that he'd have asked me out that very day, if it weren't for my cross. Don, you see, is Jewish. He was in a relationship at the time anyhow, and so was I. I knew he was attracted to me, as I certainly was attracted to him, but neither of us acted on that attraction.

We went inside after about twenty minutes of chitchat. Don was looking for someone he could trust. At this time, Boulder had quite a few Russian, Hispanic, and Asian cleaning companies, and most had bad reputations. This home was one that he had split into two separate apartments, one nice apartment for grad students and a small basement apartment, not so nice, more of a studio setup. The grad students always rented the nice places in Boulder.

The house was a dark-brown shingle home on the outside, surrounded by large oak trees, shrubs, and flowering bushes. Now I was pleasantly surprised at how bright the house was on the inside, lots of white walls. The kitchen was remodeled in the main apartment with granite countertops and beautiful cabinets, light fixtures, and bamboo flooring. It was quite small but opened right into the living room.

The living room sported a beautiful grand stone fireplace that rose to the ceiling, about thirty feet high. There were sliding glass doors showing a magnificent view of the Flatirons along the mountain, the view was *hypnotizing*. If I lived there, I would have a hard time leaving in the morning because I would have my coffee right there, looking at that view. But back to reality, not many people can afford to live in Boulder; it has always been for the rich, unless you bought property there, like a million years ago.

Students rented rooms around Boulder for around $1,100 a month at this time, and it just went higher from there. It was not rare to see five to eight students renting one house. This house rented for at least $3,000 a month, just for the upstairs apartment. To this day, property owners rake in a small fortune by renting to students.

There were wooden beams in the ceiling, an older home, about sixty years old I would say, filled with tons of character. The upstairs bedroom had a balcony overlooking the living room with doors that you could shut for privacy. All of the rooms had large windows in which to enjoy the views of the foothills and all those beautiful trees that are so abundant in this small old college town.

Boulder Colorado has a 1-percent growth law, meaning you cannot build there, that is, unless you tear something down and build on the same spot. When you tear down a structure in Boulder County to build another, or just to tear it down, you have to recycle 100 percent of it. Let me tell you, the restore business there is insane, you can find anything you want for your home, used of course, but I mean anything you're looking for, you'll find at the restore.

The studio apartment in the basement was a different story altogether. Like I said, a studio with a bathroom, no kitchen, just a countertop with a sink, microwave, and a small refrigerator, this, no doubt, probably rented for about $1,400 a month. This was a move-out clean, easy peasy, not too dirty at all.

Over the next few years, I would return to this house to clean quite a few times until Don decided to sell it.

This job led to cleaning Don's home in Louisville, not too far from Boulder. Don had a live-in gal friend who had just moved out, and he wanted everything spic and span. He said, "All the gals that have lived with me are never clean freaks by any means. In fact, they all seem to quit doing anything after they move in, you are going to charge me an arm and a leg for this one." Don seemed to go through quite a few girlfriends, looking for Ms. Right.

Don was smoking a cigarette on his front porch at his home in Louisville when I arrived to take a look, in his typical T-shirt-and-jeans attire that I had become acquainted with. This home had been a show home. In Colorado, when they are building a new neighborhood, they build all the home models that they are going to sell first, this way buyers can go through them and see what they look like finished, complete with all the upgrades. This way one can imagine for their new dwelling. This particular house sat on the golf course with a view of the mountains if you went out back, or out front on both porches. The views blew me away, just beautiful.

The home was quite open. As I walked in the front door, there was an office off to the left with French doors sporting glass panes, a nice-sized office. About ten feet in front of me was the staircase, and off to the side of that, an open dining room with large windows and the mountain view, no furniture there.

Walking beyond the dining room and down a hallway was the half bath and a small laundry room. The half bath had slate flooring, which is up and coming in the West. The laundry room had counter space and a sink, most women would kill for a sink in the laundry room. This laundry room was quite large.

The kitchen was right off the dining room with a large island and a living room open to the kitchen. This house definitely had the open floor plan. The kitchen had a large window over the sink overlooking the golf course. There were granite countertops. All the appliances were stainless steel. I could already tell that this home had many upgrades. This house had a wonderful flow to it. Sparsely decorated, of course, being Don was a bachelor his entire life, and his latest girlfriend had taken all of her things.

We went upstairs to a small open loft area where there was a coffee bar, it was unique. Get up in the morning, hit the on button, take a shower, and *bam*, your coffee was right there, perfect. What coffee drinker wouldn't love this?

There were two bedrooms and a full bath. These rooms were beautiful because Don had bought the furnishings. The drapes and bedding all went together and coordinated with the wallpaper in the bathroom. Then there was the master bedroom, and man, alive was this room huge. Don had a king-size bed with an armoire for his television, a chaise lounge chair, and in the corner were weights. Over an entrance way, there was a small living room off his bedroom. There was a bar over your head going into this room so that he could do pull-ups. Definitely a bachelor pad. In this room, there was a piano, television, stereo, large stuffed chair and ottoman, and some guitars as well. I could picture Don having his coffee in this room while watching the local or national news in the mornings. It was just too perfect, I mean who doesn't want a living room right off your master bedroom? This was quite the master suite, let me tell you, complete with large windows and views to die for of the golf course.

The master bath had a large soaking tub with jets and a window over it that went the entire length of this tub. There was a humongous shower with a built-in bench, double sinks, granite countertop, of course, and a large walk-in closet. Plantation shutters were in every room that had windows, great for insulation in the summer and winter months and really pretty to look at, just beautiful and expensive!

The house has a full unfinished basement to boot, where an entire gym was set up for Don's workouts. There was a three-car garage. There was plenty of storage.

Don was attracted to what I would call biker chicks. A rough type of woman who usually smoked, not only cigarettes but marijuana, and who would drink heavily, at least this is the impression I got from the picture of his gal friend who had just moved out, very rough-looking. Don said he wasn't ready to take her photo out of his office yet, he needed a grieving period with this one. He said, "I'm tired of going through this all the time. I think I have found the right gal, and then it all goes south, they never want me to play or watch hockey, and I love the sport, I don't understand women." Of course, I just listened like I do with all my clients.

One fall day, Don called me and asked me if I would go talk to his new gal friend in Longmont who needed a move-out cleaning. He said, "She has a large townhome up there, and it's pretty dirty, as usual she doesn't clean either." Then he dropped the bomb. "She will be moving in with me, I have been seeing her for a year now, it's time, and she isn't like all my other gal friends, she's short and brunette." I thought, *Good for you, Don. I mean, maybe this one was the one.*

I met Trixie on a cold fall day, end of October, when Colorado could get a large snowfall. I drove up to Longmont to a newer townhome community on the west side of town, out by the airport.

Typical townhome community, two-car attached garages and front of homes facing each other. As I walked up to the patio, I thought it to be impressive with shrubs and a large wrought iron fence and gate around this particular patio.

Trixie saw me coming because I barely knocked when the door flew open. "You're the cleaning gal Don sent me? Well, you don't look like a cleaning gal."

I replied with, "What exactly is a cleaning gal supposed to look like?"

She said, "Well, you're skinny and pretty to boot."

I replied, "Thanks, I'm also a mother and a grandmother, and I work my ass off every day, you're lucky to see me in the morning, honey". Then we both laughed. Trixie seemed a little different than all Don's gal friends before her. First of all, the others were all tall blonds, and Trixie was a short petite Jewish girl, brown hair, brown eyes, and built athletically. I could tell by the deep wrinkles on her face that she had either had a hard life or abused the sun. Right away, I thought, *Biker-type chic to a degree*, but she also seemed a little uppity, I couldn't put my finger on it.

Then out came, "I found Don on a Jewish dating site. I figured this would be the last attempt at trying to find a man to spend the rest of my life with." And then right outta that mouth came, "Have you slept with him?" Yep, just like that.

I said, "Oh no, Don and I have never been like that, just business with him is all."

"Well, he said you would help me out today." Just like that, she wanted that topic taken care of, I was quite shocked, to say the very least. Trixie's face was so weathered for a gal in her early fifties. Her face had wrinkles so deep that it looked as if there were curtains hanging on her face, but somehow, she was still cute. Trixie explained to me that she was an avid skier and had been a ski bum at one point in her life, hence the weathered face. "I have skied all over the world, and I will never stop, how 'bout you, do you ski?"

I said, "Yep, and each time I do, I end up in physical therapy, even when skiing the bunny trails." And we both busted out laughing.

In the next moment, she took a deep breath and asked me if I would like to smoke a joint with her before seeing the house. I declined while she took a few hits off the joint which she pulled out of her vest pocket. It was 9:00 a.m. I thought, *Okay, whatever floats your boat.* But I always hated the smell of marijuana. I hoped the smell wouldn't follow my every move I made for the rest of the day, ugh.

Now don't get me wrong, I liked her right off the bat. She had spunk, and I could tell she was easy to talk to, the real deal. I try not to judge people for their habits, let's face it, people are downright interesting, to say the very least, especially in Colorado, and most have always smoked the mighty weed. It was not unusual to see it growing in people's yards or on their porches in Boulder or mountain towns. That's just how it is back there.

We stood there in the living room, which was right in the front door. No entrance way in this house, you just walked in the town-home, and you were right in the living room. This room was small and had a fireplace which rose to the top of the fifteen-foot ceiling in the corner. A large window with a view of Twin Peaks Mountains adorned the front of the home. All of the contents of the home were already at Don's, it appeared, because the home was empty, except for a few small pieces of furniture. Right away I knew it was gonna be a real hard job, the carpet was filthy. I could see where each piece of furniture had been. *No, don't ask me to clean the carpets, please!* And just as the thought entered my mind, she asked, "Do you clean carpets? It's not a big place, ya know, and hardly dirty at all." Ah, no, no, thank you. This place had three floors; it reminded me of a treehouse.

Trixie was there getting the rest of the things from her kitchen. There were steps going up to the kitchen and dining area. The kitchen had upgraded cherry cabinets, granite countertops, and shiny black appliances. Above, where a dining room table would go, there hung a large crystal chandelier. This seemed to be a mountainy style town-home so the chandelier stuck out to me. On the other side of the kitchen would be a breakfast nook with a much-smaller table, and then a large pantry. This was a large kitchen.

Then there was a flight of steps off the kitchen going to the basement bedroom and bathroom and another set of stairs going upstairs. The master bedroom was quite large with a master bath. There was another bedroom, one more bath in the hall, along with laundry room. We women love our laundry rooms on the upper level. The perfect set up, laundry right off the bedrooms. It just seemed that there were steps going everywhere, treehouse!

The townhome was pretty dirty, but I got through it. Trixie seemed shocked at what I charged, but this was yet another gal who never cleaned. I would work my tail off this day. This townhome was going to be her income property. She was entering into the awful world of renting your home. Never seemed to work out with many in Colorado, as they would turn your home into a grow house or a meth house. Just awful.

Trixie moved in with Don, and just one year later, she would sell her townhome as the renter wasn't working out. She went through two renters in one year's time. I would keep cleaning Don's house after she moved in as she did not clean at all.

Trixie would teach children to ski in Breckenridge in the winter months, while staying at an apartment she had near there, in Dillion. Don would go up on weekends from time to time. I was wondering where all the money came from, as she never worked full-time. I mean, who can afford an apartment in Breckenridge when they don't work full-time? Maybe she acquired it in her divorce prior?

It wasn't long before Trixie would have a back injury from teaching, then came the pain pills. Trixie had an extremely difficult time getting over this injury, and the house got worse and worse, and so did her mood. She complained to me continually every time I was in the house.

She continued smoking her marijuana while I cleaned, and she would ask me if I wanted any wine, I always declined. She would say she needed the marijuana now more than ever. Alcohol, pills, and marijuana don't mix well, hence her horrid moods.

After about six months, Trixie decided she would get into pho-tography, being unable to ski. She showed me her portfolio, and the pictures were not of good quality, yet she was charging people a fortune, like $800 for the sitting, and then she would charge for the pictures they wanted printed. It was ridiculous to me because my daughter would have a college professor take her family photos and get the CD with all the pictures on it for only $135. This included a two-hour sitting fee, and then my daughter could take the CD and get whatever photos she wanted printed. Everyone was doing this at the time. I knew she wasn't going to make this business work.

Sometimes Don would meet me at the house when Trixie was not there. They seemed to not want me there unless one of them were present at first; Don had never been like that before. Maybe the marijuana made her paranoid.

Don would go outside to smoke and beg me not to tell Trixie that he was still smoking. I thought, certainly she must smell it on him. He would say, "I don't get why women want you to change everything about yourself after you are in a relationship, can you tell me why?"

I would reply with, "I think she just wants you to be healthy, she loves you, so she worries."

"But what about my clothes? She thinks I should change how I dress when we go golfing, she says I embarrass her."

And my reply to that one was, "Dress how you feel comfortable, Don, if she truly loves you, it doesn't matter." Don was just that white-T-shirt-and-jeans kind of guy, and then the black boots and belt. It was hard to believe sometimes that he was a judge.

It was fun to see how Trixie had decorated the house. The living room off the kitchen now had a small red sectional, two purple chairs and glass tables. It was like an artist moved in the house. But of course, there was Don's lounge chair with a computer table on the front of it, along with the photo of himself and George Clooney on the fireplace mantel. Trixie hated that chair. "He is either on the computer or watching hockey! It is as if I don't exist since I moved in here." Oh boy.

Same thing as usual, Don watched hockey too much according to all his women. There was beautiful glassworks from Arizona scattered throughout the home. The bedroom had the same furniture, but she added a huge painted picture of a penis on the wall, her daughter had painted it. She said, "What does that look like to you?"

I replied, "A penis."

She said, "Yeah, that's what I think, but it's supposed to be a mountain." Then we both busted a gut laughing. It was definitely a penis. Gawd. Don had to sleep in his bedroom looking at a huge penis now.

Trixie would always ask me if I had seen Don smoking, and I would, of course, deny that one. I mean Don was the one who paid me, I wasn't not going to give him up. Trixie was trying to get him to eat healthy, you know, taking care of her man. I mean he smoked, but he worked out too, and he golfed, played hockey. He just liked junk food and cigarettes. The guy didn't even drink.

Their third Valentine's Day rolled around, and Trixie had me clean on that day. She was excited because Don was taking her to a fancy restaurant, and she thought he was going to propose. She said, "It's been three years, if he doesn't propose tonight, I'm finished."

I said, "Maybe give him a little break, he's been a bachelor his entire life." She looked at me like I was the enemy.

All the meanwhile, when he was there or when we would talk on the phone about when I would be coming again, he would constantly complain that she did nothing and that now she was just playing with photography and did not have a real job. I would tell him to try to get her back at selling real estate. He told me she had never sold real estate, but that she was an assistant to a Realtor in Phoenix many years prior, and that she lived off her dad's money her entire life. Don told me that they would not marry because of money. I never asked him exactly what he was talking about. And whatever Trixie told me from that point on, I took with a grain of salt because why lie to me about being a Realtor?

Well, let me tell you, the cleaning after that Valentine's Day was a humdinger. Trixie was livid because Don did not propose to her. "I wonder what he thinks this whole deal is here with me living with him. He doesn't even dress up for me anymore. I can't recall the last time he went golfing with me either." Then she took the vase with flowers in it and threw it up against the wall. I was a little shocked, but just kept right on cleaning. I just listened. She cleaned up the mess, apologizing all the while. "I don't believe I just did that."

Well, honey, maybe quit mixing, marijuana, wine, and the pills.

Within a few months, a huge porch was added on to the back of the house, not just some simple porch, this one had a hot tub on it with an outdoor sectional couch and a firepit. It was covered with wide-striped material as an awning. It was beautiful, stunning, you just wanted to sit there with a glass of wine and look at the mountain views. I thought that perhaps Don added it on just for her to go out there and relax, nice. And no ring, how about a nice outside room instead.

Trixie was now healed, and the next thing you know, she was off to Canada for a skiing trip. You know, the ones rich people go on. It would be six women staying at a lodge and going out each day being dropped at the top of mountains. This particular trip was for the very avid skier that was experienced in this kind of skiing. The trip must have cost her a small fortune. I thought her father must treat her very well because she wasn't making any money on the photography business. She was even trying to get me to lure my daughter her way. That was when I told her what my daughter paid to get her family pictures done. People today cannot always make the money they used to doing the same job, like photography; she didn't get it. Her photos were horrific, she had no idea what she was doing; therefore, no clientele.

Before I knew it, Don had bought a condo in downtown Denver, sold his law firm in Boulder, and took a job with the federal government as an attorney. He said he just wanted out of all that responsibility of having his own firm, and that it would be much easier to just work for someone else. Well, it didn't turn out the way he planned. He couldn't just take a day off to go ride his bike whenever he wanted, and he hated the commute to South Denver where the federal center is located. That is why he bought the condo.

So now Trixie and Don were seeing each other on weekends, and she would go down and stay at the condo with him when there were hockey games. Trixie didn't like the whole setup. She said it was nice that he had a condo in downtown Denver, but it was not a real nice condo or a good location. And guess what, it was close to the hockey arena where Don spent all his time. "I will make it comfy and cozy for me to stay there," she said. "And he will quit going to all the hockey games and practices, you'll see." I thought nope, he bought the condo near the hockey arena; otherwise, he'd have bought south of Denver near his work.

Then the phone call came. "Angel, it's Don, I need the house cleaned out soon. Trixie's dad died, and she is moving in to a house she bought up in Silverthorne. I'm selling my house, and I will just be living in Denver now, it's easier."

So that whole thing went down without a catch because his house sold in what seemed like minutes after it went on the market. Trixie's dad had left her a fortune. She was buying a mediocre older home near the golf course in Silverthorne. She had sold her condo down the road in Dillon that she once told me her kids fought over whenever they wanted to go up skiing. I had never met Trixie's son or daughter. Daddy took really good care of her, obviously. Or perhaps she got a pile of money in her divorce from her children's father, I have no idea. I just knew she never worked for all that money. Her new house she bought was sold for $975,000; ridiculous to me, for what the house was. I know this because I knew a Realtor who looked it up for me.

Trixie and I kept in touch over text and e-mails. She referred me to several people. I opted out of cleaning the new home she had bought so far up in the mountains, not enough pay to get me up there. The house was small, not good-enough pay. I would meet her for coffee when she was in town from the mountains, and she would invite me up to a cookouts and things of this sort. The day came when I finally made it up to see her new house while I was staying in Breckenridge.

I was dating a Fox News reporter at the time who had a $5,000,000-house a friend let him stay at from time to time. This house belonged to a millionaire friend of his who had been one of the fellas that started the Hallmark Channel. We would go up and stay for the weekend when the house was not occupied, and he would ski while I shopped. I've never been a skier. The few times I did ski,

I would fall, have physical therapy for weeks on end due to ankle injuries, and vow to never do it again. I mean, I even fell and hurt my ankle on the bunny trail once! Those mountains in Colorado, they scare me to death.

So one day, I texted Trixie and told her we were in town, and my guy and I went over for wine and appetizers. It was fun. But the weird thing about that night was that my guy had no idea who he was going to see until we got there. I mean, I gave him a brief description—an attorney and his gal that I became friends with through my business. Turned out, he had known Don for years. It was embarrassing for Don, I could tell, he was a nervous wreck that night, and I could not figure out why. I had no idea what was going on until we left. All my guy said that evening was, "Oh, Don, how you doing, old buddy?" But both men seemed to be in shock.

Don had dated one of my guy's closest friends, a tall gorgeous blond Amazon gal who lived in Boulder. The kind always hanging on to my guy's arm. That was one of the reasons I ended that relationship, along with his fast-paced lifestyle. Every blond Amazon chic within miles would want to be on his arm. Why? He wasn't that great-looking at all, but he had the lifestyle that every woman thought she wanted. We got into every event in town that one could imagine with VIP passes, everything free of course. At one point, I was two feet from John Elway golfing.

Every band we went to see, well, we were in the green room with the band before they went out to play, enjoying conversation and great food. We were at the theater in downtown Denver one night, watching a play. As soon as the lights came on, we stood up, and when my guy turned around, I heard, "Manny, oh my god, it's Manny." These women would come running down the aisle to grab hold of him. I hated it. I was always standing off to the side, watching while they got their pictures taken with Manny. It wore me down, yet he loved every minute of it.

When we started dating, I had told Manny, "Why date me, I clean houses for a living for Chrissake. You're a bigwig, and it won't work."

He replied with, "I'm ready for you, you're my normal, you'll keep me grounded."

Well, Don's ex, and Manny's friend, we three had had a few dinners together prior, and she was this quiet, shy, sweet lady, retired school teacher, her entire face loaded with fillers. I thought she could not have been Don's type whatsoever. She had never moved in with Don, according to my guy. In fact, Don had lived in her home with her for a few years up the Canyon from Boulder. My guy said, "She was the one that broke Don's heart, she was the one that got away." Now I knew why Don had been nervous that night; it wasn't like him at all. It was funny.

Trixie wanted to come up and see the big house we were staying in, but my guy said, "No, it's just too weird for me to be around him now." I had to come up with excuses not to let her come to the house to see it. This wasn't Manny's house anyhow, we just had the privilege of getting to use it from time to time.

I moved to New York State a year later and have stayed in contact through texts and Facebook with Trixie. I am happy to say that Don married Trixie at a small ceremony in a field outside of Breckenridge. Turns out Trixie didn't let Don get away.

Tiffany

T IFFANY JOINED THE FISHER Divorce Group when I was volunteering there, her divorce attorney had recommended the group for her. She was short, hourglass figure, flat chest, brown hair that resembled a broom, just straight and damaged-looking, and here was yet another woman who looked like she was wearing thrift store, tattered-looking clothing, and no makeup. She appeared like she had been through hell and back.

Tiffany was in my group and, at first, did not have a lot to say. It was difficult to get her to talk in small group, except when everyone gathered together for dessert. Dessert is when she would open up and mingle pretty much with the men in the group, but not the women.

Tiffany's ex-husband had been an alcoholic who abused her both mentally and physically. It was her second marriage, and she was not taking it well. She preferred to stay in the marriage, and it was her ex who wanted out. She had a daughter and a son, the daughter in high school and son, working. These children were from her first marriage. They lived at home with her, but she never talked about them like all the other group members talked about their kids. You would never know she had kids, except she gave her background at the first meeting she attended.

She was quite distraught because she was a graphic artist who had been laid off after contracting Home Depot to remodel her entire kitchen, and she could not get out of the contract. She said that the payments were enormous. How was she making it, I wondered. She later disclosed that she received a small severance when she left the company.

Now when all of the gatherings took place away from the class, it was always Tiffany who wanted to be near the men and have all of their attention. She was not interested in forming friendships with any of the women in the group whatsoever. It would not be long before her appearance changed dramatically. For instance, she showed up for hiking with short shorts on and high heels on! Yes, I said high heels, I'm talking at least four-inch heels. We planned a picnic at the bottom of the mountain prior to a hike up the mountain, and that is all she stuck around for. I myself thought it to be hilarious, her intentions were so obvious. Of course, the men in the group were captivated, and that was her plan. Perhaps she thought one may leave with her that day, I don't know how someone like that thinks.

One night, Tiffany discovered one of the men in the group was terribly distraught over his wife leaving him; she gave him all of her attention. This guy was a .com fella who sold the website address to Pepsi for millions of dollars. He was loaded with money and would no doubt never work another day in his life. This fella just wanted his wife back, who had now begun an online clothing business, and was doing quite well with it. He cried at meetings almost every week.

This guy had passed me a note, asking if he could get closer to me by meeting away from the class. I turned him down, reminding him that we were not to date while in this group. I would never be attracted to him anyhow, he looked just like a young Danny DeVito. He was that guy, looking for someone to make him feel better while he somehow—if ever—got over this divorce. I had great empathy for him because he cried often and seemed desperate to have someone in his life. He was genuinely grieving his divorce like it was a death. Basically that is what divorce is, a death, the end of a relationship that we all thought would go on forever. There needs to be a mourning period, but for some men and women, this period is skipped over and replaced by a person that they can latch onto, at least for some people, for a while.

It would be at our final farewell outing at Sing Sing in Boulder, a piano bar, that Tiffany would appear dressed to the hilt in a tight dress with high heels on, full-on makeup, and hair done. It was a bitter cold winter night with about eight inches of snow falling down, and supposed to continue through the night. Most of us gals had on sweaters, hats, and boots fit for maneuvering in the snow and ice, but Tiffany was on a mission.

Mr. Vulnerable and Tiffany would begin drinking quite heavily, and the next thing you know, they were heading out the door together before the party was over. And so, we didn't see Tiffany come to gatherings any longer because she threw herself into this relationship—two people looking for someone to take the pain of divorce away, two very clingy desperate people.

To me, these are the people who are not willing to do the work that would benefit one after divorce, such as finding yourself again and learning how to grow in different ways in order to be in a healthy relationship one day. These two wanted the quick fix, and it was obviously going to be a rebound relationship, but I am sure that Tiffany had other plans in her mind. I was thinking, her third husband perhaps.

One day Tiffany called me and wanted to have coffee. Tiffany had just gotten a job again and wanted her home cleaned, her kitchen was almost finished after an entire year of remodeling. Seems Home Depot had a contractor that did not move fast at all. I declined on meeting for coffee. We decided on a date for me to go to her house to give her an estimate prior to cleaning. I didn't meet with her for coffee because I knew what the story was going to be. Mr. Vulnerable probably wasn't so great anymore. I figured I would get in, give a fast estimate, and exit.

Upon arriving at Tiffany's home, I was shocked to see what condition the front yard and surrounding area of her home was in on the outside. There were weeds growing among the tall grass, and there were empty boxes lying in the yard, along with soda cans. It seemed as if nobody had taken care of this lawn for quite some time. The tall rubber trash cans were sitting on the side of the driveway, one tipped over on its side; obviously it was not trash day, or they would be out on the curb. I was already thinking that I was getting myself into a mess.

When Tiffany answered the door, she was right back to where her appearance was when she first began the Fisher Group—awful-looking, as if she had been through hell and back again. "Hello, Angel, I can't tell you how happy I am to see you again, it has been too long."

I'm thinking to myself that there was never a real friendship between her and me; she was more interested in the men in the group, this was just business.

As I entered this house, I was right smack-dab into a small living room that was decorated in Victorian-type furniture and decor, very old-looking, very small room with big furniture. All the photos on the walls were of old people—black-and-white photos—I'm talking old here. There was an open staircase between this room and a sunken living room. This living room was a completely different style, more modern with two overstuffed love seats in front of a fireplace, barely room to walk around. Right behind the couches were barstools for the kitchen counter. I could not figure out how anyone could even move the barstools out to sit down in them. There was no space.

The kitchen was still not completely finished but very modern and pretty. There was a ton of dog slobber all over the sliding glass door in the kitchen, and you could barely see the countertops because of all the clutter; this was a filthy kitchen. I could see the floor had not been cleaned in many months, and there was black tarry dirt around the handle on the refrigerator. I was getting gaggy from the smell of dirty dog, my head was spinning. I can't stand filth, especially in a kitchen, and this house was just filth.

As we went upstairs, the bedrooms appeared extremely small. Tiffany's room had a king-size bed in it with posts. I, again, could not figure out how you could walk around the bed and get in and out of the closet, so small! The small bathroom had been remodeled, but the floor was not yet finished. The second bedroom was an ironing room, dressing room, with tons of clothes all over the floor. It reminded me of a teenager's room. Tiffany informed me that this room was her dressing room and her room only.

As we made our way down the basement stairs, I was cautious due to all the clutter and clothes scattered on the stairs. Certainly no embarrassment or apology for the condition of her house whatsoever.

Her daughter's bedroom was a complete disaster. Tiffany struggled to get the door open as there was so much on the floor. The son's bedroom we did not go in, and I was instructed to never go in that room. But the smell that came from that area, it would knock you out.

The laundry room floor was not to be seen with all the clothes on it, along with empty laundry bottles scattered about. I had never been in a house like this prior. Shocking, to say the least. It was as if every person who lived here was a drunk or just plain lazy.

As we went back upstairs Tiffany showed me an office that she used for her graphic design business. This room appeared to be a bedroom that she had converted. I couldn't believe she worked in a dark room with piles of clutter everywhere you looked. I mean, how could any person be creative in this room?

As we sat down at the kitchen table to discuss cleaning dates, we had coffee and blueberry-lemon scones that Tiffany had bought at my favorite bakery just a block away, Das Meyers. Oh, Das Meyers, one of my favorite places to hang out and drink coffee.

I had always bought cakes from this bakery to take to the divorce group gatherings. But then the price went up to thirty-six dollars for a six-inch cake, and so I quit getting the cakes. It was fun to go there at Christmastime and buy all the cookies. As you walked up to the bakery, you felt as though you had stepped back in time and gone to a forest somewhere because of the cottage feel in the little house. There was a small wooden bridge you walked over to get to the front door. There was also an old Victorian house next to the bakery where the owners had weddings, and the grounds were just beautiful. In the fall, they set up a haunted house there, which was quite popular.

In the bakery were tables and chairs for sitting and eating your baked goods and sipping coffee or tea. You could buy their homemade scented candles, heavenly, along with knickknacks. The bakery was family-owned, and the entire family worked there. Never unusual to see a baby crawling around on the floor or a playpen set up in the back. You could watch the award-winning baker decorate a wedding cake right before your eyes.

People came from all around to pick out their wedding cakes on Saturdays when they had the cake tastings. For years, I would go just to taste the cakes. There was raspberry-champagne-filled cakes, chocolate mousse, apple-pie-filled cakes, and on and on. The tasting was so wonderful, my mouth waters just thinking about it. And then they caught on that people were just coming in to taste the cakes and not order for a wedding, and so they quit letting you taste unless you had an appointment to do so and were actually planning a wedding. My wonderful Saturday mornings at Das Meyers vanished right before my eyes. I must say, my heart was broken.

When there was a winter festival in the mountains, like Georgetown, Das Meyers would always have a booth set up. The line to their booth was always at least thirty minutes long. I was always known for knowing where all the bakeries were up and down the front range, and I am learning where they are in New York State, such fun!

Well, let me tell you, Tiffany knew what she was doing when she brought out those raspberry-lemon scones; she actually remembered how much I loved Das Meyers! But then it began. "I don't know what to do, Angel, Dan and I are having problems, and I don't know why, I have done everything in my power to make this relationship work, and suddenly he has no time for me."

Well, that was the end of me enjoying the scone. I replied with, "Oh, you are still seeing Dan, that's nice."

"Well, it was at first, but now I don't know what is going on. I have jumped every time he calls me. I have gone to his house in the middle of the night to see his son through an awful fever. We took our kids to the zoo together and included him in all the family outings, the sex has been good. I don't know what to do now," she said with a pouty face. Oh gawd, here I was again—a therapist.

I told Tiffany that she needed to ask Dan if he needs a break from the relationship, or if he wants it to end. She began crying and telling me that she thought they would be married by now and that he had misled her. I turned the conversation around by telling her that perhaps he was her rebound man after her divorce. I was doing my best to make her feel like she needed to let go of this, like he was just a short-time fella and perhaps concentrate on the new job.

I took on the job and got her house up to par as much as I possibly could, but this gal didn't care much about keeping her house up inside or out, and her kids walked all over her, or else they were just following in her footsteps as far as picking up and organizing went. I thought that Tiffany just couldn't concentrate on anything domestic. It was always the man or the job. It would not be long before her son moved out and into his girlfriend's apartment. And still, I never went in that room of his.

Well, time went on, and Dan continued to ignore Tiffany's every move to get together with him, so she went into counseling. Tiffany's daughter would follow me around the house, complaining to me that her mother did not care about her or her brother but was always interested in finding the next husband. I would listen, that's what therapists do, and every now and again, I would throw in a comment like, "Well, maybe if you did something together with your mom, plan an outing with just you and her, let her know you want to spend time with her."

But whenever I saw Tiffany, it was clear that she was just desperate to get out there and find the next man. She would tell me how she stayed at bars late at night with coworkers. "All the guys at work are after me, you know." I suspected she got jobs because of her looks. I felt bad for her. It was so obvious that she was not interested in learning how to be alone, which was exactly what she needed. Like I said before, there are some people who cannot be alone, and they have no desire at all to try. Who are you right now at this age, alone? It's pretty exciting finding out. I've said it many times, it's like being eighteen again, very freeing.

One hot summer day, I came into the house and began my work. Tiffany's bedroom door opened, and she screamed out, "Please come and help your mother, please!" She was crying and sobbing. There was no sign of the daughter, and I asked what was going on. Out the door came Tiffany, crying out, "Well, I have apparently been deserted when I need help the most."

I was not believing what I was seeing. Tiffany had some kind of corset on, and her face looked as though it had been burnt. I said, "What happened to you?"

"I had a laser job on my face, and I got new boobs, I'm going to get back online and find a new man." *What?*

Then she burst into tears, screaming, "I am in so much pain right now, I can't begin to tell you." It was all I could do to maintain a straight face. I am sure I had to pick my jaw up and carry on at that point. My daughter has always told me to watch my expressions, stating, "They show exactly what you're thinking, Mom."

And then for some reason, I blurted out," Why on earth would you have so much work done all at once?"

She replied with, "I figured I may as well feel all the pain at one time. I used my bonus from work. Now my daughter is angry with me that I did this, telling me I am the most self-centered and selfish person on earth. I don't really give a damn what she thinks because she is off to college soon, and I will not be left all alone, I am determined to find the right man.

"I'll be in my bed. If she comes in, please tell her to come up and see to my needs, oh, and please bring me a glass of wine, the bottle is on the countertop in the kitchen"—sobbing—"thank you, Angel, you are such a good friend. I truly don't know what I would do without you."

Somebody, I beg you, please save me from this narcissist, please! I had heard those words from clients before.

Over the next few months, Tiffany's daughter would tell me that her mother had found someone who had a huge home in Denver and that her mother would be moving in with him and leaving her alone in the house. She was nervous, confused, and scared to death. I told her that that would not happen that quickly and not to worry. Her daughter liked the new man but didn't trust him because they met on the Internet.

There were times I would go upstairs to Tiffany's room and find notes on the post of her bed, saying, "If you're hot, and your name is Ger, jump in." It kind of grossed me out because she was sleeping with a man that quickly, right in front of her daughter. Her daughter obviously needed her. And so, it would not be long before Tiffany told me that she was moving out, leaving the house to her daughter to live in. That this man was incredibly wealthy and had a house that would blow my mind. "This one is going to work, Angel, it's a chance of a lifetime." Well, okay then.

And that is exactly what she did. She moved out, pretty much just taking her clothes and leaving the responsibility of her home to her recently graduated senior high school daughter, who would be going off to college in a few short months. There didn't seem to be a real plan going on here. Unbelievable!

And so the job there ended abruptly, and I would be watching Tiffany travel to places like Paris and Greece on her Facebook page, with a man who looked at least twenty years older than her. Before long, she disappeared from Facebook. I never heard another peep out of her. It was a whirlwind client relationship, and to this day, I wonder how her daughter is doing in life. I hope she is doing incredibly well. I look back lovingly at this relationship with Tiffany because I always stopped at Das Meyers on my visits to her house.

Lana

I ATTENDED A LARGE CHURCH in Louisville, Colorado, for many reasons other than worshiping. I loved all the women's groups, volunteering wherever needed, and joining in on the book clubs that met there on occasion. I was also cofacilitator in the grief workshop, although I do have to say that the church seemed to be more geared toward the men than the women, and as I still follow online, it remains the same.

While attending a Saturday morning women's Bible study, I would be greeted by a lady handing out the fliers at the door. Her name was Lana, and as she introduced herself to me, I began to feel quite welcome at the meeting. I remember her beautiful broad smile. She looked at me with a strange curiosity. Lana asked me if I was single. "I see you don't have a wedding ring on. I am just newly divorced, or at least I will be in a few short weeks," she said.

I replied with, "Single for many years now." And that was how it all began with Lana.

Our divorce stories would be totally different from each other. I had already been divorced for about twelve years at that time. Before I left the meeting that day, Lana asked me if I would be interested in cleaning her home. I had left a pile of my business cards on the table with many other cards. At all of these get-togethers at church, it would be an advantage to market one's self business, and so many of us did just that; it was profitable, and I would always meet new friends. What a diverse variety of women showed up at these meetings.

My church held 4,500 people in the main worshiping section of the building, then the entire lobby would fill up, watching all the large-screen monitors covering the service. There were days I would pull up, park, go inside, and see that I would not be able to walk in, let alone hear the service. So I would leave and watch it online later in the week. It seemed so strange how quickly the church grew; it started out in an old gas station in Boulder. Now there are three or four branches throughout the front range.

And so I set up a meeting to look at Lana's home, and it turned out that she lived in a neighborhood directly across the street from my home.

Lana lived in one of the larger homes on the golf course. It was my neighborhood golf course, which wrapped around the road and through her neighborhood.

I was shocked when she opened her door with a bath towel on. I thought, *I know she was expecting me*, but Lana was unnaturally—and I mean this for Denver people—down to earth. She'd fit right in in Boulder, I would soon find out. It was one of those meetings with someone when you feel like you have known them your entire life, you don't come by that much, like a gal friend you had always known and had slumber parties with growing up, that kind of thing.

Her hair was soaking wet and still had some soapsuds in it. Yes, I just said that, soapsuds. She had no makeup on, and I barely recognized the woman I had met at church who had been so dressed up, like a high-class businesswoman, the executive type. She was quite chunky and short, but she modeled a certain amount of class, even in a bath towel, lol. Thank God she ran upstairs and threw some sweats on!

The house stunk like a cat litter box was lurking around the bend that had not been cleaned in quite a while to the point of me almost gagging while walking around, looking at the rooms. I kept putting my hand over my nose nonchalantly. To this day, I cannot stand that smell.

The pictures on the walls were crooked, as I walked through the front or formal living room I could have written my name on the top of the end tables and coffee table. Carpet had not been cleaned in what seemed to be a few good hard years, the bathrooms were filthy.

Oh, what you sometimes find inside the walls of these big stately homes!

I could not see the tops of the kitchen island or counters. The large corner window over the sink and overlooking the golf course was broken on both sides. "Those damn golfers did that, why replace them when they just do it again and again," she said. I could hear the traffic across the way from I-25, suddenly I wondered why they had not put in a water feature to hide that noise, just saying. I mean they had the beautiful view of the mountains and the golf course, but then all you noticed was the heavy traffic noise.

And then of course, my mind goes to thinking about all the toxic fumes people living here must breathe in daily from that high-way. Her neighborhood was across a four-lane road from my house. My neighborhood was glorified with large old trees. This neighbor-hood had barely any large trees, and there were none between the houses or across the golf course to that busy highway. The homes here were about fifteen years old, newer, thus no trees. It was a neigh-borhood where they plowed out all the vegetation in order to build these homes, not good.

Lana kept apologizing for the state of the home. "I just have not been myself as of late, you know, the divorce and all." Well, no, I didn't know, because my home had never been in such disarray when I was getting my divorce or at any one time in my life. But whatever, everyone is different, and we all handle what life throws at us dif-ferently. This home had not been cleaned in a very long time, and I mean a very long time indeed.

"It doesn't really matter at all," she said. "Come to find out, my husband has not made the payments in over a year, and they are going to foreclose on me, but that's all right because I am going to take that bastard to the cleaners." And then she went on to say, "He is so stupid, he is going to sign the papers I have written up without an attorney present." Followed by, "I put him through college, you know. He couldn't have done it without me, that's why he is going to pay me the big bucks for the rest of his life." Then she giggled with this evil smile on her face, I found it odd but understandable once she told me her story.

A date was set for a thorough cleaning, a deep clean, a deep, deep, deep clean. And Lana was there ready and able to tell me her story while I cleaned, and yes, this was one of those days where I should have been making $250 hourly. "My husband of thirty-six years left me for his younger assistant, seventeen years younger," she said, as she began to cry this angry almost-maddening cry. This gal was very sad, and strikingly angry at the same time, that lasted for approximately five hours off and on.

"Hold on to that anger, honey, that will get you through this for a time," I said. I would later discover that this may have been the wrong thing to say to Lana.

Apparently the affair had begun seven years prior. Lana said, "The assistant saw the life we had had and wanted it for herself. Booking myself and my husband all over the world for extravagant vacations. The little bitch wanted it all, and she has taken it all from me and my three sons, she destroyed my family." Now I had heard this story prior by women in my divorce group. But I had never had to hang with them for five hours while they ranted about it over and over again.

Lana had three sons, one who lived with his wife and two daughters in the Midwest; he was a race car driver, and his father, Lana's soon to be ex, fully funded his life. Another son was a businessman with a wife and daughter in Denver. And then the younger son, he was a pizza delivery man whose wife was a dental assistant, and they had three children, well, two with one in the oven. As Lana told it, this was the son that she was the closest to, and he was an abusive husband who had actually pulled a knife on his own mother. "His meds were all messed up, and of course, he was drinking," she said. "He will be just fine when he gets off those pills, he just fell apart over what his father has done to us."

I began to see a very complicated life of a woman who was going through one of the most painful, if not the most painful, thing that could have been thrown at her—her husband had left her for a younger woman. This is a somewhat common story if you attend singles groups. And let me tell you, it isn't always the man that leaves his wife but vice versa.

Now Lana was laid off for well over a year at this point. She had been the gal who drove from bank to bank all over Colorado selling ATM machines along with a service plan. This gal had raked in $150,000 a year, had a company car and great benefits, and at that time, her husband had been making $350,000 a year overseeing food operations at colleges across the country. So here you had this couple making $500,000 a year between them, not to mention all the bonuses he and she pulled in, and living quite the high life for many years prior. This was why Lana was making sure she could keep living the life she was accustomed to after the divorce.

I couldn't blame her one bit. Lana had put her husband, her high school sweetheart, through college. She often said, "If I had not done all his papers, he would never have graduated." Then she would say, "Look how stupid he is, he signed the divorce papers without an attorney, I'm the one with all the brains." Now I have known quite a lot of women who put their spouses through college but usually by working, not doing their papers for them. She was now pulling in $7,000-a-month alimony for life, plus half of all his bonuses he would receive, along with health insurance. Unbelievable! I thought she had it made, but she didn't really. This gal had lost the love of her life, the father of her three sons. The money seemed to be revenge.

She told me stories of how she had busted her husband and his mistress in Aspen at a convention; she had driven up to surprise her man, and oh, what a surprise she got. She and his mistress had gotten into a shoving fight right there at the entrance of the fancy hotel. It was quite a story she had to tell. Her husband would be gone for weeks on end, saying that he was working and going from state to state. All the while, he was with his mistress at her home in Northern California, building a life together. The day came when she told him to get out, and that's just what he did and with the greatest of ease. And then, Lana began to fall apart. She didn't think he would take her up on it.

Lana and myself were always volunteering in the kitchen at church on Friday evenings for the free dinners, music, and sermon, followed by a multitude of meeting groups that one could fall into. Groups from divorce, fighting cancer, codependency, single parenting, arthritis pain, loneliness, loss of a child, loss of a parent, sibling, and just anything you could imagine. Then everyone would come together again for dessert and coffee before leaving. It was quite a good place to be on Friday night when you were a single woman and didn't want to stay home alone. I was flying solo at this point of my life.

Preparing the dinners in the kitchen was a blast. The meals were fabulous, the band before the sermon, all amazing. I had made such good friends there. It was a place to look forward to volunteering every week.

Some nights, well, I would just help out in the kitchen and then leave, no sermon, no group. Why? Because some of the groups would bring you down on a Friday night, and who wants to start their weekend that way? I had already had my counseling.

There were some attractive men that came every week. Marlboro men, I would call them. We all had dinner together, and there were great conversations. I thought to myself, fabulous, I can have dinner and conversation with men and not have to date them, really cool.

And then one night, I was leaving early, and a man asked me if he could walk me to my car. It was autumn, getting dark earlier. I insisted that I was fine. He then informed me that it was policy because of the men brought in from the work ranch up north near Fort Collins. And then for the first time ever, I saw the pistol hanging from his belt when he went to get his handkerchief.

This fella was security hired by our church. I inquired about what work ranch he was talking about while he walked me to my car. This was when he informed me that they were men just getting out of prison and living on the ranch for a year, a halfway house of sorts. At the end of their six-month stay, they were then rewarded for good behavior and transported back and forth on Friday nights to our church. I was shocked. The man told me he was one of many guards posted around the area on Friday nights. I had no idea!

I went a few more times, just to help prepare all that food in the kitchen, but I never felt comfortable again or, should I say, never felt safe again. Now these men were not there for the entire evening. Just the free dinner and sermon, and then they left. But still, it was never the same for me.

Lana continued going, and lo and behold, she met one of those men, Adam, and he would soon become a huge part of her life. A huge part to the point where she moved him into her home within weeks of meeting. I talked to her endlessly about how she was making a mistake and risking her life. "Risking my life! Why, Adam hasn't murdered anyone, he just stole money from old ladies because he hit hard times." Yeah, I couldn't believe my ears either! He was a felon, he had been in prison not one but several times. This information she would disclose to me later. How could she think anything of a man who had stolen from old ladies?

Lana was showing me a huge character flaw on her part. Her judgment was lacking, to say the least. Was it her low self-esteem from her husband cheating on her? I didn't know, but to me, there was no excuse for dating this kind of man. I took a few steps back and kept my distance from Lana. I told her I was no longer able to clean her house and that she would have to keep it up herself. She was getting the cleanings because she had thought she could somehow sell the home. The bank had different ideas, the home was going into foreclosure.

Lana and Adam would show up together at Bible studies other members of our church would have in their homes. Lana was changing, and I didn't like what I saw, and she had no ears for my comments. I was petrified for her. I started contemplating all the horrid things that this man may do to her.

Then the real problems began. Her sons did not want this man in her life. So what did Lana do? She rejected her sons and started supporting this ex-con financially. One son, the younger son, soon got into a fistfight with Adam and pulled a kitchen knife on him. Well, needless to say, I never went in to her house after hearing this. I would go to pick her up out front. She would tell me stories of how Adam's daughter was moving in with her boyfriend, and neither worked. Lana's life became a train wreck. Soon she was tossed out of her home by the bank, and she would rent some farm property down the road, just three miles down the road.

We met for shopping one day at a furniture warehouse just north of Denver. At the warehouse was a set of steps that go up quite a ways, and Lana had to stop midway. She could not breathe. I told her, "Honey, you need to lose the weight you have put on, you're going to have a heart attack on me!"

She replied with, "I know I am quite heavy, it's all the candy and sugar I seem to need 24-7. I just crave sweets." It was true. Lana always had ball jars filled with candy all along her countertops. And there would always be the Coca-Cola sheet cake that she brought to every gathering. Lana had many Bible study meetings at her home before she moved out, and there would never be anything healthy to eat. Truth is, I wouldn't eat there anyhow because the cats would be all over the countertops.

By now, at each Bible study Lana would begin to fall apart and talk about her ex-husband, how she wanted her old life back. My time with her became less and less because she was not getting any counseling on how to go on with life after divorce. She just had that bitter bitch syndrome that I was simply tired of listening to. And there was the ex-felon, Adam. She was stuck, and she did not want to be unstuck.

It was difficult to be friends with someone with such expensive taste in the first place. I mean, we would go out to dinners that would run me $65. Lunches that went up to $40. I couldn't keep up nor did I want to. Such a waste of my money!

To me, Lana had everything to live for. She had a nice place to live, children, and grandchildren. I mean she was pulling in $7,000-a-month alimony, plenty enough funds to continue her lifestyle. Her privilege of having her grandchildren at her home were now taken away due to her choice in a partner. Turns out that before Adam had moved in with her, she kept her granddaughter overnight without telling the mother that Adam would be spending the night. Her daughter-in-law was livid and no longer trusted her judgment.

I could not believe that she was seeing this awful man. I mean, she was a mess! I kept telling her that she needed to be alone and learn how to live on her own without a man around. She was so needy to have a man, and this so-called man was being supported financially by her, what was the point? "Oh, he fixes things around the house for me," she would say. He never worked a real job.

And then the call came. "Angel, I fell off my backsteps and broke both of my ankles. Can you come out here and clean for me at least once?"

"No," I said, "I just don't have any room on my schedule, I'm so very sorry to hear you have broken both ankles."

"Well," she said, "they are going to operate on one of my ankles, I have pre-op tomorrow, could you at least drive me there?"

Oh, how badly I did not want to go to her house, and I did not. I mean, how could I possibly get her in and out the door, both ankles were broken. She said Adam was busy, but I stuck to my ground. I recommended she call one of her big strong sons to help her get there. And when I look back, the narcissist Adam began to pull away from her from this point on, at least that was what Lana was telling me. A woman that suddenly needed him for support in every way, he wasn't having that, he wasn't the type.

It would be a few calls in the next two days, and then the big call came. "Angel, they are taking me in for surgery on my ankle and my lung. They found a mass on my lung when they took the X-ray for surgery. Doctors would be doing a biopsy."

A few more days passed by, and then another call came. "Angel, they found lung cancer, stage 4, I don't know what to do. Adam is never here, can you please come over?"

And so I went because Adam was in the mountains, and her daughter-in-law would be there. I had made up my mind that if Adam appeared while I was there, I was out the door. While driving, I began to wonder how a woman who never smoked had stage 4 lung cancer, all kinds of things started to go through my mind. I had heard such horrific panic in her voice, desperation.

When I entered the house, it was in such a disarray that I could not believe my eyes. There lay Lana, on a mattress thrown onto the living room floor, and to top it all off, she did not smell like she had had a bath for quite some time. There she was, crying, surrounded by three of her grandchildren and her daughter-in-law. She begged me to come and do a deep cleaning on her house, I just couldn't. I told her my schedule was completely full, and it just wasn't possible. I stayed only a few moments, gave her a hug. I told her I had a former commitment to go to. It felt wrong to do that, but I had promised myself to not go there again, and it appeared that she now had plenty of support from her daughter-in-law.

Then six weeks later, the phone call came, the worst phone call yet. "Angel, it's Lana, please call me back as soon as you can." All the while, she was sobbing to no end. And so I waited till the end of my workday and called her back. Why did I wait? Because over the previous weeks, every call was of her complaining that Adam was never there but always off with his daughter somewhere. I could not convince her to get him to move out. I was pretty much over the constant drama of this awful man who she let into her life. She was like talking to the wall.

It had all come to the point where her sons told her they would not bring her grandchildren over for her Sunday dinners any longer, not until she moved Adam out of the house. The Sunday dinners were a tradition for Lana. These dinners would host fifteen family members each and every Sunday, and they were extremely important to Lana. But she was willing to give those up for this loser as well.

She was telling me awful stories regarding how he had stolen money from her and taken things to the pawnshop that had belonged to her grandfather. She was phoning me every other hour. I am sure because she couldn't do anything but sit; I couldn't answer, it was all too much.

I called her back at the end of my day. It was one of those bone-chilling conversations that I will never forget. Lana had brain cancer that had metastasized from her lung. I think I went into shock for a brief moment, I recall not being able to talk but only listen. And listening is what the friendship became, because it did not matter how big a mess her life was in, she didn't want to hear advice from anyone. Lana became extremely blunt in regard to this. "Don't tell me how to live my life, Angel, you don't have a damn clue what I am going through!" she had shouted at me in a restaurant one sunny afternoon. She was right, I didn't have a clue, but I had had enough.

Lana had become even more angry and was even threatening to kill her ex and his new wife. Yes, her ex had married the younger assistant, and to top it all off, well, he bought her a big beautiful brand-new four-thousand-square-foot house just up the road, a $550,000 palace.

This newfound deeper hate started well before this. Lana had me meet her in a coffee shop, showing me pictures of the engagement ring that her ex's gal friend had posted on her Facebook page. It was a huge diamond. And how were they celebrating their engagement? Well, thanks to her daughter-in-law, Lana was informed that they were all being flown in to the Gulf Coast of Florida for a ten-day vacation. Something I had always thought that Lana did not need to know.

Lana was dying inside because her grandchildren were being exposed to this woman, and they were also calling her grandma. It was as though someone had stuck a knife in Lana's heart. It all made me so sad for her. She would say, "She stole my entire life from me, I should be in that house, not her." It was scary because she was driving by their home all the time, it was all eating her alive.

I couldn't be in her life at all for a few months. I couldn't take the drama of Adam, and I really thought she was going to hurt the ex or his new wife. It would be about four months later that I would run into her daughter-in-law at Walmart. She would say, "Angel, Lana needs you, Adam is completely out of the picture now, please call her."

I told her I didn't know if I could at that time. I just had seen and heard too much, and I was tired, the relationship with Lana had drained me.

And then it happened, I ran into Lana at a coffee shop. She began to cry and begged me to be her friend again. Now she was bald and looked like a homeless woman. The clothes she had on were shocking. An old scarf around her head, old boots, baggy clothes. I was blindsided by her appearance. And so, I decided to let her in my life but not without huge boundaries.

Mostly we just met up at cafés to have lunches. At this point, she had moved into the apartment complex just across the lake from my house. The boundaries had to be strong, she was now too close for my comfort level. I was not sure what she was capable of. I mean, really, what did she have to lose? I had heard harsh and damaging words come from her mouth, time and time again, and I had not forgotten. I mean she wanted to kill her ex and his new wife; she had spoken about that.

Soon Lana would wreck her truck. She began doing crazy things. Her daughter-in-law would call me time and time again. "We can't let her drive anymore, we don't know what to do, we all work." They wanted my help, but I couldn't help, not now, my workload was huge. Lana was now dating a nudist, and that was okay, except he was one of the strangest people I would ever meet, scary strange. The family did not want him around their children as well.

Lana kept forgetting things, not being able to talk correctly, her apartment was a complete wreck, things thrown everywhere, you couldn't even see the living room floor. She told me it was the laser treatments on her brain, that for two days after, she was disoriented. "Oh, Angel, I'm going to be just fine. "They're treating it, it will all be okay soon, the tumor is small," she would tell me.

She had thrown herself into a new relationship instead of spending time with her children and grandchildren. It was hard to watch, and so I was not around to watch it. Her daughter-in-law would call me and tell me that they just wanted her to get well alone, without this strange man in their lives. I felt badly for her kids and the grandkids.

There were phone calls from Lana, but not too many after she found the new man in her life. I had to step way back, once again. I needed the break from all of the drama, it was so draining to me. The fall came and went, and soon winter was upon the lake, so beautiful. I wondered how Lana was. I didn't even frequent the coffee shops we used to meet at. I was avoiding her, and I felt guilty about it, but I wanted to protect myself from all of it.

I was getting ready to fly to New York State to visit my son and his family on Christmas when Lana's daughter-in-law called me, asking if I could go visit her at the hospital, she wasn't doing good. Not doing good? I mean there was never a clue that Lana was going to be hospitalized. She was still quite plump and going strong, dating this man. I hadn't seen her for several months at this point, though.

I had witnessed people in my life pass from cancer. They became frail within only six months' time. I never thought Lana was that sick, she never looked frail, her face had never been drawn. She had always assured me that her cancer was curable with the laser treatments, although I had my doubts. The entire illness was confusing to me.

I drove across town to the east side of Denver to see her. I was shocked when I went into her hospital room. She looked quite healthy, except that she was not taking care of herself. There were spots of hair on her head. Her hair was growing back, but in small sections, and some were longer than others. I felt it odd, Lana had always taken such good care of her looks when I had first met her. She had worn wigs after she began losing her hair, earrings. She seemed disoriented, not able to talk and make sense.

She said, "Please, please…it's the medications."

I felt she was embarrassed about her appearance, but I didn't care, she was sick. She changed the subject a few times, and I couldn't follow what she was saying.

I left the room to answer a phone call from my son. I was flying out the next day to visit him. I was quite taken aback and in shock by what I had just seen. I recall quite well not being able to breathe, trying to explain to my son what I had just seen. It was difficult for me to go back into the room, and there was this smell, this awful smell. After the death of my daughter, well, hospitals were not my favorite cup of tea at all. I got dizzy and had difficulty breathing almost every time I had to be in a hospital. I was sure I was having a panic attack.

I went back into the room, and Lana pulled me down to her bedside, telling me, "Go, go away and start a new life somewhere that you can be happy, go." Then she began to jabber on about I don't even know what, nothing she said after that made any sense. It was as if she were coming in and out of sanity.

There was that strange odor about her that I couldn't get out of my nose. I rubbed essential oil all around my nose and up inside my nose; it burned, peppermint oil. That strange smell, it lingered on for days. You know, your mind recalls smells, and it can be just as strong as the day you smelled it.

When I left her room, I had a little trouble getting down the hall. I had to stop and cry, my legs didn't want to hold me up, I couldn't believe what I had just seen. There was something very wrong with her, something strange and unexpected. I didn't understand what was going on.

I had had two aunts pass away from breast cancer when I was in my early twenties, and they both melted away to nothing. Here Lana was, still so plump. I was confused. I just kept thinking it was the medicines and the laser treatments. Lana seemed as though she was losing her mind, insane to me. I kept telling myself that it had to be the laser treatments and the medications. Yes, that's what it was.

I went on to New York to see my son and had a wonderful visit. I recall flying from LaGuardia Airport to Syracuse. We flew low in a smaller plane. The view was incredible. There was green at Christmastime, I couldn't believe the beauty. Bodies of water all along the way, something you don't see much in Colorado, where I had lived for thirty-seven years. I had forgotten how beautiful the East was, all the trees and water. I recall thinking that it was just such a beautiful part of the country. The visit was so very nice. My first visit to my son's home at Christmastime. Such joy it brought to my heart.

When I returned home, I was unpacking after the seven-day visit when I received a call from Lana's daughter-in-law, asking me to please go visit her at her boyfriend's house. "We need you to convince her to come back home, please, Angel."

She told me she was not sure how Lana was doing, that she had left the hospital and gone right to his home. Her daughter-in-law did not want to go there because she had gone there before. She was disgusted at the filth and did not like to be anywhere near this man. She told me how she had run out the door as quickly as she could.

She said Lana was not making any sense over the phone. She had called the nurse that was coming in and out to check on Lana, and that the nurse stated that her mother-in-law wanted to be there and not to go home. That nobody could force her to leave, it was her right to be where she wanted. The nurse was delivering medicine when needed. Lana's daughter-in-law seemed confused at what was going on. This is a young mother that worked full-time as a dental assistant while juggling three small toddlers and a husband that was completely losing it over his mother's choices and, clearly, her illness.

Oh, how I did not want to go there! But I went. I went to help the family, to try one more time to talk some sense into her and see what was going on. Perhaps talk her into going back to her apartment. I was mortified, to say the least. As I approached the home, about two miles from my home, the yard was overgrown with weeds. This property had not been kept up at all, especially for the neighborhood it was in. I was afraid to knock on the door, to tell you the truth. That door looked like it had been hit with a tornado. This house had not been painted in years, I couldn't believe it was in this neighborhood. Surely the HOA had fined this fella over and over again for violations.

As the door opened, her boyfriend asked me to come in. My hair stood up on the back of my neck; it was one of those moments where every inch of my being told me not to proceed, but I did. I was on a mission for Lana's family, I had to help somehow. I followed him through his kitchen and into a sunken living room. A living room that had long cobwebs hanging from the beams. Black cobwebs, this place had not been cleaned in years. The smell was overwhelming. There lay Lana on a small bed of sorts, up against the wall, with a portable toilet next to her.

"I need to go to the store, please stay here for me a short while so that I can do that. I have not been able to leave her at all," asked the boyfriend.

"Of course," I said, "but I have somewhere I have to be in sixty minutes, so please hurry." I never even knew this guy's name, but I began to be thankful that he left and prayed he would return very soon. How could Lana have chosen to be with this man instead of her family? Was he now making all of her decisions for her?

I think Lana knew who I was, I am not sure, she was out of her mind, clearly. She lay on the bed, tossing and turning, mumbling all kinds of things that I could not make sense of. The smell of her body was overwhelming, and I had to get out my peppermint essential oil right away. I tried my best not to let her see it. I didn't want to make her feel self-conscious of the smell, or did she even know she smelled? I was not sure. Brain cancer, I kept thinking to myself, she doesn't know what is happening.

As I looked around the room, I began to cry. I began to have a feeling that she would die in this room, this awful filthy dark place from hell. Lana asked me to help her onto the toilet by saying, "Toilet, toilet."

And so I did, and then I promptly ran to the kitchen sink and washed my hands. I could not believe that there were no rubber gloves to be found near her bed. I tried to say things that would comfort her, like, "Your family loves you so very much, and they really want to be here with you, have you contemplated going home for them? We could get you home, your sons will come and get you, I can take you home right now."

"Fuck them," she said, very clearly.

It was as though a demon had taken over her entire body. There was no talking to her, it seemed Lana was not there in her body any longer. I just sat there, bewildered, crying my eyes out in silence for what seemed to be hours. Lana kept tossing and turning on what seemed to be more of a cot than a bed. She kept mumbling, as if she were crazy. I didn't know what to do. I was panicking because I knew I couldn't get her out of there. I had put myself in a situation of which I had literally no control of whatsoever now. What if this man did not return? How long was I trapped in this awful place?

I think I was there with Lana for around thirty minutes before a nurse came knocking at the door. She told me it was bad, that the end was near. I didn't understand how it could all be happening like this. "Why isn't she clean?" I screamed out.

"There is nothing more we can do to get rid of the odor," the nurse told me.

I told the nurse, "We need to move her to her home for her children's sake. They should be with her and not this man that had only been in her life a few short months. This is why I am here, they sent me, we need her to go home." I tried my best for the family. The nurse informed me that Lana had the right to stay there, that there was no power of attorney for the children to take over her decisions.

Suddenly I began to hate this man, how could he not make sure that she was surrounded by her sons at this time. Well, there was no staying around to try to talk to him, for all I knew, he wasn't coming back anytime soon. And could I stand to have a conversation with him? Probably not. This man looked like he lived under a bridge both times I had met him. Just awful.

I left, I felt my way to my car, with tears running down my face, my entire body shaking, my legs giving out underneath me. I don't remember the drive home, except I recalled that I had not said goodbye to my friend. When I got home, I collapsed for hours on end, not being able to move. I had already had my fill of death in my life. I know this sounds selfish, but I learned early on to take good self-care of myself years prior. I was on my own in this life, a single woman. All I had was myself, my self-employed self, that had to keep moving on.

Lana's daughter-in-law called me and had left several messages. I finally called her back, telling her how shocked I was by it all. I told her how badly I felt that I could not convince her to leave there. She seemed to understand, the family had done all they could. Lana was determined to stay in this man's home.

In the middle of the night, that next day, they would move Lana to a hospice in Louisville, Colorado, by ambulance. She would be there for only six hours before her death. Lana's three boys were by her side when she left this earth. She had completely lost her mind, and they were convinced that she did not know they were there at her side. I want to think she knew, somehow, she knew she was surrounded by family.

To me, Lana had gotten ill because she had a broken heart. I have met many women who soon were diagnosed with cancer after a divorce. My aunt died of breast cancer when I was only twenty, and she once said, "I am not dying from cancer, I am dying from a broken heart."

My uncle had left her for a gal that was only two years older than myself. Protect your heart. I often think of Lana, and when I think of her, I see her with her long dark hair in a crisp white blouse, sitting in an expensive restaurant toasting with her wine glass in hand, and that beautiful smile on her face. This is the friend I choose to remember.

Bill

I MET BILL WHEN I moved to New York State and was still trying to build a cleaning business here. I was introduced by Bill's neighbor, who lives next-door. But it was Bill's wife, Donna, who had called me to go and look at the home.

What can I say about Bill, he is simply wonderful, like most people his age, just full of knowledge. To this day, I could sit in his living room, or on his front porch, and talk with him for hours and hours.

Bill opened his front door, and in front of me stood the most handsome ninety-three-year-old man I have ever seen. I could not believe my eyes. I mean seriously, most ninety-three-year-old men do not stick out in the way of their looks; this man does. The Clint Eastwood type.

Bill was a bit bent over but explained that he has a back problem from a recent surgery. I thought he could have been a movie star in his younger days, and yes, I told him that. I mean who doesn't like to make a senior citizen feel on top of the world? Senior citizens are quite wonderful, at least most of them are. I try to always compliment them as couples when I am out and about, tell them how cute they are together, I always get a huge smile, you can tell it just makes their day. Seniors have amazing stories to tell, and they make me want to get up out of bed and keep moving on those days when I don't want to; at least Bill had this effect on me.

Bill lives in a ranch-style home with a large yard, magnificent trees all around the yard, no flowers anywhere, a simple upkeep for an older man. As I came into the living room, there was a baby grand piano with an antique stool to sit on. The piano was amazing, it sparkled in my eyes. The antique stool had beautifully carved legs with brass eagle claws holding glass balls, just breathtaking.

The living room was large enough for the piano, a couch, which had several books on health scattered around, and two lounge chairs. There were beautiful mineral rocks on the mantle, cabinets full of stones and glassware from Steuben Glass (pricey). The wall was covered with photos of the four children he had raised, along with photo albums on the bookcase below. I wondered what ages his children are now. The kitchen was a large one with a dining table at one end and a large window overlooking the massive backyard.

As we walked through the kitchen, we came into a laundry room with a half bath and an enclosed porch out back. The enclosed porch had Floridian windows, you know, the kind you crank out, with slats of glass. *Hard to clean*, I thought to myself. The room sported a large antique wooden table with photo albums and candles, chairs all around and a summer bed, and again, bookshelves with lots of books, mineral rocks, and bookshelves with more photo albums. What a wonderful place to hang out three seasons out of the year.

There were three nice-size bedrooms. In the first bedroom, one wall was covered with more pictures of his children, along with his wife who had passed from cancer, and there were war photos. Obviously Bill was a young man in those pictures, extremely handsome. The second bedroom was furnished with newer furniture and lavender walls with decorations of flowers. On the dresser was a picture of Bill with his current wife. This wife was not pretty like his first. These two had separate bedrooms, and I could see in the photo that his wife was much younger than him, I'm talking twenty-plus years younger. There was one full and one half bath off of these two bedrooms. The third bedroom was Bill's office, and there were bookshelves with many books and a drawing table. Bill was an engineer, retired for thirty years now. I could see he still stayed busy in his office and with all of his books.

We worked our way to the fully finished basement which had shelf after shelf of mineral rocks in which his former wife had collected during her lifetime, through all of their travels together. I thought that perhaps all of these mineral rocks were what kept this man so vibrant and healthy all of these years. Frankly I couldn't believe this ninety-three-year-old man could go up and down all those stairs. This house has never been updated and was built approximately forty-five to fifty years ago. I could tell that Bill was a man who was frugal with his money over the years and had lived a simplified lifestyle.

When I asked Bill what day would be a good time to schedule a cleaning for him and his wife, he explained to me that he lived alone and that his wife of twelve years lived a few houses up the street. Bill explained to me that his children were not that happy with him remarrying, and words were spoken. He said he would like it if Donna lived with him, but that she had her own home and was quite happy up the road. It was obvious that the grown children did not approve of the new marriage, perhaps because the new wife was so much younger? I don't know.

Bill said to me, "Well, I guess I'm messy, according to my wife, and she wants my house cleaned twice a month. I had a gal cleaning for a small bit, but my wife decided she did not like her here any longer, perhaps she will like you more."

As the months rolled by, I realized that Bill did not need me more than once month, but Donna insisted I come twice a month, stating, "The house is always just a mess, and those bathrooms are the worst." Not so. Bill was quite clean and kept his house up very well. I spent at least an hour and a half chatting with Bill on each visit. It was obvious to me that he was lonely, and oh, how he enjoyed talking, he would use his hands and arms to express himself and really get into the conversation.

Bill shared with me that Donna would come a few days a week and that they would go have breakfast together at a local restaurant if the weather was permitting. Bill did his own cooking, making meals with salmon and frying up a steak on occasion. When I asked Bill how often he went to dinner up to Donna's house, he told me that dinners don't happen anymore, and he could not remember when all that stopped. "She used to cook for me," he said sadly.

Donna only had dinners with him to celebrate something, and that it always had to be in a nice restaurant that served good quality wine. Bill did all his own cooking and his own laundry as well. I was impressed by all he could do. Honestly I always felt like I was talking and observing a man in his early sixties.

While talking one day, he told me that a Tuesday would never work because he goes to the VA on Tuesdays to teach recovering alcoholics and drug addicts how to play tennis. Bill had played and taught tennis his entire life, and actually one of his sons lives in a high rise in New York City, on the forty-third floor, and teaches tennis on the forty-first floor there. This ninety-three-year-old man teaches tennis, I couldn't believe what I was hearing!

One day, while dusting photos in the living room, I had asked Bill what a picture was of, and he had told me it was a view of his vineyard overlooking Keuka Lake. Bill had owned a vineyard for many years with his older son, who lived twenty-seven miles away. He explained to me how to grow grapes and what wonderful conditions it was to grow up above a lake. "Perfect conditions," he said. "Very hard work with many workers." He and his son had come to the decision that it was time to sell once he had turned seventy-nine. Bill still had a large garden that he and his son did together every year on a lot that they rent. He would send me home with tons of leeks and tomatoes. He drove his tractor in the garden while plowing and planting. It was hard work, but he said he loves it.

Bill also still drove his car anywhere he wanted to go in town. He said the trips to New York City were now over. "Too far for me to go now, just too far." So, the son in New York City would frequently come and visit. Bill also has a daughter who lives in Alabama and owns her own store selling beautiful glass pieces that she makes herself. Bill's daughter comes once a year, in the spring, and spends two weeks with her father. She goes to the Corning Museum of Glass, just twenty-five miles down the road, to make all her glass pieces that she will take home and sell in her shop. While she is in town, she organizes and cleans out things for her father. *Sweet daughter*, I thought to myself. Bill loves her visits but says he doesn't hear from his daughter much when she has a boyfriend. When he said that, we both looked at each other and giggled. I thought she must be in her sixties or seventies. Bill also has another son whom he does not see often. This son lives in North Carolina. Bill says this son is very busy with his life.

Bill was in World War II from 1944 to 1946. He was the radio man in the B12 bomber airplane. He said, "I sat in the back of the plane toward the bottom where it was extremely cold, so cold that I could barely move my fingers." Bill flew thirty-five missions over Germany. I told Bill my son was in the Iraq and Afghanistan wars. We talked about many things regarding war, and he said he had always wondered how very difficult it must have been for the men fighting on the ground, that he admired them. After his thirty-five mission, Bill was flown to South England and came back to the United States from there on the *Queen Elizabeth*. He had so many wonderful stories to tell me.

I told Bill about the honor guard because I knew my son was a veteran who helped out there. I had already told my son about Bill, and he said he would be a perfect candidate to go to Washington. The honor guard flies World War II veterans to Washington to see the monuments and the memorial wall for the World War II war. A younger veteran, like my son, escorts them throughout the entire trip. My son holds it as a high honor to do so, there are not so many World War II veterans left. I asked Bill if he may be interested in making the trip, and he said it sounded wonderful. When I got home that evening, I called Donna and told her all about the honor guard and the trip to Washington, that it was a simple application to be filled out and mailed in so that Bill could go, that he would have an escort the entire trip.

Donna said, "Thank you for telling us about this, I will look into it."

When I asked Bill later if he would be making the trip, he said, "No, Donna says it is not a good idea, big trip for me, you know." Broke my heart a little.

I would be busy cleaning and come down the hall to see Bill sitting on his couch, reading a book on good health, something like eating more omega-3s and how to do so, and then thirty minutes later, I would see him on the same couch, sitting with his arms on his knees and hands held together, looking down at the floor. I would come back maybe ten minutes later, and he would still be sitting and looking down at the floor. This was why I would stick around and chat with Bill, I knew he needed some company.

Bill would tell me all the wonderful stories of raising his children, the vineyard he owned, and how he and his first wife traveled the world together. His eyes would light up, and he would smile from ear to ear when telling me his stories. In the winter, I would sit in his living room and listen to him, and in the warmer months, we would sit on his front porch. I would not have traded this time with Bill for anything.

Bill would tell me how he loved to dance, but that Donna would not dance with him any longer. Bill gave me a beginner's class on how to play the piano one afternoon. Other days, from time to time, he would play for me while I was working. It was delightful, to say the least.

To this day, I cannot understand why Donna had married him and now never spent much time with him. Perhaps the age difference grew too big, she being seventy-two and he ninety-five now. But then Donna was no spring chicken herself and not much of a catch, nothing special to look at, and at least eighty pounds overweight at a height of about four feet, ten inches. But oh, how Bill would light up if she happened to stop by, even if it were just to refill his pill dispenser for the week. There was an occasional meal here and there, church on Sundays, but they didn't even watch television together in the evenings. Strange, I thought, because they had only been married for twelve years when I met Bill.

There was the time Donna would go off at Thanksgiving and Christmastime to visit her daughter in San Diego and stay for weeks on end, leaving Bill behind. I thought it to be cruel. There were never any decorations, no Christmas tree, not even one that stood on a tabletop. I have seen elderly people just quit decorating. it is as if they have quit living, quit celebrating life. But not Donna. Up the street, at her home, there were Christmas lights around all the bushes and trees and many decorations in the yard. I could only imagine what the inside looked like because I was never at her home, except to drive by. One would think she would at least bring a small tree to her husband's home.

Then there was the time Bill told me that Donna had driven up to Rochester to buy herself a beautiful ring on Bill's credit card. This is one of those cases where you just begin to think that the woman married the man for his money, but I tried to just think that they grew apart because of the age difference. It was painful for me to tell Bill I would not be cleaning his home any longer. I think about him often, and it leaves me with a huge grin on my face. What an honor to have met him and to get to listen to all his stories!

In Retrospect

W HEN ONE STARTS OUT their life, we never know where we will go, down which life's path, who we will encounter, what, if any, accomplishments we may or may not achieve. How, or if, our choices result in our dreams or desires.

When my life's course changed and thrust me into my new profession, I would never have guessed it could turn out as it has.

Now that I have documented my most memorable clients, I must sit back, take a deep breath, and exhale slowly, followed by a very sound, "Holy crap!"

Overall, I'm happy of the way my life has progressed upon this writing.

People would often comment on how they wish they could live in that big beautiful home!

I would gaze at them and respond with, "Be careful of what you wish for, there are a lot of unhappy people behind those walls."

I would like to thank all of my past clients and friends for keeping me going, by allowing me to exercise my mind and body through college and fitness, as I worked out each and every day for you with results which everyone truly appreciated. Being self-employed truly makes one's life their own.

About the Author

ANGEL CHRISTINE IS A first-time author of this book. She has worked as a waitress, aerobics instructor, body-firming coach, reservations agent at airline, secretary to judges and lawyers, small business owner, and school bus driver. She is a brown belt in judo. Her lifelong interests include exercising, sewing, crocheting, upholstery, classic movies, and interior design. She lives in Upstate New York.

CPSIA information can be obtained
at www.ICGtesting.com
Printed in the USA
LVHW110528051021
699551LV00001B/23